HISTORY OF AMERICAN THOUGHT AND CULTURE
Paul S. Boyer, *General Editor*

Portrait of John Winthrop by Charles Osgood, 1834. Photo courtesy of the Massachusetts Historical Society.

John Winthrop's World

HISTORY AS A STORY; THE STORY AS HISTORY

James G. Moseley

The University of Wisconsin Press

The University of Wisconsin Press
114 North Murray Street
Madison, Wisconsin 53715

3 Henrietta Street
London WC2E 8LU, England

Printed in the United States of America

Library of Congress Cataloging-in-Publication Data
Moseley, James G.
John Winthrop's world : history as a story, the story as history /
James G. Moseley.
204 pp.   cm.—(History of American thought and culture)
Half title: John Winthrop's world.
Includes bibliographical references (pp. 187–190) and index.
ISBN 0-299-13530-6 (cloth) :   ISBN 0-299-13534-9 (paper)
1. Winthrop, John, 1588–1649.   2. Puritans—Massachusetts—
History—17th century.—3. Massachusetts—History—Colonial period,
ca. 1600–1775.   I. Title   II. Title: John Winthrop's world.
III. Series
F67.W79M67   1992
974.4′02′092—dc20   92-20629

For Candace

Contents

Preface   ix

Introduction   3

Part One: HISTORY AS A STORY

1. English Roots   13
2. Laying Foundations   41
3. A Time of Testing   70
4. Looking Steadily Forward   94

Part Two: THE STORY AS HISTORY

5. The Perils of the Text   121
6. Ways of Making History in Early New England   130
7. The Governor and the Historians   148
8. Coming Home Again   169

Notes   179
Selected Bibliography   187
Index   191

Preface

SEVERAL individuals and groups helped me to understand John Winthrop and to see connections between his world and ours. For ideas, insights, and critical suggestions, I am indebted to Giles Gunn, Marilyn Harran, Martin Marty, Amanda Porterfield, and Rowland Sherrill. I have learned much from colleagues in a series of colloquia, directed by Conrad Cherry and supported by the Lilly Endowment, at Indiana University's Center for the Study of Religion and American Culture. Perhaps most significantly, the participants in the Summer Seminars that I have directed for the National Endowment for the Humanities complicated my thinking with refreshing observations drawn from their engagement with Winthrop's journal and other American texts. Carolyn Denton, Curator of Special Collections in the Library at Transylvania University, helped design the cover. Finally, Paul Boyer's encouragement was crucial to the completion of a manuscript that Barbara Hanrahan, Raphael Kadushin, Carol Olsen, Angela Ray, and many others at the University of Wisconsin Press helped to become a book.

As a symbol of my intellectual life, this book is dedicated to my wife, Candace Chambers Moseley, without whose learning and love little would have been ventured. To her and to our children, Emily and Jamie, I repeat what John Winthrop wrote to his firstborn son about the early stages of the Puritan migration: "God sende a good ende to these happie beginninges."

John Winthrop's World

Introduction

JOHN WINTHROP led the Puritans who came to America in the early seventeenth century. While serving as the first governor of the Massachusetts Bay Colony, an office he held with few interruptions for two decades, he worked to establish a society in which true Christianity could flourish, beyond the reach of the unfaithful Church of England. Winthrop also recorded the daily events in which he found himself—the political infighting and religious quarrels, as well as the Puritans' relations with other colonists, their dealings with the Indians, and their disputes with England. As our primary source for understanding the early years of this important settlement in New England, Winthrop's journal is a window into a world that, while unfamiliar, continues to influence our sense of the meaning of America.

By all accounts Winthrop was an extraordinary man, the first citizen of early New England. Generations of historians have mined his journal for information about the Puritans. Little attention has been paid, however, to the connections between Winthrop's political activity and his writing. In fact, he learned much about himself by describing his world. As both a politician and a historian, Winthrop was an interpreter of foundational events in American history. Within his journal, therefore, lie resources for understanding the nature of leadership and the meaning of liberty in our past. Because of the ongoing Puritan legacy in American culture, Winthrop's journal may show us our own world, and possibly our future, in new ways.

Yet access to this vital resource is not easy. On the surface, occasionally the Puritans' spelling and use of the English language, to say nothing of their medieval calendar, are unlike our own. Following their usage, though, frees us from a facile translation of the Puritans' thoughts into our own terms and allows us to avoid altering the works of historians who quote them, without posing serious difficulties for a modern reader. More significantly, because deep differences underlie the enduring connections between their world and ours, we have created images of the past that make the Puritans seem either

3

safely quaint or mercifully irrelevant. To enter Winthrop's lively world, therefore, requires removing the blinders of the present and seeing through the traditional images that have been used to domesticate the unsettling remembrance of early New England.

An age devoted to simple questions has difficulty hearing complex answers, especially when complicated truths reveal the dangers of simplicity. When the subject is unavoidably part of our history and experience, caricature becomes an accepted way of evading the disturbance such answers cause. Stereotypes soften the difficulty by providing reassuring images, particularly when the matter lies at the foundation of our cultural identity. Small wonder, then, that John Winthrop, the man who led the migration and oversaw the establishment of the largest, most successful English colony in the New World, the man who told his people that their undertaking was so important that in the eyes of the world "wee shall be as a Citty vpon a hill," the man who upon reaching the New World not only governed his people but also wrote their history for succeeding generations, has been portrayed so variously, sometimes by those who seek to explain away his accomplishments and more often by those who appeal to his achievements to legitimate their own desires. With such a figure, it may be impossible to avoid misperceptions, especially when misunderstanding has been so staunch an ingredient in the Puritan legacy.

Recognizing that all readings include misreadings, acknowledging that the writing of history, like its making, is irretrievably a matter of the conflict of interpretations, we should preface Winthrop's story by reviewing some of the caricatures and stereotypes through which we have inherited this remarkable man. We will then be prepared to enter the world he shaped as a leader and described as a writer, and able thereby to understand the ways historians and others have used Winthrop to shape the future by interpreting the past. There is no simple way to understand a complicated man and no other way to reclaim what is of lasting value in what he learned about himself, the nature of leadership, and the promise of America. In some ways we still live in Winthrop's world, and in many ways we do not. We begin to discover the true difference between his world and ours and to appreciate the difference such difference makes when we sort out some of the images through which, rightly or wrongly, John Winthrop has continued to be a presence in American culture.

Authors with an ax to grind, whether on or with the Puritans, tend to portray Winthrop as a one-dimensional character. Such straightforwardly positive or negative characterizations inevitably miss Winthrop's natural ambivalences and slip into caricature. When images of the same person stand in clear contrast to each other, their authors' intentions are easy to read. For example, to novelist Anya Seton, Winthrop is a moralistic, self-denying, humorless father-in-law and father figure who is given to sermonic harangues and disapproves of all that her strong-willed, passionate, life-embracing heroine Elizabeth seeks in life. Elizabeth marries Winthrop's appealing, ne'er-do-well, tragically short-lived son Henry. Though supported and cared for by Winthrop, Elizabeth, like virtually everyone else in the novel, fears the guardian whose rectitude dominates her conscience. In Seton's *The Winthrop Woman,* published in 1958, John Winthrop is a theocratic villain in whose world the vibrant Elizabeth "suffered the handicaps peculiar to her sex and her time." The domineering governor's firstborn son, John, Jr., relieves the caricature toward the end of the novel by telling Elizabeth, "You misjudge my father as usual. You see but one side of him!"[1] But Jack's rejoinder provides merely momentary resistance to the stereotypically authoritarian view of Puritanism expressed in a novel written about a woman by a woman on the eve of the sexual revolution of the 1960s.

If Seton created a caricature from one aspect of John Winthrop's character, then Cotton Mather had done so, much earlier and with perhaps an even heavier hand, from another. As a third-generation American Puritan, Mather sought to inspire "a glorious resurrection" of true religion by portraying the greatness of the founders of New England for the instruction of his decreasingly theological and increasingly commercial contemporaries.[2] Mather's reforming zeal and daunting industriousness were matched by the bombastic verbosity of his devotion to the founders, evidenced by the incantation introducing his matchless governor, John Winthrop:

Let Greece boast of her patient Lycurgus, the lawgiver, by whom diligence, temperance, fortitude and wit were made the fashions of a therefore long-lasting and renowned commonwealth: let Rome tell of her devout Numa, the lawgiver, by whom the most famous commonwealth saw peace triumphing over extinguished war and cruel plunders; and murders giving place to the more mollifying exercises of his religion. Our New-England shall tell and boast of her Winthrop, a lawgiver as patient as Lycurgus, but not admitting any of his criminal disorders; as devout as Numa, but not liable to any of *his* heathenish madnesses; a governour in whom the excellencies of Christianity made a most improving addition unto the virtues, wherein even without *those* he would have made a *parallel* for the great men of Greece, or of Rome, which the pen of a Plutarch has eternized.[3]

When we consider Winthrop's story as history, we shall look into Mather's exaltation of himself, by implication, as the American Plutarch.

In Mather's rendering of Winthrop, "*this* eminent person was, by the consent of all, chosen for the Moses, who must be the leader of so great an undertaking: and indeed nothing but a *Mosaic spirit* could have carried him through the temptations, to which either his farewell to his own land, or his travel in a strange land, must needs expose a gentleman of his education." This Winthrop "was a very religious man; and as he strictly kept his *heart,* so he kept his *house,* under the laws of piety." As "our New-English Nehemiah," Winthrop was not vexed by small-minded troublemakers as he led the people in building the colony; likewise, as "the Joseph," he saved them from starvation "with his open-handed bounties." Winthrop encountered difficulties, in Mather's view, solely because "goodness it self will make enemies." All his trials show "the exemplary skill of this wise man, *at giving soft answers*" to his adversaries.[4] Little wonder that historian Sacvan Bercovitch finds "the Puritan origins of the American self" in Mather's hagiography of Winthrop.[5] Such a saintly leader hardly seems to be drawn from the same figure as was the narrow-minded tyrant who oppresses the heroine of Seton's novel.

Not all of the popular images of Winthrop are cast in such stark relief as those of Seton and Mather. Yet vestiges of caricature also color some less extreme characterizations, both positive and negative, of Winthrop's life and legacy. Thus Louis Auchincloss, for example, introduces virtues of wisdom and patience to mitigate somewhat the governor's authoritarianism in a collection of short stories, *The Winthrop Covenant,* published in 1976. Nevertheless, stereotypes persist, as when Auchincloss imagines Winthrop saying in conversation with William Hutchinson, "There is a time to be lenient and a time to be strong. Tell your wife, Master Hutchinson, and tell your brother Wheelwright to learn respect for the leaders of our colony and to *show* it. Or else, sir, let me assure you that they will be banished. Banished for sedition!" To this Hutchinson inwardly responds, "Ah, there it was . . . there it was, the same hard little light in the eyes, the same fixed, sinister gleam." As Auchincloss's series of stories moves through generations of Winthrops toward the present, a noble but narrow-minded Puritan sense of mission toward others declines steadily, until the final, modern Winthrop figure is simply an amoral "survivor" who enjoys running other people's lives. As attitudes harden, certain images persist. The "long hard look" endures, and in the last scene of the final story "John's lips formed a tight straight line."[6] By retaining the family name and linking the descendants through such images, Auchincloss makes Governor John Winthrop's Puritanism seem responsible, three and a half centuries later, for the unbending opportunism the writer found characteristic of American life in the 1970s.

If Auchincloss's examination of the Winthrop legacy is finally unbalanced in one direction, then the editorial commentary of Robert C. Winthrop, who published *The Life and Letters of John Winthrop* a century earlier, ultimately tips the other way. This later Winthrop sought "to form a just portrait of the old Puritan leader" in order to correct "some false impressions" of his character. "We all knew [they] were men of piety and prayer," Robert Winthrop notes. "But not a few of us had doubted how far these old Fathers of Massachusetts were men of charity." Winthrop's editorial purpose with respect to his forefathers is clear: "They have been associated, certainly, with an austerity of disposition, a sternness of character, and a severity of conduct, which have often subjected them to the reproach of history, and which have sometimes rendered them repulsive even to their own posterity. We are glad to believe, that the Life and Letters of Winthrop, as thus far given, have done something to mitigate, if not to dispel, this prejudice. They have served to exhibit at least one of the foremost of the Massachusetts Fathers as abounding in tenderness and love. If any thing of severity, or any thing of bitterness, shall be developed in what remains of his life, it is plain that he brought no root of either of them with him. We have seen him severe indeed, but towards no one except himself." In this editor's eyes, John Winthrop "was a man of practical wisdom, as well as of refined sensibility; a man of decision, resolution, and energy, as well as of piety and charity," whose career in the New World was an "exhibition of vigorous effort and manly endurance."[7] Along with his desire to dispel misperceptions of his great ancestor, perhaps Robert C. Winthrop, who had served as congressman and Speaker of the House in the 1840s and as senator during the Fugitive Slave Bill debate, felt that Americans especially needed such remembrances of their cultural forefathers at the conclusion of the Civil War.

If authors and historians have been captive to the caricatures of John Winthrop that seemed appropriate to their own times and purposes, we should not be surprised to find the boldest and least credible clichés employed in the rhetoric of presidential self-assurance. In the final televised address of his presidency, for example, Ronald Reagan evoked Winthrop to authenticate the vision of America that he believed our children should know more about. "Because he was . . . an early 'Freedom Man,'" President Reagan explained, Winthrop came to America "looking for a home that would be free." When he saw that same "shining city" in his own mind, the president said, it was "teeming with people of all kinds living in harmony and peace—a city with free ports that hummed with commerce . . . [with doors] open to anyone with the will and the heart to get here." Winthrop's "city on a hill," Reagan asserted, is "still a beacon, still a magnet for all who must have freedom, for all the Pilgrims from all the lost places who are hurtling . . . toward home."[8] Virtually everyone, of course, conflates the Puritans and the Pilgrims; in addition, President Reagan's espousal of pluralism and free trade bore little resemblance to the freedom Winthrop sought for the Massachusetts Bay Colony. However much one may quarrel with the historical accuracy of Reagan's citation, though, it seems understandable for a president in the late 1980s, at the unsettling end of his second term in office, to attempt to put his own work in perspective by referring back to a time of origins, when goals were clear, purposes widely shared, and the authority of leadership unchallenged. Or so clichés and caricatures allow one to think!

We create images of the past to help us endure the ambiguity of the present, to sustain our efforts to imagine, and perhaps to manage, the future. Hence we are susceptible to "illusions of innocence."[9] Some of the attractions are obvious. As one writer put it, "Massachusetts in the seventeenth century. You weren't afraid to walk the streets."[10] Debunking such clichés is easy work for historians; caricatures of pristine beginnings are natural grist for the mill of critical inquiry. Yet somehow the images persist, perhaps because, at least to some extent, they enable us to make affirmations which, if impossible to realize, nevertheless seem vital to our common identity. The radical simplifications of experience that caricatures entail, however, are dangerous insofar as, by nurturing illusions of perfection, they permit us to avoid dealing practically with the complications of everyday life. For example, while current events are always revealing the all too human limitations of political figures, we continue a pattern of inordinate expectations followed by dismayed condemnation of their failings. Given such a pattern, Lewis Lapham asks, "Who could bear the thought of being governed by human beings, by people as confused and imperfect as oneself? If a politican confessed to an honest doubt or emotion, how would it be possible to grant him the authority of a god? Better to remain numb, to applaud mediocrity with a feeling of relief because nobody onstage has raised any troubling questions, to buy books for the same reason that one buys cocaine or tickets to *A Chorus Line*—as anesthetics against the fear of death or the unpatriotic suggestion that maybe all stories don't have happy endings."[11] We use historical stereotypes for refuge from contemporary complications, and by providing such shelter, they use us. As the runaway slave Jim says in response to Huck Finn's vision of freedom, while their raft drifts south of the Mason-Dixon line, "it's too good to be true." To see beyond the stereotypes, for the better understanding and conduct of our present life, we need to look both through and behind our caricatures of the past.

One apparent way to avoid the lock that stereotypes hold on access to the past might be to look through a different door, not so much to see how historical acts have been remembered as, instead, to explore the actual places where they occurred. But the acids of modernity stain even hard physical evidence. John Winthrop's first dwelling in the New World and the original seat of the Bay Colony's governance in Charlestown, before the governor and the court moved to Boston, are now the site of an underground highway project. And the archives in Bury St. Edmunds have been searched for quaint names for the streets of a real estate development at Groton Manor, the Winthrop family seat in old England. Evidently in none of its forms can the past be appropriated without interpretation.

If it proves impossible to see the past without looking backward consciously through the images in which it continues to live, then we must also remember that past events were themselves informed by conflicting interests, perceptions, and beliefs. The founding and early history of New England dramatically illustrate an ineluctable conflict of interpretations. A recent cartoon shows one Englishman saying to another, as they step ashore in the

New World, "My immediate interest is religious freedom, but in the long run I want to get into real estate." No one lived amid such conflicts more actively than John Winthrop, and no one recounted the events they shaped more faithfully than he. Indeed, the journal he kept is the primary record of the early history of the Bay Colony. Whether in or out of office, Winthrop was embroiled, sometimes to his detriment, in the events his journal describes. Writing about events in which he was often centrally involved may have heightened Winthrop's sensitivity to the interplay of interpretations that defined relationships within the colony and between the colony and other people and parties, in both New and old England. We will see him learning from observing his own actions and shaping himself as he wrote. Though a proud, resolute man, Winthrop, as his journal will show, was often more able than his compatriots to sustain the drive of his original vision by making crucial adjustments to the demands of the new situations in which he found himself.

If we misread Winthrop's journal as a simple chronicle of events, without paying attention to the ways that making history involved both writing and acting, then we lose a vital dimension of Winthrop's life, along with an important part of his significance for the subsequent history, and to some degree the future, of American culture. In exploring this double role, the present work moves beyond Edmund S. Morgan's *The Puritan Dilemma: The Story of John Winthrop,* an otherwise fine book, which tends to assume that Winthrop's consciousness was fully formed before he stepped on board the *Arbella* for the voyage to New England.[12] The Puritan contribution to American culture was neither imported wholecloth from England nor inaugurated de novo in the "howling wilderness" of Massachusetts. Rather, as a compound of original vision and accommodation to circumstance, it was worked out along the way. The text of Winthrop's journal is perhaps uniquely able to reveal the initial stages in that process. Therefore, we must turn to the text itself, where Winthrop is more often than not the hero and always the writer, in order to understand his history as a story. Then we shall be prepared to appreciate what happened to the story as history, in the hands of historians and other interpreters of America. Only then shall we be ready, in conclusion, to learn what John Winthrop has to teach about the possible future of American culture.

Part One

HISTORY AS A STORY

1

English Roots

JOHN WINTHROP'S journal, *The History of New England,* begins auspiciously on Easter Monday, 29 March 1630, when Winthrop was aboard the ship *Arbella,* riding the sea just off the Isle of Wight. Four English ships of Puritan emigrants faced the contrary winds together, with with six more still in port. Such an undertaking had naturally required considerable preparation. The enterprise of emigration began well before the ships set sail, and the story of Winthrop's personal journey begins even earlier still. Who was this man who was chosen to govern these voyagers to the New World and who, while leading the movement, also wrote its history? What brought him to this point of departure?

Certain patterns emerge from his family history. The Winthrop family name can be traced back through the records of English history for at least seven centuries. Villages in several counties bear, or bore, the name. The first definite reference to John Winthrop's direct ancestors appears in the parish register of Lavenham, in the county of Suffolk, with the birth of Adam Winthrop in 1498. "This Adam was the eldest son of Adam Winthrop and Joane (or Jane) Burton," and as Robert C. Winthrop notes, "he seems to have been a person of pretty decided character."[1] At the age of seventeen, Adam left home and went to London, where he learned the trade of making cloth, the most important industry in early sixteenth-century England. After serving out his apprenticeship, he was given the freedom of a citizen in the city of London in 1526. The following year he married Alice Henny (or Henry), who bore a daughter and four sons within six years, while Adam established himself as a clothier. Adam Winthrop's desire to carve out a career for himself, to make a place in the world for himself and his growing family, marks the birth of an enterprising spirit that would be inherited and enhanced by his son Adam and given even larger scope by his grandson John.

13

Alice soon died, and within a year, in 1534, Adam married Agnes Sharpe. Soon Adam had become a steward of the Clothworkers' Company of London. Advancing through positions as quarter-warden and upper-warden, he became the master of the company in 1551. Thus he was a man of considerable standing, income, and family—for Agnes delivered five daughters and three sons, two of whom were twins, by 1552. Once during these years Adam was imprisoned for negotiating with foreigners, perhaps pursuing less restricted trade or corresponding with religious reformers, and fined six hundred pounds. His ability to pay such a large fine indicates that Adam had become a man of considerable means, and whatever sort of trouble he had been in did nothing to slow his progress in business and society. Adam's ability to work his way to a position of leadership in the Clothworkers' Company suggests a desire for responsibility and also a certain savvy about human relations, coupled with a willingness to risk engaging in international affairs. These characteristics helped to establish his family and would flower even more fully, two generations later, in John Winthrop's governorship of the Massachusetts Bay Company.

Within a year of his scrape with the law, Adam was granted the manor of Groton, in 1544, "in consideration of the sum of four hundred and eight pounds eighteen shillings and threepence, of lawful English money."[2] Having officially dissolved and confiscated the monasteries, Henry VIII was selling them to fortify the royal treasury, and Adam Winthrop knew how to turn a connection between religious reform, politics, economics, and real estate to the lasting advantage of his substantial family. Located just six miles from his native Lavenham, Groton Manor became the Winthrop family seat, and Adam was appropriately made an esquire by Henry's successor, the young Edward VI, in 1548. Having established the family fortune, Adam Winthrop died in 1562. Agnes remarried well, and the Winthrops' daughter Alice married Agnes's new husband's son, who contributed much, including a title, to the ongoing Winthrop extended family.

A portrait of Adam Winthrop, attributed to Holbein, "portrays a man of adventurous and fearless spirit," according to Robert C. Winthrop, who notes with approval that Adam Winthrop, lord of the manor and patron of the church, was characterized as a man of faith who loved religious truth.[3] Adam's last will and testament reveals additional characteristics which were inherited, along with his considerable estate, by generations of Winthrop descendants. After bequeathing his soul to Almighty God and ordering that forty shillings be distributed "to the most needest" among the poor of Groton, Adam gives his mansion and its land, along with the income from the other properties he had purchased or acquired through trade, to Agnes, his wife, for the remainder of her natural life. Some lands are given to a son from Adam's first marriage, all of the children of his marriage with Agnes are well provided for, and upon Agnes's decease the principal residue of the estate is to go to Adam's eldest surviving son, John, "and to his male heirs of his boddie lawfully begotten." Adam showed a shrewd knowledge of his children's ways, for John died without heirs who fit these terms. Hence, as the will stipulates, "for lack of such Issue males of his boddie lawfully begotten," John's substantial inheritance passed with the same condition to his younger brother, another Adam, whose life did not disappoint their father's hopes. After ensuring that Agnes had use of his other houses as well as continual access to a chamber in his house in London, old Adam concludes his will with two conditions that reveal his insight into the domestic hazards of a newly acquired fortune. First, if any of his sons or their heirs or anyone in their name or on their behalf "doe molest or troble Agnes my wief her executors or assignes, or doe attempte or otherwyse goe about to disproue or adnichillate or disanull this my will," then whatever has been given to them is "to be frustrate and voyde and of none effecte" and will be given, instead, to Agnes and her heirs. Second, he names Agnes as the executor of his will and instructs her, in fulfilling its conditions, to "take lerned councell in the lawe, from tyme to tyme to make them perfecte and formall according to the law."[4] The sense of serious partnership with his wife seen in the conditions of Adam Winthrop's will was inherited by his namesake and expressed more fully in the relationship between John Winthrop and his remarkable wife, Margaret Tyndal.

Although the distance from Lavenham to Groton Manor was only six miles, along the way Adam Winthrop had learned much about business, politics, law, and love. If sufficient records existed, his biography might reveal as much about negotiating the changing currents of English life in the first half of the sixteenth century as his grandson's does a century later. Old Adam brought the Winthrop family out of obscurity into potential prominence. His success established a foundation upon which his son Adam, Governor John Winthrop's father, was ready to build. Yet however much he inherited, the younger Adam, born the year his father was made an esquire, was his own man and contributed much to the making of John Winthrop.

Although Adam of Lavenham had done what was needed to acquire Groton Manor, the next Adam Winthrop was not quite, as the saying goes, to the manor born. Lordship of the manor, as we have seen from the will, bypassed the only son of old Adam's first marriage and went, instead, to John, the first surviving son of his marriage to Agnes Sharpe. John failed to produce a lawful male heir, however, and when he undertook a new plantation in the south of Ireland, he relinquished his interest in Groton. In accordance with the will, in 1594 a license of alienation transferred the manor to John's younger brother, Adam, who had for some time been living on and managing the family estate, where his own and only son, John, had been born six years earlier. Squire Adam inherited his father's ability to acquire and oversee real estate, and he was well prepared by the year or so he spent at Magdalene College, Cambridge, by his legal training, and by his experience as a lawyer to negotiate the tangled process through which he inherited Groton Manor.

Like his father, Adam married twice, increasing his wealth and social standing each time. After Alice Still died in childbirth, Winthrop married Anne Browne, who delivered three daughters who survived infancy, as well as a son, John. As his family grew, John Winthrop's father managed the business of farming well, with income from the lands he worked often exceeding what he derived from rents. Given his status as a barrister, evidence of his prudent management, and perhaps a little help from the fact that the father of his first wife had been master of Trinity College, Adam Winthrop was appointed auditor of Trinity, and somewhat later of St. John's College. In this capacity he served Cambridge University for almost two decades. While overseeing accounts for the colleges, Adam also helped keep order within his community, where as a justice of the peace he held frequent courts, both at Groton and elsewhere, and served on various grand juries and local commissions. In addition to keeping accounts for others, he maintained careful records of his personal business, domestic events, and the public service into which he was increasingly drawn.

Indeed, by his own account Adam Winthrop was something of a man of letters, maintaining an active correspondence with family and friends, loaning and borrowing books, annotating many volumes in his own library, writing occasional poetry in both English and Latin, and keeping track in a written diary of the history of his family and of important political events in England. He listened intently to the sermons he regularly heard, and his evaluation of them suggests a man who took religion seriously, if not with the passion that occasionally consumed his son. A practical as well as a literary man, he paid careful attention to his son's education and helped to arrange a marriage that brought John a substantial new estate.[5]

When Adam Winthrop died in 1623, he had added a literary sensibility, the legal profession, and an active commitment to public service to the strong sense of personal initiative and family responsibility that his own father had bequeathed to later generations of Winthrops. As these characteristics passed from father to son along with increasing and well-managed landed wealth, John was more than simply the first Winthrop actually to the manor born. Indeed, if such an inheritance were given to a person of acute religious sensibility and if the circumstances of English public life moved in certain problematic directions, then truly remarkable possibilities for leadership would emerge.

The "Latin Pedigree" compiled by Adam Winthrop to record the most significant events of his lifetime contains a single entry between the years 1585 and 1590: "1587. John the only sonne of Adam Winthrop and Anne his wife was borne in Edwardston aforesaide [being the home of Anne

16

Browne] on Thursday about 5 of the clocke in the morninge, the 12 daie of january anno 1587 in the 30 yere of the reigne of Qu: Eliz:"[6] Public events of the time were noteworthy: "Less than a year had elapsed since the tragical death of Mary, Queen of Scots," as Robert C. Winthrop observes, and "before another year should pass away, the grand Spanish Armada would be hovering on the coast of England."[7] But we have few details of the boy's early years, although we can surmise that the son of Adam Winthrop witnessed the comings and goings of the lawyers and judges with whom his father had business, the ministers from nearby parishes whom the family entertained, neighboring landowners and tenants, and the members of the growing extended family who visited at Groton Manor.

Some insight into John Winthrop's childhood may be gained from a document, "John Winthrop's Christian Experience," that he wrote when he was almost fifty years old. He remembers that "in my youth I was very lewdly disposed, inclining unto and attempting (so far as my yeares enabled mee) all kind of wickedness, except swearing and scorning religion, which I had no temptation unto in regard of my education. About ten years of age, I had some notions of God," he says, and "after I was 12 years old, I began to have some more savour of Religion, and I thought I had more understanding in Divinity then many of my years." But noble thoughts had little effect, for "I was still very wild, and dissolute, and as years came on my lusts grew stronger." Thankfully, such tendencies were "under some restraint of my naturall reason; whereby I had the command of my self that I could turne into any forme. I would as occasion required write letters etc. of meer vanity; and if occasion were I could write others of savory and godly counsel."[8] We hear of the boy's natural wildness and occasional pious self-reproach from no other source, however, and his "Christian Experience" should be read more for the light it sheds upon Winthrop's role in the crisis in which the entire Massachusetts Bay Colony was embroiled when the document was composed than for an accurate picture of the governor's boyhood.

Nothing is known of John's early education, but Adam's diary for 1602 records that "the 2d of December I rode to Cambridge" and that six days later "John my soonne was admitted into Trinitie College." On "the 2d of Marche my soonne went to Cambridge," where he studied at the college his father served as auditor of accounts.[9] Adam notes John's comings and goings between Groton and Cambridge over the next two years. In 1604 he records an important public event: "24 Octobre. The same day it was proclaymed that England and Scotland shoulde be called great Brittaine." The next entry marks the beginning of an equally auspicious private event, "the vth of Novembre my soonne did ryde into Essex with William Forth to Great Stambridge." In January, William's uncle, John Forth, came to Groton, and in March "I and my soonne viewed ouer Mr. John Forthes land at Carsey and Hadley." The drama concludes succinctly: on 26 March "I and my

17

soonne did ride to Mr. John Foorthes of great Stambrige"; two days later "my soonne was sollemly contracted to Mary Foorth by Mr. Culverwell the minister of greate Stambridge in Essex" with parental consent; and on 16 April 1605 "he was maryed to her at Stambridge in Essex by Mr. Culverwell."[10] Having completed the year or two of college that sufficed as higher education for many English gentlemen of the time, John Winthrop was a married man at the age of seventeen, with increasing responsibility for managing two substantial estates.

Although the Forths were an important family, John Forth had acquired vast landholdings in the counties of Suffolk and Essex largely by way of his marriage to Thomasine Hilles, the childless widow of two husbands. Mary was their only child and heir. The prudence of young John Winthrop's marriage is summarized well by Robert C. Black III: "That the fortunes of English families have been frequently and profitably advanced by way of the altar is too well known to require elaboration. But the effectiveness of the technique becomes particularly clear in the presence of a maiden like Mary Forth. Mary was a most unusual young lady in that she was the sole heir of profusely landed parents. It was in fact difficult to consider her otherwise than in terms of acreage. That her age exceeded by four years that of Adam Winthrop's son John was a matter of indifference."[11] But John's interest lay not merely in land. In less than ten months, as Adam's diary records, "my soonne's first soonne was borne in Groton." On "the 23 of Feb: beinge sunday my soonne's first soonne was baptized and named John."[12] Recalling how Adam's own inheritance had depended upon having a lawful son of his own body may explain his somewhat dynastic rhetoric. His first grandson became a remarkable man, as we shall see, ending his life as the longtime governor of Connecticut and one of New England's leaders in science and technology as well. Adam's own son John, the new baby's eighteen-year-old father, developed an understandably strong sense of responsibility for the welfare and well-being of his growing family.

The future inheritor of Great Stambridge and Groton needed to master the intricate details of managing the manorial lands, many of them worked by tenants. Traveling sometimes with his wife or his father, or occasionally with his mother, John moved from one estate to the other and, somewhat less frequently, to London. His young family settled initially at Groton, where in January 1607 Adam notes "my soonne's second soone Henry was Christened." No reason was given when, the following October, "my soonne and his wyfe departed from Groton to dwell at Stambridge in Essex."[13] Travel and correspondence between the estates continued, with John Winthrop returning to Groton to hold his first manorial court when he turned twenty-one. As the future lord of the manor, he would dispense local justice, and a knowledge of the law also smoothed somewhat the crabbed details of manorial management. Like his father and perhaps under his tutelage, John

Winthrop read and studied law, both privately and in London at Gray's Inn in 1613. By 1617 Adam turned the lordship of Groton Manor over to John, who by then was serving as one of the justices of the peace in Suffolk. Along with managing the estates, such judicial duties, together with his legal work in London in subsequent years, became John Winthrop's principal business, or, in the religious terminology he was beginning to adopt, his calling. For religion, always present to some degree in his mind, was now capturing John Winthrop's heart.

While living at Great Stambridge, Mary delivered another son, named Forth, in 1609, and a daughter, Mary, in 1612. Despite his prosperity, John Winthrop was vexed during these years by religious doubts, unmanageable desires, illness, and an apparently overbearing father-in-law. Liberation from all of these came together, as he noted in an introspective notebook he had begun to keep:

May 23 1613. When my condition was much straightned, partly through my longe sicknes, partly through wante of freedome, partly through lacke of outward things, I prayed often to the Lord for deliverance, referring the meanes to himselfe, and with all I often promised to putt forthe myselfe to muche fruitt when the Lorde should inlarge me. Nowe that he hathe set me a great libertye, givinge me a good ende to my teadious quartan [recurrent malarial fever], freedome from a superior will and liberall maintenance by the deathe of my wifes father (who finished his days in peace the 15 of May 1613) I do resolve first to give myselfe, my life, my witt, my healthe, my wealthe to the service of my God and Saviour, who by givinge himselfe for me, and to me, deserves what soever I am or can be, to be at his Commandement.[14]

Having given substantial legacies to his daughter and her husband in their marriage settlement, and through them to their firstborn son, John Forth named John and Mary coexecutors of the will in which he also provided liberally for his grandchildren Henry, Forth, and Mary.[15] After Mary's father's death, the Winthrop family returned to Groton, where in the summer of 1614 Mary delivered a daughter, Anna, who soon died. Mary herself died in childbed, along with a second Anna, the following summer. While married to Mary, John Winthrop moved from adolescence into maturity. She bore him four children who survived—three sons and a daughter—and left him greatly enhanced wealth with which to manage his growing responsibilities. Moreover, she introduced him, through the Reverend Ezekial Culverwell, who married them and served the parish at Great Stambridge, to something of perhaps even greater significance—a form of religion that would increasingly inspire his thinking, constrain his desires, satisfy his heart, and direct his life.

Culverwell was a Puritan, and John Winthrop was becoming one too. Years later, in his "Christian Experience," Winthrop recalled: "About 18 years of age (being a man in stature, and in understanding as my parents conceived mee) I married into a family under Mr. Culverwell his ministry in Essex; and living there sometimes I first found the ministry of the word to come to my heart with power (for in all before I found onely light) and after that I found the like in the ministry of many others. So as there began to bee some change which I perceived in my self, and others took notice of. Now I began to come under strong excersises of Conscience: (yet by fits only) I could no longer dally with Religion."[16] The minister whose sermons inaugurated this great change had served as rector at Great Stambridge since 1592, so we may assume that his message was well received by the Forth family.

The hierarchy of the Church of England, however, found Ezekial Culverwell's reformist convictions less satisfactory. He had been suspended for nonconformity in 1583, and the year following John Winthrop's decision to move his young family to the Forth estate, Culverwell was deprived of his office at Great Stambridge.[17] But the seed he sowed grew in the soul of John Winthrop, who began to listen intently then to other ministers, in other places, whose new words had escaped Anglican notice or who had as yet avoided the episcopal ax. One reason for moving his family back to Groton, following John Forth's death in 1613, was to hear the inspired, reformist teaching of Henry Sands in nearby Boxford.

The unquenchable desire of such ministers to purify the Church of England had troubled the settlement Queen Elizabeth devised in hope of pacifying England's quarrelsome religious factions. Although promising peace, King James had less patience. His churchmen moved to secure the standing order by stifling dissent. Sometimes suppression exacerbated the tensions, though, and battle lines were being drawn. Yet whatever was subsequently accomplished in society, politics, and the church by the people whom less idealistic Englishmen disparaged as "Puritans," John Winthrop's early Puritanism was wholly a matter of intensely private spiritual experience. Significantly, his desire to find a way of making workable sense of his life took the form of self-examination in a private diary.

At nineteen years of age, with his first son almost one year old, John Winthrop found it hard to fulfill his increasing duties at Groton Manor and his new responsibilities at Great Stambridge. Daunted by the notion of all he was expected to accomplish and at the same time distracted by the pleasures available to a young gentleman, in February 1606 he began a notebook titled simply "Experiencia," in which he could examine his experiences: "Worldly cares thoughe not in any grosse manner outwardly, yet seacreatly, togither with a seacret desire after plesures and itchinge after libertie and unlawfull delightes, had brought me to wax wearie of good duties and so to forsake my first love, whence came much troble and danger."[18] Winthrop recorded his thoughts in this notebook at odd moments over the next thirty years. The solution he finally discovered was not so much an answer to a question as a way of living purposefully in an uncomfortable situation. Life could be satisfying, but the basic problem of reconciling physical and spiritual desires remained the same.

The first section of Winthrop's notebook covers the years from 1606 to 1613. Some of the difficulties Winthrop records here are quite mundane, such as "one morninge a great fitt of impatience, for matter betwixt my wife and my mother, for which I pray God forgive me." Many have been widely shared. On one Sunday, for example, "beinge at sermon at Groton, I let in but a thought of my iornie into Essex [a forthcoming journey to Great Stambridge], but strait it delighted me, and beinge not verie carefull of my heart, I was suddainely, I know not how, so possessed with the worlde, as I was led into one sinne after an other, and could hardely recover my selfe, till taking myselfe to prayer before I was too farre gonne, I found mercie." A repeated theme is expressed when on "the 20 of Aprill, 1606, I made a new Covenant with the Lorde which was this: 'Of my part, that I would reforme thesse sinnes by his grace, pride, covetousnesse, love of this worlde, vanitie of mind, unthankfulnesse, slouth, both in his service and in my callinge, not preparinge myselfe with reverence and uprightnesse to come to his word: Of the Lords part that he would give me a new heart, joy in his spirit, that he would dwell with me, that he would strengthen me against the world, the fleshe, and the Divell, that he would forgive my sinnes and increase my faith. God give me grace to performe my promise and I doubt not but he will performe his. God make it fruitfull. Amen.'" Later in his life, after reading over the entries in this notebook, Winthrop added a chastened insight to its early pages: "In these following Experiences, there be diverse vows, promises to God, or Resolutions and purposes of my heart, occasioned throughe the ofte experience of my weaknesse in such things, and my great desire of keeping peace and holdinge communion with God, many of which I have in tyme observed that I have great need to repent (in some of them) my unadvisednesse in making them, consideringe that they have proved snares to my Conscience, and (in others of them) my wretchednesse and sinne in not carefully observing them."[19] Thus by reviewing the ways he described his experiences, Winthrop detects his tendency to fall into a certain rhetorical pattern of "covenants" with God, and the older, more self-reflective man sees the danger of such promises.

The more mature Winthrop must have found some of his early covenants humorously revealing. In 1611, for example, after citing eight arguments against shooting a gun—it is against the law since shooting spoils more creatures than it gets, it offends many people, it wastes time, it requires too much physical effort, it endangers one's own life, it brings no profit, it has substantial penalties, and it brings one's character into contempt—he notes that "lastly for mine owne parte I haue ever binne crossed in usinge it, for when I haue gone about it not without some woundes of conscience, and haue taken muche paynes and hazarded my healthe, I haue gotten sometimes

a verye little but most commonly nothing at all towards my cost and labo-
ure." Chiefly because he turns out to be a bad shot, therefore, he has
"resolved and covenanted with the Lorde to give over alltogither shootinge
at the creeke;—and for killinge of birds, etc: either to leave that altogither or
els to use it, both verye seldome and verye secreatly. God (if he please) can
giue me fowle by some other meanes, but if he will not, yet, in that it is [his]
will who loves me, it is sufficient to uphould my resolution."[20] His spiritual
reasoning, like his shooting, could sometimes miss the mark.

Other entries suggest a more mystical side. Thus in January 1611, "after
I had bine visitinge Jesus Christ in his faithfull servant, old Hudson," Winthrop recalls that "in my sleepe I dreamed that I was with Christ upon earthe,
and that beinge very instant with him in manye teares, for the assurance of
the pardon of my sinnes etc: I was so ravished with his love towards me, farre
exceedinge the affection of the kindest husbande, that being awaked it had
made so deep impression in my hearte, as I was forced to unmeasurable
weepings for a great while, and had a more lively feelinge of the love of Christ
than euer before." Naturally, some of his observations were more prosaic.
Thus in February of the same year he concludes "that the profitt of sinne can
never countervaile the damage of it, for there is no sinne so sweet in the
committinge, but it proves more bitter in the repentinge for it." He also
considers that "it is good to beware of Custome in sinne, for often sinninge
will make sinne light."[21] Such moralistic platitudes could overwhelm the
young writer's religious sincerity.

Sometimes Winthrop commits himself to more than his later experience
will show him to be capable of achieving, as when he resolves that "I will ever
walke humblye before my God, and meekly, mildly, and gently towards all
men, so shall I haue peace." Occasionally he simply catalogs his good
intentions. For example, after virtually rejoicing over the death of his father-
in-law, as we have seen, he lists twelve promises regarding such topics as more
prudent spending, family prayers, the education of his children, banishing
profanity, and diligently observing the Sabbath. An entry in 1613 records
Winthrop's meeting with seven other men and some of their families at the
home of the Reverend Henry Sands, "where we appointed all to meete
againe the next yere on that frydaye which should be neerest to the 17 of
September, and in the meane tyme every one of us each fryday in the weeke
to be mindefull one of another in desiring God to grante the petitions that
were made to him that daye."[22] But Winthrop primarily recorded private
experiences and reflections. Most entries portray the ups and downs of
spiritual life as a tug-of-war between the world, with its distractions of
business and pleasure, and the religious life, with its duties and rewards. In
the early section of the "Experiencia," this pattern usually concludes, as
Winthrop later noted, with a "new" resolution or covenant between the
writer and his God.

Between September 1613 and December 1616 Winthrop made no entries in his notebook. In 1613, in addition to moving his family back to Groton Manor and managing the two estates, he studied law at Gray's Inn in London. During the next two years, as subsequent reflections in the diary show, he was almost undone, and certainly much changed, by two tragic deaths. In the summer of 1615 Mary Forth had been laid to rest beside two daughters named Anna. In a short time Winthrop married again. But soon there was to be another burial at Groton Church.

On 6 December 1615, less than six months after the death of his first wife, Winthrop married Thomasine Clopton, from one of Suffolk's most distinguished families. Except for the death of his new bride's father, the wedding would have been even sooner. Five years older than John, Thomasine was a Puritan, and she soon proved to be an admirable new mother for her husband's four children. On 30 November 1616 she gave birth to a daughter, who lived only two days. Thomasine's own death followed the infant's by one week. Thrown into grief, Winthrop resumed writing his "Experiencia" on the first anniversary of his second wedding.

Underneath the previous section of his notebook, Winthrop drew a heavy black line. As if to summarize its content, he wrote in a large, round hand, "Security of heart ariseth of over much delighte in the things of the world."[23] In contrast to the vigorous moralism of his earlier self-analysis, the new entry begins with a sense of acceptance: "God will have mercie on whom he will have mercie, and when and how seemes best to his wisdom and will." The lesson of pain is clear: "Surely the Lord hathe shewed me . . . that there was never any holye meditation, prayer, or action that I had a hand in, that received any worthe or furtherance from me or anythinge that was mine. And untill I sawe this and acknowledged it, I could never have true comfort in God or sound peace in mine owne conscience, in any the best I could performe." Even when he prayed for comfort, Winthrop found a tendency "to cast an eye towards myselfe, as thinking myselfe somebodye in the performance of such a duty in such a manner"; then "such a thought would presently be to my comfort and peace as colde water caste upon a flame; whereby I might see that God by such checkes would teache me to goe wholly out of myselfe, and learne to depende on him alone. . . . For it is not possible that any good thinge should come from me as of myselfe." Such honesty about himself opened Winthrop to new spiritual resources: "In this tyme of my sorrowe for my wifes weaknesse, I founde it a speciall meanes for the humblinge and cleeringe of my hearte and conscience, even to meditate upon the Commandments and to examine my life past by them, and then concludinge with prayer, I found my hearte more humbled and Gods free mercie in Christ more open to me then at any tyme before to my remembrance."[24] Acceptance of Thomasine's death clearly marked a turning point in Winthrop's religious life.

Thomasine's ordeal lasted several days. Tortured with fever, at times she wrestled with her conscience and strove with temptation, "defying Satan, and spitting at him, so as we might see by hir setting of hir teethe, and fixinge her eyes, shaking hir head and whole bodye, that she had a very greatt conflicte with the adversarye." In lucid hours she conversed with family and neighbors, dispensing deathbed advice to all comers, praying with her husband and listening to him read from the Scriptures until late at night. "When I spake to her of any thinge that was comfortable," Winthrop writes, "she would lye still and fixe her eyes stedfastly upon me, and if I ceased awhile (when hir speeche was gone) she would turn her head towards me, and stirre hir hands as well as she could, till I spake, and then she would be still againe." After death finally came, "she was buried in Groton chancell by my other wife, and hir childe was taken up, and laid with hir." Winthrop characterizes her as "a woman wise, modest, lovinge, and patient of iniuries," and his concluding words are full of pathos: "Hir lovinge and tender regard of my children was suche as might well become a naturall mother: For hir cariage towards myselfe, it was so amiable and observant as I am not able to expresse; it had this onely inconvenience, that it made me delight too much in hir to enjoye hir longe."[25] Out of such pain came new, deeper spiritual understanding.

The long narrative of Thomasine's death notes the passing of days but is not broken into separate daily entries. Likewise, subsequent passages of the "Experiencia" are more fluid in form and more coherent in reflection than Winthrop's previous record keeping. The accompanying change in the writer's character is suggested by a new tendency toward meditation on the Scriptures, instead of the formulation of moral resolutions. This new direction of spiritual discipline required careful, sometimes painful, self-scrutiny.

Acknowledging that "it is a hard thing to love Christ as well in contempt as in glorye," Winthrop confesses that while "it was an easye thing to think gloriously of the martirdome of such as were glorious in worldly respects, as learninge, honor, eminency of place, or great birth," he had previously found it "on the other side no easye thinge to read the histories of such as were vile, and base, and had no other ornament but naked truethe, without some contemptible thoughts abating the worth and estimation of their cause and sufferings." He was troubled by his response to the example of such saints until he considered that "Christ's Kingdome is not of this worlde, and that a Christian as he must beare the Crosse, so he must denye himselfe, which is the harde thinge." But now as with the stories he read, so with the writer himself. "Before I beleeved these things," he observes, "my heart would ever be readye to attribute somewhat to its own worthe and power, in the well doeing of any dutye, notwithstandinge that I have founde the contrarye by much experience." Experience had shown Winthrop that "when I have been forced with wearinesse to give over, even in the very partinge Christ hathe shewed himself unto me, and answered all my desires. And hereby he hath taught me to trust to his free love, and not to the power of selfeworthe of my best prayers, and yet to lett mee see that true prayer, humble prayer, shall never be unregarded."[26] Reflection on years of moral struggle, induced by a period of personal suffering, had brought Winthrop to see his own need for grace.

His double encounter with death produced an insight that would continue to be Winthrop's most characteristic response to life: "It is a better and more safe estate to be prepared to die then to desire deathe, for this commonly hath more selfe love with it then pure love of God: And it is a signe of more strength of faith, and Christian courage, to resolve to fight it out, then to wish for the victorye."[27] The battle between the world and the spirit will continue, but Winthrop no longer seeks its resolution. While still using the term *covenant*, Winthrop now understands it as the mark of an ongoing relationship with God, rather than a moralistic bargain between two parties. Thus instead of castigating himself for moral failure or imagining himself spiritually victorious, he has begun to view Christian selfhood as a process toward an end that God alone controls. Now progress depends on divine grace and love, rather than on a man's effort and estate. In place of a premature grasping for the goal, Winthrop's focus has become the process of Christian life itself.

By virtue of his new understanding of his personal spiritual life, Winthrop acknowledges for the first time that he has become a Puritan. Conversing with God as he writes in his diary, Winthrop admits that "in this way there is least companie, and that those which doe walke openly in this way shall be despised, pointed at, hated of the world, made a byworde, reviled, slandered, rebuked, made a gazinge stocke, called puritans, nice fooles, hipocrites, hair-brainde fellowes, rashe, indiscreet, vain-glorious, and all that naught is." He is assured, however, that "I am in a right course, even the narrowe waye that leads to heaven." Winthrop finds himself now "farre more fitt and cheerefull to the duties of my callinge," not when he denies the world but, instead, "when I hould under the fleshe by temperate diet." Temperance turns out to cut both ways, saving one not only from excessive self-denial but also from unmerited self-assurance: "The unspeakable comfort that I had in the former sweet communion with my Lord Jesus Christ filled me with such ioye, peace, assurance, boldnesse, etc, as I was many tymes readye to incline into the other extreme of lightnesse and securitye, but God gave me grace, when I beganne to wax wanton, to looke into my sinnes and corruptions, and by the consideration of them I was kept under." Too much joy, he finds, leads to melancholic discontent, which in turn renders joy burdensome. Hence "I thinke it good wisdome for me to keepe to a meane in my ioyes, especially in worldly things; moderate comforts being constant and sweeter, or saufer, then suche as beinge exceedinge in measure faile as much in their continuance; for they beinge wasted by passion, are resolved into paine, even as the bodye is most sensible of could, when it hathe beene thoroughlyest warmed by the heat of the fire."[28] Soon he would be seeking a woman with whom to share a lifetime of such sensible warmth and constant comfort.

Knowing that "an unruly horse will more weary himselfe in one miles travaile then a sober horse in 10" and that "so it is when we goe about any dutye where our hearts looke for their libertie," Winthrop was prepared to put on the Puritan harness. For he was learning that "he which would have suer peace and ioye in Christianitye, must not ayme at a condition retyred from the world and free from temptations, but to know that the life which is most exercised with tryalls and temptations is the sweetest, and will prove the safeste. For such tryalls as fall within the compasse of our callinges, it is better *to arme and withstande them* then to avoide and shunne them."[29] Pursuit of his calling would indeed lead to trials and temptations beyond Winthrop's present capacity to imagine. He would need to rely on a strong wife's constant love, and his personal sense of life's direction would have to broaden to encompass a sense of social purpose. But he had discovered the spiritual resources that would enable him to endure new challenges and to prevail in larger conflicts.

The complete manuscript of the notebook Winthrop called his "Experiencia" no longer exists. The passages that have been recorded from this period in his life, though, enable us to see that the act of writing a journal had become his way of discovering the meaning of his inward life. Other English Christians were keeping such journals and, like Winthrop, reading books and treatises by such learned ministers as Thomas Cartwright, William Perkins, Richard Rogers, and William Ames. Their discoveries, and the changes of life their journals record, were the common spiritual experience of Puritanism.

Without any apparent sense of such brotherhood, Winthrop in his conclusions in 1617 might have spoken for them all. Reviewing his early life, "amongst other sinnes which I founde in my selfe, I sawe my great unbeleefe was one of the cheifest." As he summarized the great change he had experienced, Winthrop saw that "whereas before all my care was to gether peace to my heart from the smalnesse of my infirmities etc, nowe my comforte was in bringinge them (smale or great) unto the bloud of Christ," and he felt his "faithe beginne to revive as a man out of a dreame." While previously he had been discouraged from undertaking new duties by such considerations "as the iudgment of the greatest parte, the unlikelyness of success, the evill acceptation of others, the feare of losse, disgrace, health, etc," Winthrop now "perceived that these and suche like rubbes to our faithe were the offences that Christ doth partlye meane there, and I see that they that will take offence from the opinion of others, their owne corrupt reason, common experience, etc, shall never enjoy the comforte of livinge by faith."[30] Given the right set of challenges to face, such an understanding of the "comforte" of living by faith might prepare a man to undertake great things.

Winthrop's more immediate need was to find a woman to love, a mother for his children, a spiritual companion, a source of enduring comfort and strength. He found them all in the remarkable Margaret Tyndal. Even for John Winthrop, however, making her his wife had challenges of its own. Although their family fortunes in land and social standing had risen for three generations, the Winthrops were not yet in league with the Tyndals. Margaret's distinguished father, Sir John Tyndal, had been murdered in 1616 by a man deranged by a verdict in Sir John's court and was considered by Sir Francis Bacon, then attorney general of the crown, to be a martyred saint in the pantheon of English justice. Margaret's siblings and friends, concerned for her welfare and perhaps also for the security of the family estate, seem to have argued against her marriage to Winthrop, on the grounds of his being older, being less well established, and having four children to support. Hence Winthrop made his case to Margaret's mother on the basis of his affection for her daughter, the sincerity of his religious convictions, and the promise of a growing fortune.

There were many journeys between Groton Manor and Much Maplestead, the Tyndal family seat. When the case was finally decided in his favor, Winthrop wrote to Margaret, celebrating her perseverance in "that vnequall conflicte which for my sake thou didst lately sustaine, and wherein yet (although the odds were great) God beinge on they side, thou gatest the victorye." Without God's help, Winthrop believed, "such an invincible resolution could not have been founde in a poor fraile woman," and he urged his beloved to see their triumph as a sign of divine blessing on their marriage. "Let worldly mindes that savour not the things of God," he enjoined, "make sure of great portions with their wives, and large Joyntures from their husbands." Even if "God lettes suche many tymes catche what they can scramble for," in the end "he sends leannesse into their soules." The divine message to Margaret, "whom God hathe ordayned to a better ende," is different and, in Winthrop's transcription, unconsciously prophetic: "He telles you that you are a pilgrime and stranger in this life." Knowing "it is the dearest purchase that must cost a man the losse of his sowle," Margaret has refused the bargain of the fool who "was of the opinion that our common protestantes are of in these dayes (who in the depthe of their devise, wilbe wiser than Christ and his Apostles,) he thought he had found an easier waye to heaven then other men, he thought to save his soule, and yet keepe and love the world too: but he was deceived, and so shall they be also, for the mouthe of the Lord hathe spoken it, let them please themselves never so muche with their owne conceites in the mean tyme."[31] For Winthrop, as for the Puritans more generally, self-denial could be a step toward a more profound self-affirmation, matched with a sense of divine reward more certain than the ephemeral security of the merely self-seeking world. Sometimes, as when mixed with the promises of love, such faith could be expressed in decidedly materialistic terms.

Because she has chosen wisely, Winthrop writes, Margaret need not fear for her well-being. In casting her fate with Winthrop, "havinge mett with (at least in thy perswasion) sufficient assurance of holynesse, thou canst be content to conceive hope of outward happiness even from doubtfull conditions." Indeed, although "by this which I have allreadye written I may seeme to confirm those obiections which they freindes have moved, and to grant that there should be great causes of discouragement offered thee in outward respects," Winthrop closes his letter with reassurance—"I trust I shall make it appeare that thou shalt have no wronge, no disparagement by matchinge with me"—and with a touch of humor—"I confesse it is possible that I may die verye soone, and then they maintenance for a while may be somewhat lesse then convenient, but it is more likely that I may live a fewe yeares with thee, which will certainly better thy condition." While Margaret is to know that "with a little patience, they meanes may be better than 80 li. [pounds] a yeare," she is not to inform her friends, for "I had rather that they should finde it then expect it." Even Margaret's assertive suitor could not have forecast the changing fortunes their future would bring, but the conclusion of his bargaining metaphor begins to express the love they would share for almost thirty years: "Whatsoever shalbe wantinge of that which thy love deserves, my kindest affection shall endeavor to supplie, whilst I liue, and what I leave vnsatisfied (as I never hope to be out of they debt) I will sett over to him who is able, and will recompence thee to the full."[32]

As the wedding day approached, John Winthrop addressed Margaret as "my onely and beloued spouse, my most sweet freind, and faithfull companion of my pilgrimage" and confessed that, "wantinge opportunitye of more familiar communion with thee, which my heart fervently desires, I am constrained to ease the burthen of my minde by this poor helpe of my scriblinge penne." Margaret was a "comely" woman, and to discuss such "trifles" as proper wedding apparel, Winthrop took refuge in writing, "for when I am present with thee my speeche is preiudiced by thy presence, which drawes my minde from it selfe." Yet even from a distance, she has unbalanced him, for his hope that she will dress soberly so that "there might be no discouragement to daunt the edge of my affections" is followed by a fulsome retraction and a touching declaration of the writer's love: "Onely let thy godly kind and sweet carriage towards me, be a fuell to the fire, to minister a constant supplie of meet matter to the confirminge and quickninge of my dull affections: This is one ende why I write so much vnto thee, that if there should be any decaye in kindnesse etc throughe my default, and slacknesse heerafter, thou mightest have some patternes of our first loue by thee, to help the recoverye of such diseases."[33] He need not have worried.

Margaret, an attractive, discerning, strong woman, was wise and loving, and her correspondence when she and John were apart in future years was as warm, practical, insightful, and supportive as her presence evidently continued to be. She bore four sons—Stephen in 1619, Adam in 1620, Deane in 1623, and Samuel in 1627—bringing the number of Winthrop's living children to eight. On the last day of March 1618 Adam Winthrop had assured his new daughter-in-law "that yow shal be happye in matchinge with my soonne, I do heere faithfully promise for him, in the presence of almighty god, that he will alwaies be a most kinde and lovinge husbande vnto yow, and a prouident stuarde for you and yours during his lyfe, and also after his deathe." Ezekial Culverwell's marital invocation, "Let him therefore have your hearts and he will give them back ech to other," was also an auspicious blessing.[34] Their love was an enduring source of strength as John Winthrop, Esquire, lord of the manor of Groton, was drawn deeply into the problems of a wider world.

The 1620s were at once disheartening and enlivening for Winthrop. Even as he saw the economy depressed, the state in turmoil, and true religion besieged, he was also pulled directly into the struggle against the general decline. Winthrop's growing involvement in the Puritan movement and his rise to leadership of the faction that was deciding to leave England reveal a spirit of negative capability, a capacity for invigoration over against the entrophy he and others perceived to be spreading throughout English society. The ability to draw energy for the struggle from the very spreading of the disease is peculiarly characteristic of both Winthrop himself and the Puritan movement to which he was increasingly devoted. His life to this point had prepared Winthrop almost ideally for the large challenges he now faced. For Winthrop and other Puritans, the 1620s were a decade of decision.

The initial catalyst was economic in nature, for a depression in the textile industry soon upset the world the Winthrops had built at Groton Manor. For almost a century the rise of the Winthrop family had depended on a growing textile industry, at first directly with old Adam Winthrop's prominence in the Clothworkers' Company and then indirectly through the rents received from the lands he and his son and grandson had acquired. Hitting hard in the county of Suffolk and soon affecting the country as a whole, the depression could not have come at a worse time for John Winthrop's large family. His eldest son and namesake was ready to enter college and would come of age in 1627, and the other boys would soon be seeking their place in a world of diminishing resources.

With a strong sense of responsibility for those whose welfare and futures depended on him, John Winthrop responded to hard times by turning to his training in the legal profession for additional income, at first locally and then in London. He worked as a private attorney and found some employment drafting legislation for a parliamentary committee, and finally in 1627 Emmanuel Downing, husband of Winthrop's sister Lucy, helped Winthrop secure an appointment as one of three common attorneys in His Majesty's Court of Wards and Liveries. The work was potentially quite lucrative, for this court oversaw the management of estates that had reverted to the king. If an estate that had originally been acquired from the Crown, such as Groton Manor itself, was inherited by an eldest son who was yet a minor, the inheritor became a ward of the Crown, giving the king the right to use all of the estate's lands or, more often, to sell such rights to the highest bidder. The possibilities for misuse and abuse were rife, with litigation and the revenues from it naturally likewise abundant. Here Winthrop's Puritan conscience was exposed firsthand to the corruption he was also witnessing in the sharpening struggles between Parliament and the Crown and, indeed, throughout the metropolis of London.

The Court of Wards required Winthrop to be in London four times a year, for several weeks per session. Because of this responsibility, together with other business and the difficulties of travel, Winthrop was frequently separated from his family. Prevented from establishing a family residence in London by the expense of maintaining two households, Winthrop had quarters with the other lawyers in the Inner Temple. He visited the Downings often and spent time too with the family of Thomas Fones, surviving spouse of Winthrop's deceased sister Anne. But the company of a wide circle of relatives and friends did not lessen his deep affection for his own family. He returned to Groton whenever work permitted and came to rely on regular correspondence to stay in touch with his beloved Margaret. Their letters, along with those passing between Winthrop and his son John, away at Trinity College in Dublin, offer a window into Winthrop's tender affections, his perceptions of the religious, political, and economic ills troubling England, and his growing resolve to discover a way of life beyond the corruption and constrictions of "this sinfull lande."[35]

Like many parents writing to children away at college, Winthrop in his letters to his son John dealt with such mundane matters as arranging payment for tuition, books, fees, and clothing, and he also revealed an abiding concern for his son's spiritual well-being and devotion to learning. With this son he had no cause for alarm, for "I heartyly rejoyce, that [Christ Jesus] hathe withdrawne thy minde from the love of those worldly vanityes, wherewith the moste part of youthe are poisoned, and hathe given thee to discern of and exercise thy selfe in, thinges that are of true worthe." Sometimes he related sad news, as with "the departure of your Grandfather," who "hathe finished his course and is gathered to his people in peace, as the ripe corne into the barne, he thought longe for the daye of his dissolution, and wellcomed it most gladlye. thus is he gone before and we must goe after in our tyme, this advantage he hathe of vs, he shall not see the evill which wee may meet with ere we goe hence: happie those who stande in good termes with God and their owne conscience, they shall not feare evill tydinges and in all changes they shalbe the same." Indeed, given the grievances of England, his son's residence in Dublin even led Winthrop to "wish oft God would open a waye to settle me in Ireland, if it might be for his glorye."[36] However understandable, this wish was not pursued.

Winthrop's letters characteristically express a parent's love and support: "I shall continue to pray for you, and will not be wantinge, to my power, to further your good in every thing, and knowe this, that no distance of place, or lengthe of absence, can abate the affection of a lovinge father towardes a dutyfull well deservinge childe." Evidently John, Jr., reciprocated his father's affection, for Winthrop on occasion had to admonish a homesick son: "Commend me heartyly to your Reverend Tutor: and think not of seeinge England till you may bringe a hood at your backe."[37] Like other parents, Winthrop often hoped his son would experience more fervent religious convictions and sometimes wished his namesake's wide-ranging intellect would settle on some particular profession. Yet although he never became a passionate Puritan, John Winthrop, Jr., was a brilliant, responsible eldest son upon whom his father could always rely. A few years later he even oversaw the sale of the family estate and brought Margaret safely to join her husband in New England.

Winthrop's letters to Margaret, often written at the weary end of a busy day, are full of tender, thoughtful affection. He thanks God for "the constancie and increase of thy true Loue, wherein (I seariously professe) I doe more reioyce then in any earthly blessinge," and misses her companionship: "I am heere where I haue all outward content, most kinde entertainment, good companye and good fare etc: onely the want of thy presence and amiable society makes me weary of all other accomple[men]ts, so deare is thy Loue to me, and so confident am I of the like entertainem[en]t my true affection findes with thee." Unlike more ethereal believers who seek to invest an earthly relationship with the sublime love of Christ for his church, Winthrop tells Margaret of his hope "that we could delight in him as we doe in each other." His letters frequently end with a physical image and pledge: "I embrace thee in the love of a faithfull husband and will ever remaine Thine onely." With Margaret he shared not only the warmth of his feelings but also the depth of his concern for their land: "We have cause to feare the worst, in regarde that all thinges are so farre out of order, and that the sinnes bothe our owne and of the whole lande doe call for iudgmentes rather then blessinges."[38] Such a combination of private affection and public concern led Winthrop to increasingly direct action.

In the winter of 1621–22 Winthrop wrote to his brother-in-law Thomas Fones to express his joy in the recovering health of both of their wives. But his personal joy was clouded by public events: "We might reioyce greatly in our owne private good, if the sence of the present evill tymes, and the feare of worse did not give occasion of sorrowe. The Lo: looke mercifully vpon this sinfull lande, and turne vs to him by some repentance, otherwise we may feare it hath seene the best dayes." Within two years a document written largely in Winthrop's hand detailing "Common Grieuances Groaninge for Reformation" was circulated during the last Parliament of the reign of King James.[39] The authors apparently looked to Parliament for redress of a variety of religious, social, and economic woes: the daily increase of multitudes of papists; the arbitrary removal of local indictments by the Crown; lackadaisical punishment of adultery, whoredom, and incest; unjust charges of sedition levied against groups of believers meeting for prayer and devotions; the scarcity of wood and timber; the extraordinary devastation caused by careless fires; the poor condition of highways; the growing mischief of horse stealing; the decay of the honorable trade of saddlery; the misuse of funds collected by the Crown from the churches; the profusion of scandalous and ignorant ministers; the prohibition of marriages without payment of fees for licenses; great delays in legal proceedings; the holding of appointments in multiple parishes by ministers; punishment of believers who go to another parish to hear sermons when there are none in their own; unfair taxation of the poor and undue loopholes for the rich; the silencing and suspension of many learned ministers who disdain minor ceremonial regulations; the pitiful conditions of orphans and the poor; the strictness of oaths required of church wardens; ministers who practice medicine for profit; the depletion of pheasants and partridges caused by the disorderly sport of hawking by gentlemen; abuse of authority by clerks of weights and measures in the markets; and the manifold oppression of the poor by arrests and imprisonments for every small debt and trespass. Even with such a laundry list of problems, Winthrop wrote to his son that "our Parliament heere is begunne with exceedinge muche comfort and hope." Seeing the problems of the age addressed publicly made him optimistic: "God sende a good ende to these happie beginninges."[40]

Yet while friends thanked Winthrop for his expression "of so many good purposes in the howes of Commons," in private moments he was less sanguine about reform. If "our livelynesse in Christianytye . . . meanes the world shall disclaime vs as none of hirs, and shall refuse to hould out to vs suche full breastes as she dothe to others, this shall not need to trouble vs, but rather may give vs matter of ioye in beinge strangers heere," he confided to Margaret, and "we may looke for our inheritance in a better life." The same faith through which Winthrop continued to look heavenward for final relief from the trials of life released him from any ultimate anxiety and freed him to live confidently in this world. Theirs was "a tyme of much businesse and distraction" given "what the carriage and issue of these late affaires hath been in our countrye," he told his son; hence their trust was in the Lord to "guide vs all wisely and faithfully in the middest of the dangers and discouragementes of these declininge tymes."[41] Indeed, as England's troubles intensified, Winthrop began to consider carefully what to do for the sake of his family and his beliefs. When an alternative did appear, he would be ready to help shape it into a real possibility. Discussing his frustrations with other Puritans who owned estates and held government offices, Winthrop seemed to draw strength from the mounting problems they faced.

The succession of Charles I to the throne in 1625 quashed Puritan hopes for parliamentary reform. Already suspect by virtue of his marriage to a Catholic, Charles disappointed the Puritans further by turning the power of the Church of England over to men who held to what the Puritans saw as the heresy of Arminianism, the belief that faith and, therefore, salvation depend upon human will power more immediately than upon divine grace. If the Puritans sought to tie Charles's hands by refusing to authorize the funds he needed until his policies could be discussed in Parliament, then the king knew what to do. He dissolved Parliament in 1625, then called another and suspended it in short order. In place of legal taxation, Charles attempted to raise funds through a forced loan and imprisoned those who resisted his authority by refusing to pay. Encouraged by their ministers, the Puritans in the House of Commons grew bolder, denying the king's right to dismiss Parliament and calling for the repeal of illegal taxation and the suppression of Arminianism. By 1629 Charles had had enough. Again he dissolved Parliament, this time irrevocably. Like the Hugenots in France and the Protestants in Germany, Puritans in England seemed to have lost the battle.

Winthrop's sons responded to desperate times in ways that exemplified alternatives and, in various ways, concerned their father. Henry adventured to Barbados, where he produced some tobacco so foul that not even his aunts and uncles would buy it. Then he returned to London, forced himself and his riotous companions on his sickly uncle Fones, ran into debt for sumptuous clothing, and hastily married his cousin Elizabeth, without poor Fones's consent, on the grounds of a pretended pregnancy. An exasperated John Winthrop cut off Henry's financial support and then had to tell Margaret to make room for the newlyweds at Groton. The scholarly Forth went the other way and, at an expense that now became a concern, continued to study at Cambridge toward his intended vocation as a minister. John, Jr., joined his father in London, where he studied law until he, too, felt the urge to go abroad to seek his fortune. In 1628 he wanted to sail with an early party of Puritans to New England, but his father's feelings were divided: "Seeinge you haue a resolution to goe to sea I know not wheare you should goe with such religious company and vnder such hope of blessinge, onely I am loth you should think of settlinge there, as yet, but to be goinge and comminge awhile and afterward to doe as god shall offer occasion. you may adventure somewhat in the plantacion at the present, and heerafter more, as God shall giue enlargment."[42] In other words, in the midst of an economic depression, his father needed to sell land to raise capital. Independent but dutiful, John, Jr., delayed traveling until they could get an acceptable price, finally 590 pounds, for the estate at Great Stambridge. When the negotiations dragged on, he left instead for a grand, expensive tour of the Mediterranean.

In private as well as public affairs, these were hard times for true Christians. Winthrop must have responded sympathetically to a letter from the famous Puritan scholar and clergyman John Wilson, who exclaimed, "But alas! what times are these! No man knows what is his owne, or whither that he hath, be not kept for the enemies of god? and of our peace. The good lord turne our hartes to him, and prepare vs to meete him, in true Repentance, and hear the Sighes and Teares of his people, (so many thousandes,) for Christs sake, what hope is left vs, but his mercie?"[43] In short order, a way appeared or was created by men like Winthrop in response to the emergency they felt themselves in. Soon John Wilson and John Winthrop would be leaders of church and state in New England.

By 1629 Winthrop had come to see his family's welfare, even his concern and affection for his wife, in the context of public affairs. "It is a great favour," he wrote to Margaret, "that we may enioye so much comfort and peace in these so euill and declininge tymes and when the increasinge of our sinnes giues vs so great cause to looke for some heauy Scquorge and Judgment to be cominge vpon us." The linkage he felt between private and public experience is shown in his use of first-person pronouns to reflect upon the condition of England, where the Lord's warnings were being disregarded: "We sawe this, and humbled not ourselues, to turne from our euill wayes, but haue prouoked him more then all the nations rounde about vs: therefore he is turning the cuppe towards vs also, and because we are the last, our portion must be, to drinke the verye dreggs which remaine: my deare wife, I am veryly perswaded, God will bringe some heauye Affliction vpon this lande, and that speedylye." Yet he sustains a biblical hope that a remnant of God's people may be saved from the approaching debacle. "If the Lorde seeth it willbe good for vs, he will prouide a shelter and a hidinge place for vs and ours, . . . if not, yet he will not forsake vs." Although he nurtures keen hope against the much deserved retribution, Winthrop counsels Margaret and perhaps himself to adjust their desires to the scale of their trust in God: "If he seeth it not good, to cutt out our portion in these thinges belowe equall to the largnesse of our desires, yet if he please to frame our mindes to the portion he allottes vs, it wilbe as well for vs."[44] Yet however unwise it would be to expect events to match human hopes, the Winthrops' belief in God's active role in history worked strongly against any lasting sense of resignation.

Evidently they discussed the possibility of emigration during one of Winthrop's brief stays at Groton, for he wrote to Margaret that "I am still more confirmed in that Course which I propounded to thee, and so are my brother and sister D[owning] the good Lo: direct and blesse vs in it." He also surmised that he would lose his appointment as attorney to the Court of Wards and Liveries, a loss confirmed, along with the loss of his chamber in the Inner Temple, in mid-June 1629.[45] Winthrop responded to adversity characteristically with action rather than despondency; the next month he and Emmanuel Downing spent two weeks in Lincolnshire with Isaac Johnson and other Puritan gentlemen, evaluating the opportunity of a large-scale emigration to New England.

Winthrop's experience drafting legislation for discussion in Parliament was put to good use as the Puritan focus shifted from ridding England of its immediate abuses to a new strategy of indirect reform. If doors were closing at home, the Puritans did not give up the cause. Some of them simply decided to continue the struggle from afar. In the face of evil and declining times, their commitment to renewal of church and state came to require removal from their native land. Winthrop wrote, revised, and circulated several drafts of observations and arguments for a Puritan "plantation" in New England. The reasons he gave, together with his responses to objections raised in his own mind through discussion and correspondence with other men of substance and standing, summarize the coincidence of his personal and public frustrations.[46] In the colorful language of an early draft, Winthrop makes the following general observations:

1. It will be a great service to the church to carry the gospel abroad "and to rayse a bullwarke against the kingdom of Antichrist which the Jesuites labour to reare vp in all places of the worlde."
2. Given the desolation of true churches throughout Europe and the coming judgment upon England, "who knows, but that God hathe provided this place, to be a refuge for manye, whom he meanes to save out of the general destruction?"
3. "This lande growes wearye of her Inhabitants," so that men are worth less than the earth they walk upon and "so as children neighbours and freindes (especi[ally] if they be poore) are rated the greatest burdens, which if things were right, would be the cheifest earthly bless[ings]."
4. "We are growne to that height of Intemperance in all excesse of Ryot, as no mans estate all most will suffice to keepe sayle with his equalls," to the extent that "it is allmost imposs[ible] for a good and vpright man to maintaine his charge and liue comfortably."
5. "The fountains of learninge and Relig[ion] are so corrupted" that "most Children, even the best wittes and of fayrest hopes, are perverted corrupted and vtterly overthrowne."
6. Since "the whole earthe is the Lordes garden: and he hathe given it to the sons of men to be tilld and improved by them: why then should we stand striving heere for places of habitation?"
7. Nothing is more honorable for Christians than to raise and support a new church in its infancy, especially when it may well be ruined without the help of these particular people. And, finally:

8. If people who "are knowne to be godly and liue in wealthe and prosperitye heere, shall forsake all this to ioine themselues to this Churche, and to runne the hazard with them of a harde and meane condition, it wilbe an example of great vse" to the future by encouraging others to commit themselves to the plantation.

In the political climate of England in the late 1620s, the interpenetration of economic, social, and educational considerations lent additional force to the Puritans' thinking, as Winthrop's list of reasons shows. The breadth of these concerns helps to explain how the religious motivations central to the Puritans' evolving decision enabled them to undertake and in short order to enact the complex preparations required for a large and successful emigration.

There were, of course, objections from some who thought about joining the project, as well as from others who were more inclined to continue the struggle in England. Winthrop's legal training prepared him for arguments and counterarguments, and he seems to have considered them all in finally making up his own mind. The central argument against emigration, dealt with in this early list of reasons as well as in Winthrop's private correspondence and subsequent documents circulated and discussed among the Puritans, concerned the questionable morality of removing so many of the best people from the primary scene of the conflict to which they were so strongly committed. Of course, many more would be staying than going, as he pointed out, but Winthrop had two more persuasive responses to the nagging question of where their ultimate responsibility lay. In the first place, he asserted that they were not actually abandoning the struggle, for the true church is universal, and helping one part strengthens the whole. Moreover, he was convinced that "a future good, if it be greater, may be preferred before a present good that is lesse; and in this respecte, the members of that Church may be of more vse to their mother Churche heere then manye of those whom she shall still keepe in her owne bosome." In other words, leaving England was in truth not separation at all, and the entire emigration was actually undertaken in service to the eventual triumph of the true church at home. The Puritans could not have found a better attorney to argue their case.

Given the close links that had been forged between his private life and his sense of public affairs, Winthrop did not hesitate to publish the personal considerations that compelled him to join the movement:

1. "In all probabilitye, the wellfare of the plantation depends vpon my assistance: for the maine pillers of it beinge gentlemen of highe qualitye, and eminent partes, both for wisdome and godlinesse, are determined to sitt still, if I deserte them."
2. "My meanes heere are so shortned (now my 3 eldest sonnes are come to age) as I shall not be able to continue in this place and imployment where I now am: . . . and if I should let pass this opportunitye, that talent which God hath bestowed on me for publike service, were like to be buried."

3. "I have a lawfull callinge, outwarde, from the Cheife of the plantation, approved by godly and iuditious divines: and inwarde by the inclination of my owne heart to the worke."

4. "My wife and suche of my Children, as are come to yeares of discretion, are voluntaryly disposed to the same course."

5. "In my youth I did seariously consecrate my life to the service of the Churche . . . but it hathe ofte troubled me since, so as I thinke I am the rather bounde to take the opportunitye for spendinge the small remainder of my tyme, to the best service of the Churche which I may."

His analysis of himself and his own circumstances meshed with his reading of the general situation sufficiently to answer any less critical objections. As Winthrop noted in the margin of one draft of the arguments, "when God intends a man to a worke he setts a Byas on his heart so as tho' he be tumbled this way and that way yet his Bias still drawes him to that side, and there he restes at last." In his mind and heart, Winthrop was already on board. If one final obstacle could be overcome, then only the myriad of details remained, which his previous responsibilities on the family estates and in London had prepared Winthrop to organize and discharge.

The last challenge was substantial, and its resolution guaranteed the Puritans' control of their colony as troubled times gave way to chaos and civil war in England. That Winthrop and the other leaders foresaw the problem and dealt with it in advance shows both the enormity of what they were undertaking and also the shrewdness that underwrote its success. In 1628 the king's Council for New England had chartered the New England Company, which sent a small party led by John Endecott to establish a base settlement for the new colony. Like those of every other English colony, the affairs of this venture into the New World were to be governed by a company based in old England, the dealings of which could be easily monitored for the Crown by the council. Given their political experience, however, Winthrop and his fellow Puritans were not willing to sell their estates and cross the ocean only to expose themselves, their families, and their combined wealth to risk of such oversight, particularly in view of their firsthand knowledge of the corruption, intrigue, and enmity at work in England. So when they met and signed an agreement at Cambridge on 26 August 1629, in order that "euery man may without scruple dispose of his estate and afayres as may best fitt his preparacion for this voyage," they bound themselves "in the word of a Christian and in the presence of God" each to be ready "to embarke for the said plantacion by the first of march next . . . to passe the Seas (vnder Gods protection) to inhabite and continue in new England" only upon satisfaction of a significant condition: "Provided alwayes that before the last of September next the whole gouerment together with the Patent for the said plantacion bee first by an order of the Court legally transferred and established to remayne with vs and others which shall inhabite vpon the said plantacion."[47] Somehow in the political turmoil of late 1629 the transfer was made, and the Puritans possessed their own royal charter as The Governor and Company of Massachusetts Bay in New England.

In October a cheerful and hectically busy John Winthrop confided to Margaret: "So it is that [it] hath pleased the Lorde to call me to a further trust in this businesse of the plantation, then either I expected or finde my selfe fitt for (beinge chosen by the Company to be their Gouernor) the onely thinge that I haue comforte of in it is, that heerby I haue assurance that my charge is of the Lorde and that he hath called me to this worke: O: that he would giue me an heart now to answeare his goodnesse to me, and the expectation of his people!"[48] In the next few months Winthrop arranged the sale of his family estate at Groton Manor and the remaining property at Stambridge and agreed that Margaret, who again was pregnant, would remain along with his son John, finally returned from the Mediterranean and now deeply committed to New England, to oversee the final disposition of their affairs and would sail to Massachusetts the following year. As governor, Winthrop led the Puritans in securing ships, provisions, adequate financing, an appropriate array of needed craftsmen, and, most important, godly ministers for their settlement.

During these busy days many tender words passed between John and Margaret, and they agreed to devote the hour between five and six o'clock on Mondays and Fridays to thinking of and praying for one another until they were at last together in New England. On board ship on 28 March 1630, "hauinge tryed our shipps entertainment now more then a weeke, we finde it agree very well with vs, our boyes are well and cheerfull, and haue no mind of home, they lye both with me, and sleepe as soundly in a rugge (for we vse no sheets heer) as euer they did at Groton, and so I doe my selfe (I prayse God)." Cataloging his preparations, he summarized: "We are in all our 11: shippes, about 700: persons passengers; and 240 Cowes, and about 60: horses. the shippe which went from Plimouth carried about 140: persons, and the shippe which goes from Bristowe, carrieth about 80: persons."[49] Once again he pledged his love:

And now (my sweet soule) I must once againe take my last farewell of thee in old England, it goeth verye neere my heart to leaue thee, but I know to whom I haue committed thee. . . . oh how it refresheth my heart to thinke that I shall yet againe see thy sweet face in the lande of the liuinge: that louely countenance, that I haue so much delighted in, and beheld with so great contente! . . . I shall not auoid the remembrance of thee, nor the greife for they absence: thou hast thy share with me, but I hope, the course we haue agreed vpon wilbe some ease to vs both, mundayes and frydayes at 5: of the clocke at night, we whall meet in spiritt till we meet in person. yet if all these hopes should faile, blessed be our God, that we are assured, we shall meet one day, if not as husband and wife, yet in a better condition.[50]

Contrary winds delayed departure, perrmitting a final letter on 3 April, when Winthrop found that "for my selfe, I was neuer at more liberty of bodye and minde these many years."[51] Such freedom toward the future was necessarily complicated by the love Margaret's letters inspired:

I am neuer satisfied with readinge, nor can reade them without teares, but whither they proceed from ioy, sorrowe or desire, or from that consent of Affection which I allwayes holde with thee, I cannot conceiue: Ah my deare heart, I euer helde thee in high esteeme, as they loue and goodnesse hath well deserued, but (if it be possible) I shall yet price thy vertue at a greater rate, and longe more to enjoy thy sweet society then euer before. I am sure thou art not shorte of me in this desire, let vs pray harde and pray in faith, and our God, in his good tyme will accomplish our desire. O, how loth am I to bidd thee Farewell, but since it must be, Farewell, my sweet loue, farewell: Farewell my deare children and familye, the Lord blesse you all, and grant me to see your faces once againe. come (my deare) take him and let him rest in thine armes, who will euer remaine Thy faithfull husband.[52]

With departure so imminent, such was Winthrop's final private farewell. As now with everything in his life, fulfillment of his love for Margaret would occur in New England.

Winthrop's final public farewell was a similar attempt to separate without severing a relationship, or at least to sustain the appearance of a connection that would soon be stretched beyond resemblance by distance and new experience. The Reverend John Cotton from Boston, Lincolnshire, who was soon to join John Wilson as a minister in Boston, Massachusetts, came to Southampton to deliver "God's Promise to His Plantation," by way of confirming the emigrants in their calling to undertake God's work in New England. It was left to Winthrop and his friends in a "Humble Request" from on board the *Arbella* in Yarmouth to assure "the rest of their Brethren in and of the *Church* of ENGLAND" and perhaps to reassure themselves that in crossing the ocean they were not breaking away from the people and the institutions they were leaving behind. Acknowledging "the generall rumor of this solemne Enterprise," they sought their countrymen's prayers, for these emigrants were Puritans, not naive idealists: "Howsoever your charitie may have met with some occasion of discouragement through the misreport of our intentions, or through the disaffection, or indiscretion, of some of us, or rather, amongst us: for we are not of those that dreame of perfection in this world; yet we desire you would be pleased to take notice of the principals, and body of our company, as those who esteeme it our honour, to call the *Church* of *England,* from whence we rise, our deare Mother." Maternal imagery suggested an enduring bond, for "such hope and part as wee have obtained in the common salvation, we have received in her bosome, and suckt it from her breasts." But what they asked was already more than a religiously divided England could deliver: "If any there be, who through want of cleare intelligence of our course, or tendernesse of affection towards us, cannot conceive so well of our way as we could desire, we would intreat such not to despise us, nor to desert us in their prayers & affections." And they promised more than they would themselves be able to sustain: "Wishing our heads and hearts may be as fountaines of teares for your everlasting welfare, when wee shall be in our poore Cottages in the wildernesse, over-shadowed with the spirit of supplication, through the mainfold necessities and tribulations which may not altogether unexpectedly, nor, we hope, unprofitably befall us."[53] However necessary it was to say and however reassuring their "Humble Request" may have been, such skillful rhetoric could not disguise the facts in old or New England.

Yet the assertion was important, for unlike the Pilgrims at Plimouth, the Puritans were not idealistic perfectionists. They went to Massachusetts for the sake of England, hoping by distant example to awaken, refresh, and renew the mother they were leaving. Even when Puritans on both sides of the Atlantic became more engrossed by their own than by each other's affairs, the sense of an audience established by the "Humble Request" remained. It is no wonder that Winthrop believed that the Puritans' journey to and settlement in New England were matters of public record, in the broadest sense of the term, and that his calling was not only to lead the enterprise but also, and perhaps even more important, to write its history for the world.

The family heritage and personal experience that led to his commitment to the Puritan emigration had prepared Winthrop uniquely well for his double role as governor and historian of early New England. He knew the value of family and the importance of land, he was well educated and respected the power of reasoned argument, he had much experience in the private practice and public business of law and justice, he wrote well and was given to examining the events of his life through writing, he knew the coincidence of personal experience and public affairs, he could manage a complex enterprise and was recognized as a leader of men, and he believed deeply in God and knew the Christian life as an ongoing journey through an imperfect world. Like many other immigrants, Winthrop sought space in the New World that might be sufficient for his needs and commensurate with his desires. He was one of the first Americans to create through writing a place where the meaning of his experience could be explored and its significance discovered.

2

Laying Foundations

I N HIS eagerness to be under way, perhaps desiring to couple his story with the beginning of the sacred year, John Winthrop began his journal, *The History of New England,* on Easter Monday, 29 March 1630, with the Puritans riding the seas near the Isle of Wight, awaiting the fair winds that would finally, ten days later, enable them truly to set sail for New England.[1] The governor and other leaders are aboard the *Eagle,* designated the flagship of the eleven vessels and renamed the *Arbella* in honor of Lady Arbella Johnson. Until 8 April the Puritans are in limbo, having cast off but not really departed. Notable visitors, such as Matthew Cradock, the original governor of the company, come aboard the *Arbella* for farewell conferences. Two landsmen are disciplined for a little mischief with "strong water." Some of the gentlewomen go ashore to refresh themselves, while emigrants on board sight English, Dutch, and pirate ships. When at last an east wind enables the ships to set sail, the captain mistakes eight friendly sails for Spanish ships, and the Puritans prepare courageously for battle with the enemies of England. A shipboard militia is organized and armed, bedding is jettisoned, the women and children are sent below, until on closer inspection "our fear and danger was turned to mirth and friendly entertainment." Winthrop's playboy son, Henry, dallies on an errand ashore, finally making the passage on one of the other ships, where he would be less under his father's watchful eye. Thus it is with a mixture of delay, mischief, excitement, and merriment that the Puritans finally put to sea.

Such commonplace events fill the early pages of the journal, giving Winthrop's readers, then and now, a sense of daily life at the outset of the Puritan mission to the New World. Throughout the long voyage, the author simply recounts what occurs, rather than filtering events through the prism of a grand design. The inevitable tedium of the journey is broken by the children's play, the danger of rough weather and the intermittent frustration of calm seas, the disciplining of sailors for occasional mischief at the expense of the faithful, catechisms and weekly sermons when the ministers and people are well, encounters with other ships, sightings of whales, the deaths of two servants and one seaman, and the births of one healthy and one stillborn child. Although he gives brief advice to those who will follow about the importance of wearing warm clothing, Winthrop is more storyteller than moralist. Hence his readers share the experience of the voyage, rather than being told its meaning, and can rejoice along with the Puritans when land is finally sighted.

After two months at sea, on 8 June "we now had fair sun-shine weather, and so pleasant a sweet air as did refresh us, and there came a smell off the shore like the smell of a garden. There came a wild pigeon into our ship, and another small land bird." With minds drenched in biblical imagery, none of the Puritans would have missed the import of the fresh Edenic air or the sign of the birds: their ships, like Noah's ark, were coming to rest in a new world. To people who were coming to see themselves as God's New Israel, the Atlantic was a latter-day Red Sea. Thus for Winthrop's audience back in England, as for the seafarers themselves, the journal tells the story of the voyage as a communal rite of passage. Before setting foot in New England, Winthrop reminded the people he led of the significance of the work they had undertaken. Yet the point of it all was not made in the narrative mode of the journal but in "A Modell of Christian Charity," a sermon Winthrop wrote at sea and delivered on board the *Arbella*.[2]

By not including his sermon in the text of the journal or even referring to its delivery, Winthrop did not confuse telling about his design with showing how the events to which it gave rise unfolded. He had come to believe that the Christian life is more a process of living in an imperfect world than a matter of stamping a predetermined plan upon the vagaries of experience. He had learned to see his personal religious covenant less as a code of moral rules than as a mode of relationship with a gracious God; similarly, Winthrops records in his journal the course of public events as they happened rather than strictly in reference to particular ideas and beliefs. In the sermon he laid out both a model for the Puritan project and a series of reasons supporting it. In reading the history he wrote, we can see how soon the model came apart in the New World, sometimes with Winthrop himself leading the way, while the spiritual insights given as reasons for it became, if anything, increasingly vital to the ongoing life of the Puritan community.

The basic model of Christian love that Winthrop had inherited was static, hierarchical, and utterly traditional: "God Almightie in his most holy and wise providence hath soe disposed of the Condicion of mankinde, as in all times some must be rich some poore, some high and eminent in power and dignitie; others meane and in subieccion." No sane believer in England, or anywhere in Christendom, would have disagreed with that! Yet the reasons and conclusions on which the model was based, and especially the applications Winthrop drew from them, opened possibilities for communal life well beyond the tight system of the model itself. Indeed, although later generations abandoned the explicit model and most of the theological reasons and religious conclusions upon which it was based, some of the applications Winthrop articulated have endured as elements of the American social and political imagination.

Winthrop believed that "there are two rules whereby wee are to walke one towards another: JUSTICE and MERCY," which sustain harmonious relations between the various orders of society and, especially, among Christians. In particular, Christians are to share their bounty with one another, even to the extent of forgiving loans when a brother in Christ cannot repay them, for God's mercy and love in Christ are the ligaments that bind the body of Christians together. The direct applications of such reasoning to the Puritan mission are clear. "Wee are a Company professing our selues fellow members of Christ," who go by mutual consent, with special divine providence and an extraordinary approval of the Christian churches, "to seeke out a place of Cohabitation and Consorteshipp vnder a due forme of Goverment both ciuil and ecclesiasticall." Hence for religious reasons, "the care of the publique must oversway all private respects," and even in practical civil terms "perticuler estates cannott subsist in the ruine of the publique." The goal, then, is to improve our own lives in service to God and the church so that "our selues and posterity may be the better preserued from the Common corruptions of this euill world." Since our goal is extraordinary, "wee must not content our selues with vsuall ordinary meanes whatsoever we did or ought to haue done when wee liued in England, the same must wee doe and more allsoe where wee goe: That which the most in theire Churches maineteine as a truthe in profession onely, wee must bring into familiar and constant practise." In their new situation the Puritans were actually to do what could only be professed in England.

Together with special opportunity came a special obligation. For "when God giues a speciall Commission he lookes to haue it stricktly obserued in every Article," and "wee are entered into Covenant with him for this worke," therefore "the onely way to avoyde this shipwracke and to provide for our posterity is to followe the Counsell of Micah, to doe Justly, to loue mercy, to walke humbly with our God, for this end, wee must be knitt together in this worke as one man, wee must entertaine each other in brotherly Affection, wee must be willing to abridge our selues of our superfluities, for the supply of others necessities, wee must vphold a familiar Commerce together in all meekenes, gentelnes, patience and liberallity, wee must delight in eache other . . . allways hauing before our eyes our Commission and Community in the worke." If we do these things we shall prevail against any odds, and "hee shall make vs a prayse and glory, that men shall say of succeeding plantations: the lord make it like that of New England: for wee must Consider that wee shall be as a Citty vpon a hill, the eies of all people are vppon us." As Moses told the people of Israel, "Beloued there is now sett before vs life, and good, deathe and euill." Like the Israelites, we are commanded to love God and to do his will "that wee may liue and be multiplyed, and that the Lord our God may blesse vs in the land whether wee goe to possesse it: But if our heartes shall turne away soe that wee will not obey, but shall be seduced and worshipp other Gods our pleasures, and proffitts, and serue them; it is propounded vnto vs this day, wee shall surely perishe out of the good Land whether wee passe over this vast Sea to possesse it; Therefore lett vs choose life, that wee, and our Seede, may liue; by obeying his voyce, and cleauing to him, for hee is our life, and our prosperity." Such was Winthrop's model and his dream of how Massachusetts might truly be a new England. For better or worse, the New World provided an environment with material and spiritual seductions beyond anyone's capacity to imagine. The Puritans were "knit together" by the hardships of the early years, but they faced unforeseen challenges almost as soon as their feet touched dry land.

The first question, of course, was exactly where, and how closely together, they should live. What they saw as New England had been an Indian homeland for centuries, and Winthrop's Puritans were not even the first Englishmen to settle in Massachusetts. A more radical group had separated entirely from the Church of England, moving first to Amsterdam and then to Massachusetts in 1620. By the time the Puritans landed, approximately three hundred of these Pilgrims lived in a separate colony known as the Plimouth Plantation. In addition, two brief settlements at Weymouth, the first led by Thomas Weston and the second by Robert Gorges, had been abandoned, and a settlement at Nantasket had broken up and moved to Cape Ann, as a fishing outpost presided over by Roger Conant. A few free spirits lived for several years at "Merry-Mount" with Thomas Morton, and their sporadic licentiousness agitated their new Puritan neighbors. Several individual Englishmen already occupied lands within Massachusetts Bay: Samuel Maverick on Noddle's Island; William Blackstone at Shawmut, shortly to become Boston; and Thomas Walford at Mishawum, soon the site of Puritan Charlestown. The Puritans themselves had sent John Endecott in 1628 and Francis Higginson in 1629 to bolster a plantation begun in 1626 at Naumkeag and now known as Salem. Endecott's governorship over the three hundred souls scratching out a living at Salem was subordinate to The Governor and Company of Massachusetts Bay. Governor Cradock had been sending Endecott instructions from England, and now the authority of the two original governors was united as Winthrop arrived with charter in hand to take direct charge of the colony. Some eight hundred people came over with Winthrop, and more soon followed, thus establishing Puritan dominance in New England and also presenting the Puritans with the problem of maintaining a sense of community among so many people. The hardships of settling into a new land and the challenge of physical survival consumed the early years, and Winthrop proved equal to the task of laying the foundations for an enduring society.

"A fine fresh smell from shore" continued as the *Arbella* tacked her way along the Massachusetts coast. The Puritans saw English fishermen and were greeted on board by Isaac Allerton, one of the financial backers known as Adventurers at the Plimouth Plantation. Governor Endecott and the Reverend Samuel Skelton came aboard from Salem, and Winthrop's Puritans finally set their feet upon New England soil on 12 June: "We that were of the assistants [the governing body of the Company], and some other gentlemen, and some of the women, and our captain, returned with them to Nahumkeck, where we supped with a good venison pasty and good beer, and at night we returned to our ship, but some of the women stayed behind. In the mean time most of our people went on shore upon the land of Cape Ann, which lay very near us, and gathered store of fine strawberries." After such welcome refreshment, several Indians greeted Winthrop's party on board, and the *Arbella* finally dropped anchor in a safe harbor on 14 June, when most of the Puritans moved ashore. They were no longer leaving England or journeying to New England. Like all immigrants, their first concern was "to find out a place for our sitting down."

When the other ships in the Puritan fleet arrived in early June, some were in good condition, others had lost passengers anad livestock at sea, and many passengers of one, the *Success,* were nearly starved. On the voyage and in the months ahead, no one was immune to hardship and death. Soon Winthrop himself felt the sting. Yet a one-line observation on 2 July, "My son Henry Winthrop was drowned at Salem," dramatically underscores his understanding of the journal he was writing as a history of public events, rather than an inward narrative in which he might examine private experiences or express personal feelings. In letters to Margaret, he spoke more freely: We haue mett with many sadd and discomfortable thinges, . . . and the Lordes hande hath been heavy vpon my selfe in some verye neere to me: my sonne Henry, my sonne Henrye, ah poore childe, yet it greiues me much more for my deare daughter," Henry's wife, Elizabeth. Even privately, hardship produced courage instead of despair: "Yet for all these thinges (I prayse my God) I am not discouraged, nor doe I see cause to repent, or dispaire of those good dayes heere, which will make amends for all."[3] Henry's profligate ways would perplex his father no more; his young widow, now more than ever a member of the family, came to New England with Margaret the next year. Despite private grief, John Winthrop was a public man with a colony to begin in the face of mounting difficulties.

With the arrival of all the ships, "a day of thanksgiving in all the plantations" was kept on Thursday, 8 July. Six weeks later the Massachusetts Bay Company held its first official meeting, or court, in Charlestown, and after keeping a fast on 27 August, the first congregation of believers was organized as a church, ordaining John Wilson as their minister, Increase Nowell as ruling elder, and William Gager and William Aspinall as deacons. In this ceremony the Puritans were conscious of beginning a new church, with the congregation ordaining its leaders by solemnly laying their hands upon them. Yet they wanted to remain Puritans, not become Separatists, so "we used imposition of hands, but with this protestation by all, that it was only as a sign of election and confirmation, not of any intent that Mr. Wilson should renounce his ministry he received in England." As the people carved out farms and established towns, they soon organized additional churches and ordained other men to lead them. However much the Puritans sought to convince themselves that they were preserving ties to England while building new institutions, both the Company and the churches soon developed new patterns of organization more suited to the conditions of life in New England.

Likewise, however much the first entries in Winthrop's journal that were written on New England soil chart in a matter-of-fact manner the organization of Puritan institutions, the terseness of the writing and the long gaps between entries suggest that the writer, like the other Puritans, had more pressing business. Indeed, the subsequent entries tell a more desperate story:

September 20. Mr. Gager died. September 30. About two in the morning, Mr. Isaac Johnson died; his wife, the lady Arbella, of the house of Lincoln, being dead about one month before. He was a holy man, and wise, and died in sweet peace, leaving some part of his substance to the colony. The wolves killed six calves at Salem, and they killed one wolf. Thomas Morton adjudged to be imprisoned, till he were sent into England, and his house burned down, for his many injuries offered to the Indians, and other misdemeanours. Capt. Brook, master of the Gift, refused to carry him. Finch of Watertown had his wigwam burnt and all his goods. Billington executed at Plimouth for killing one. Mr. Phillips, the minister of Watertown, and others, had their hay burnt. The wolves killed some swine at Saugus. A cow died at Plimouth, and a goat at Boston, with eating Indian corn.

With all the sickness, the Puritans wanted fresh water, and Charlestown had only one fresh spring. Winthrop and most of the others, therefore, moved over to Boston, but the deaths increased as winter approached: "October 23. Mr. Rossiter, one of the assistants, died." More soon followed. Experience had taught them that life is a struggle, but the prospects in New England were bleaker than even the Puritans expected.

Thomas Dudley wrote privately to the countess of Lincoln, "We found the Colony in a sad and unexpected condition, above eighty of them being dead the winter before, and many of those alive weak and sick; all the corn and bread amongst them all hardly sufficient to feed them a fortnight, insomuch that the remainder of a hundred and eighty servants we had the two years before sent over, coming to us for victuals to sustain them, we found ourselves wholly unable to feed them," since some of the planned provisions had not actually been shipped, "whereupon necessity enforced us, to our extreme loss, to give them all liberty."[4] In the fearful account of the famous Captain John Smith of Virginia, after a turbulent voyage cost the Puritans much of their livestock and left many passengers sick, "in this perplexed estate, after ten weekes, they arrived in New England at severall times, where they found threescore of their people dead, the rest sicke, nothing done, but all complaining, and all things so contrary to their expectation, that now every monstrous humor began to shew itself." Endecott's advance party turned out to confront Winthrop's Puritans with additional problems rather than well-laid preparations for settlement. Yet, as Smith continues: "Notwithstanding all this, the noble Governour was no way disanimated, neither repents him of his enterprise for all those mistakes, but did order all things with that temperance and discretion, and so releeved those that wanted with his own provision, that there is six or seven hundred remained with him, and more than 1600 English in all the Country, with three or foure hundred head of Cattell."[5] The amount of work required for mere survival left little time for the pomp and circumstance befitting the foundational events of a new society and even less time, or energy, for the writing of history.

Fortunately Winthrop thrived on action, particularly in the face of adversity. Even when writing to Margaret about the "mortalitye sicknesse and trouble" in New England, he was moved from trial to affirmation: "Yet we may not looke at great thinges heer, it is enough that we shall haue heauen, though we should passe through hell to it. we heer enjoye God and Jesus Christ, is not this enough? What would we haue more? I thanke God, I like so well to be heer, as I doe not repent my comminge: and if I were to come againe, I would not haue altered my course, though I had foreseene all these Afflictions: I neuer fared better in my life, neuer slept better, neuer had more content of minde, which comes meerly of the Lordes good hand, for we haue not the like meanes of these comfortes heere which we had in England, but the Lord is allsufficient."[6] According to one eyewitness, "And for the Governor himselfe, I haue observed him to be a discreete and sober man, givinge good example to all the planters, wearinge plaine apparell, such as may well beseeme a meane man, drinking ordinarily water, and when he is not conversant about matters of justice, putting his hand to any ordinarye labour with his servants, ruling with much mildness, and in this particular I observed him to be strict in execution of Justice upon such as have scandalized this state, either in civill or ecclesiasticall government, to the great contentment of those that are best affected, and to the terror of offenders."[7] In a few years Winthrop's "mildness" would get him into trouble with the more zealous among the saints, but no one was resisting his help now.

As word of the governor's work reached England, his friend and supporter John Humfrey wrote to Winthrop of his fear, given "that you will neede time and strength for ordinarie occasions," not to "bee prodigal of your precious health." Humfrey's advice shows that he knew his correspondent well: "What the lord layes upon you, hee is able and faithful to enable you unto, and hee that knowes your strength I dare warrant you will exercise it to the utmost, but bee not barbarously cruel unto your selfe, by thinking eyther to superrogate or superinduce upon your selfe more then you have strength to beare, and then the lorde in his wisedome and mercie imposeth upon you. Some neede the spurre, but you the reine, your exesse may be of more daungerous consequence then their defect and indeede the greater sin, being this would bee greatest against the publicke, theirs cheifely against their owne private, and but with a reflexive or secondary respect against the common good."[8] The notable events Winthrop recorded during his first year in New England need to be viewed against this background of widespread hardship, sickness, and death. Winthrop's liberality in helping the sick, in dispensing his own provisions for the common good, and in resolving arguments among the Puritans, while dealing sharply with any whose actions undermined the community's reputation or its strength of purpose, helped the group survive a harsh winter and augmented Winthrop's authority as their governor.

In October Winthrop restrained the drinking of toasts at his own table, in order to quell those insincere declarations of affection that such drinking might encourage, and his example spread. But soon it was the relentless cold outside, rather than the feigned warmth within, that truly threatened the Puritan settlement. Christmas Eve was "so cold as some had their fingers frozen, and in danger to be lost." Three of the governor's servants were driven off course by strong winds and somehow survived a night without fire or food, "but the fingers of two of them were blistered with cold, and one swooned when he came to the fire." Two days later, to make matters worse, "the rivers were frozen up, and they of Charlton could not come to the sermon at Boston till the afternoon at high water." Several who tried to reach Plimouth by sea had their craft broken up by the strong winds. Upon reaching shore, "some had their legs frozen into the ice, so as they were forced to be cut out." Despite help from Indians, several died from cold and exposure. On the other hand, fire was not always friendly, for some of the hastily built houses burned to the ground.

In early February the ship *Lyon* arrived. Among its twenty passengers was Roger Williams, "a godly minister" who would soon stir up spiritual fires. The *Lyon* also carried a more immediately needed resource among its two hundred tons of provisions, for "the poorer sort of people (who lay in tents, &c.) were much afflicted with the scurvy, and many died, especially at Boston and Charlestown; but when this ship came and brought store of juice of lemons, many recovered speedily. It hath been always observed here," Winthrop could not resist noting on 10 February, "that such as fell into discontent, and lingered after their former conditions in England, fell into the scurvy and died." Concerning those who foresaw such hardship and did more than merely complain and long for former comforts, Winthrop likewise observed on 18 February: "Of those which went back in the ships this summer, for fear of death or famine, &c. many died by the way and after they were landed, and others fell very sick and low, &c." In the stalwart leader's mind, the Puritans' struggle against that freezing winter had knit the community together. Their courage and endurance, rather than the hardships they suffered, were foremost in Winthrop's thoughts as he resolutely refused to consider suggestions from Puritans in England that the colony be moved south toward a gentler climate. Yet spiritual warmth and material comforts, within a few years, would weaken the community and challenge the governor's leadership.

As 1630 changed to 1631 in March, according to the Puritan chronology, the record of events in Winthrop's journal became more positive. Starvation and sickness no longer threatened the colony. Social relations and trade with the Indians seemed to be going well. But rain and warm weather, however auspicious for planting, were of little help in coping with a shortage almost as serious as the winter's lack of food, namely, the unmet need for qualified, sincere ministers of the gospel for the churches of Massachusetts. Hence on 1 April, after commending Winthrop and two others for the service of "prophecy," or preaching, the Reverend John Wilson departed for England, to search for godly ministers for Massachusetts and to try to convince his wife to move to New England. In Wilson's absence, at a court held in Boston on 12 April, the magistrates of the Bay Colony had their first encounter with the unusual opinions of Roger Williams. They found it strange that the church at Salem had called Williams to the ministry "whereas Mr. Williams had refused to join with the congregation at Boston, because they would not make a publick declaration of their repentance for having communion with the churches of England, while they lived there." When disputes arose, Winthrop traveled to reason with the churches. He went first to Salem to help the people see that it was indeed an error to hold that the church of Rome was a true church, and then, later, he went to Watertown to disentangle more hurt religious feelings. In the first instance, he asserted that it was truly an error to believe that Catholic churches were truly Christian; yet in the second instance, it was also wrong to refuse to share Communion with a fellow Christian who had fallen victim to such errors. Fortunately, Winthrop was able to defuse many such conflicts.

Just as he had learned to see his personal spiritual life as a journey within an imperfect world, so Winthrop now mediated disputes by arguing for "a necessitye of reformation from the Corruptions of Antechrist which hath defiled the Christian Churches, and yet without an absolute separation from them, as if they were no Churches of Christ." In his view, it made no sense to castigate sincere believers, "for althoughe the most part are ignorant (the

49

more is their sinne and our greife) yet whores and drunkards they are not: weake Christians they are indeed, and the weaker for want of that tender Care, that should be had of them." Instead of name-calling, perfectionists should look to their own "spirituall pride," and honest Christians should beware of what Winthrop derided as "the Charity of these harsh spiritts."[9] Puritans in later generations bemoaned the decline of the religion, but in its early years the colony suffered more from an excess than a deficiency of religious zeal.

Perhaps his ability to negotiate both sides of such issues led to Winthrop's reelection as governor in 1631. In any event, at a general court in Boston on 17 May, "the former governor was chosen again, and all the freemen of the commons were sworn to this government." Winthrop's simple language makes a virtual revolution seem like a natural development. For the Company records show that at a previous meeting Winthrop had suggested that the assistants, or the governing board, be selected not merely by the members of the Company itself but by all the freemen, and that all of the freemen present had voted in favor of the change. In effect, the Company became a commonwealth, by consent of the governed. The freemen were bound to obey the decisions of the assistants whom they elected, yet their leaders were no longer so much the executive officers of a corporation as the legislators of a state. Indeed, when the people of Watertown objected to paying a tax for fortifying a new town, they were called to Boston, where, after some debate, they came to understand the important change that had occurred. As Winthrop notes on 17 February: "The ground of their errour was, for that they took this government to be no other but as of a mayor and aldermen, who have not power to make laws or raise taxations without the people; but understanding that this government was rather in the nature of a parliament, and that no assistant could be chosen but by the freemen, who had power likewise to remove the assistants and put in others, and therefore at every general court (which was to be held once every year) they had free liberty to consider and propound any thing concerning the same, and to declare their grievances, without being subject to question, or, &c. they were fully satisfied; and so their submission was accepted, and their offence pardoned." Winthrop writes of this momentous change as a natural progression in the New England way, rather than as a crack in the design he had propounded in "A Modell of Christian Charity." He would never be able to tolerate the idea of pure democracy, but he seems to have understood virtually from the outset that the authority of magistrates rests securely upon their election by the citizens whom they govern.

A similarly momentous change occurred in the governor's personal life in 1631, for in early November his beloved Margaret, John, Jr., and his wife, and the other members of the Winthrop family arrived in Massachusetts. Before their departure, Winthrop had written to advise Margaret: "For our little daughter, doe as thou thinkest best. the Lord direct thee in it. if thou bringest her, she wilbe more trouble to thee in the shipp then all the rest. I knowe my sister wilbe tender of her till I may send for her."[10] But Margaret brought the baby along with the rest of the family aboard the *Lyon,* which carried the Reverend John Eliot and sixty other Puritans. In his journal Winthrop noted that the ship had had a successful voyage, with none dying "but two children, whereof one was the governour's daughter Ann, about one year and a half old, who died about a week after they came to sea." Death was not a stranger in seventeenth-century England. While separated from her husband, Margaret had also borne the sickness and death of Winthrop's son Forth, just completing his studies for the ministry and engaged to be married on the eve of his turning twenty-one. Margaret had indeed become a mother to all of John's children. Fortunately, John, Jr., was there to share her grief, to coordinate the complex details of selling a manor whose lord had crossed the Atlantic, to collect debts and pay bills for the provisions so desperately needed in Massachusetts, and to arrange the family's removal to New England. Despite private sadness, their arrival was a joyful and widely celebrated reunion, for "most of the people, of the near plantations, came to welcome them, and brought and sent, for divers days, great store of provisions, as fat hogs, kids, venison, poultry, geese, partridges, &c., so as the like joy and manifestation of love had never been seen in New England. It was a great marvel, that so much people and such store of provisions could be gathered together at so few hours' warning." On 11 November "we kept a day of thanksgiving at Boston," with Governor William Bradford coming from Plimouth to join the celebration. After the reunion they had so strongly desired, John and Margaret Winthrop would be together, except for occasional brief separations, for virtually all of both their lives.

All was not harmonious in Massachusetts, though, and not all those in positions of leadership had Winthrop's balanced judgment. The quick-tempered, soldierly original governor John Endecott wrote to Winthrop from Salem of his frustration at having missed a session of the court: "Sir, I desired the rather to have beene at court because I heare I am much complayned on by goodman Dexter, for striking him. I acknowledge I was too rash in strikeing him, understanding since that it is not lawfull for a justice of the peace to strike. But if you had seene the manner of his carriadge, with such daring of mee with his armes on kembow etc. It would have provoked a very patient man." Writing of the incident, Endecott had none of Winthrop's restraint: "But I will write noe more of it but leave it till we speak before you face to face. Onely thus farre further, that he hath given out if I had a purse he would make me empty it, and if he cannot have justice here he will doe wonders in England, and if he cannot prevale there, hee will trie it out with mee heere at blowes. Sir, I desire that you will take all into consideration. If it were lawfull to trie it at blowes and hee a fitt man for mee to deale with, you should not heare me complaine; but I hope the Lord hath brought me off from that course."[11] Their colony's survival depended on men and women of strong will, and Winthrop's chief challenge as governor was to find ways of dispensing justice while keeping Puritan passions within the community's bounds. Isolation made the generally raucous character of seventeenth-century English life risky in Massachusetts Bay. Poised on the edge of a wilderness, the Puritans needed to resolve the normal disputes of everyday life without provoking unwanted oversight from England or arousing the hostility of the native inhabitants. Theirs was a precarious balancing act.

The English were capable of seeing divine providence in plagues among the Indians that eased the acquisition of land for settlements, but Winthrop's journal also records numerous Puritan attempts to treat the native inhabitants of the land fairly. Indian leaders known as sachems and sagamores were entertained in the governor's home, some trading occurred, and the Puritans and Indians attempted to deal justly with one another by punishing the crimes that contact inevitably engendered. Indians made reparations for cattle they killed, for example, and on the Puritan side, an Englishman was executed for murdering an Indian, a young man was whipped for making sexual advances toward a squaw, and a gentleman who stole corn from Indians was made to restore it twofold. He was also degraded from the title of a gentleman, and the servants who had helped him were whipped. Organized violence occurred between rival Indian groups, but not in the early years between Indians and English. On 11 October 1631 Winthrop records an amusing vignette which shows his ability as a teller of stories in which he is himself a character and also suggests some of the ambivalence of contact between the two cultures:

The governor, being at his farm house at Mistick, walked out after supper, and took a piece in his hand, supposing he might see a wolf, (they came daily about the house, and killed swine and calves, &c.;) and, being about a half a mile off, it grew suddenly dark, so as, in coming home, he mistook his path, and went till he came to a little house of Sagamore John, which stood empty. There he stayed, and having a piece of match in his pocket, (for he always carried about him match and a compass, and in summer time snake-weed,) he made a good fire near the house, and lay down upon some old mats, which he found there, and so spent the night, sometimes walking by the fire, sometimes singing psalms, and sometimes getting wood, but could not sleep. It was (through God's mercy) a warm night; but a little before day it began to rain, and, having no cloak, he made shift by a long pole to climb up into the house. In the morning, there came thither an Indian squaw, but perceiving her before she had opened the door, he barred her out; yet she stayed there a great while essaying to get in, and at last she went away, and he returned safe home, his servants having been much perplexed about him, and having walked about, and shot off pieces, and hallooed in the night, but he heard them not.

In ensuing years, ambivalence issued less in such comic relief and more often in death and destruction, when contact degenerated into conflict.

Once the very survival of their colony was no longer at issue, the Puritans turned their attention to drawing boundaries, not only between themselves and the Indians but in virtually every aspect of their common life. Even in a community that was to be knit together as one person by the love of Christ, considerable rivalry existed between strong individuals. For the sake of the community, relations between the important men of the colony needed to be harmonious, and soon it became necessary to distinguish between their rights as individuals and their authority as elected leaders. Jealousy between leading men threatened to burst into bitter words, with rivals trading charges about abuse of power, especially when Thomas Dudley was second in authority to Winthrop, which was often the case.

When provoked, Winthrop could be arrogant, and Dudley's short temper and vanity were often provocative. On 3 April 1632 "at a court in Boston, the deputy, Mr. Dudley, went away before the court was ended, and then the secretary delivered the governour a letter from him, directed to the governour and assistants, wherein he declared a resignation of his deputyship and place of assistant; but it was not allowed." On 1 May Winthrop and the other assistants met privately to consider Dudley's attempted desertion. They knew that "his main reason was for publick peace; because he must needs discharge his conscience in speaking freely; and he saw that bred disturbance." But they all agreed "that he could not leave his place, except by the same power that put him in." Nevertheless, Dudley was obdurate, even though elections would be held at the next meeting of the general court in only a week.

Then the mudslinging began in earnest, with Dudley being criticized for "some bargains he had made with some poor men, members of the same congregation, to whom he had sold seven bushels and an half of corn to receive ten for it after harvest, which the governor and some others held to be oppressing usury, and within compass of the statute; but he persisted to maintain it to be lawful, and there arose hot words about it, he telling the governour, that, if he had thought he had sent for him to his house to give him such usage, he would not have come there; and that he never knew any man of understanding of other opinion; and that the governor thought otherwise of it, it was his weakness. The governour took notice of these speeches, and bare them with more patience than he had done, upon a like occasion, at another time." The criticism of Dudley did not stop there: "Upon this there arose another question, about his house. The governour having formerly told him, that he did not well to bestow such cost about wainscoting and adorning his house, in the beginning of a plantation, both in regard of the necessity of publick charges." To this Dudley responded "that it was for the warmth of his house, and the charge was little, being but clapboards nailed to the wall in the form of wainscot." Evidently it was quite an afternoon, for "these and other speeches passed before dinner." Yet if Dudley's temper was hot, it was not lasting, for a week later "the deputy governor, Thomas Dudley, Esq., having submitted the validity of his resignation to the vote of the court, it was adjudged a nullity, and he accepted of his place again, and the governour and he being reconciled the day before, all things were carried very lovingly amongst all, &c. and the people carried themselves with much silence and modesty." Nevertheless, if Dudley did not stay mad, he did not stay calm either.

In early August, "being still discontented with the governor," Dudley complained to two leading ministers "partly for that the governour had removed the frame of his house, which he had set up at Newtown, and partly for that he took too much authority upon him." Meeting with Dudley and five elders, Winthrop maintained that he had built his house as promised at Newtown but that none of the other assistants would build there and that his neighbors in Boston, being discouraged by Dudley himself from moving to Newtown, had reminded him of "the promise he made to them when they first sate down with him at Boston, viz. that he would not remove, except they went with him." The ministers decided "that the governour was in fault for removing of his house so suddenly, without conferring with the deputy and the rest of the assistants; but if the deputy were the occasion of discouraging Boston men from removing it would excuse the governor" somewhat but not completely. In such a manner Winthrop could easily be magnanimous: "The governour, professing himself willing to submit his opinion to the judgment of so many wise and godly friends, acknowledged himself faulty." He was content to lose small battles.

After dinner things heated up. First Dudley protested "that what he should charge the governour with, was in love, and out of his care of the publick, and that the things which he would produce were but for his own satisfaction, and not by way of accusation. Then demanded he of him the ground and limits of his authority, whether by the patent or otherwise." This was the heart of the matter, and Winthrop asserted that the patent gave more authority to the governor than to the other assistants, whereupon "the deputy began to be in passion, and told the governour, that if he were so round, he would be round too. The governour bad him be round, if he would. So the deputy rose up in great fury and passion, and the governour grew very hot also, so as they both fell into bitterness; but, by mediation of the mediators, they were soon pacified." Dudley then charged Winthrop with seven particular abuses of power, involving such matters as Winthrop's lending twenty-eight pounds of his own gunpowder to help the Pilgrims at Plimouth "upon their urgent distress, their own powder proving naught, when they were to send to the rescue of their men at Sowmasett," or Winthrop's permitting "the people of Watertown, falling very short of corn the last year," to build a weir to catch enough fish to enrich their soil, or Winthrop's staying the banishment of two men because "being in the winter, they must otherwise have perished." In responding to Dudley's heavy-handed complaints, Winthrop "confessed, that it was his judgment, that it were not fit, in the infancy of a commonwealth, to be too strict in levying fines, though severe in other punishments," and argued that "if he had made some slips, in two or three years' government," then these were because he, "for want of a publick stock, had disbursed all common charges out of his own estate; whereas the deputy would never lay out one penny." Furthermore, Winthrop was accused of exceeding his authority as governor in staying the winter banishment of two men until the next court, but Dudley himself in the interim had discharged them of their need to reappear and let them go to Virginia.

Finally the real issue came out, with Dudley charging "that the governour intended to make himself popular, that he might gain absolute power, and bring all the assistants under his subjection." Winthrop found all of this "very improbable, seeing the governour had propounded in court to have an order established for limiting the governour's authority, and had himself drawn articles for that end, which had been approved and established by the whole court; neither could he justly be charged to have transgressed any of them." But Dudley was not to be pacified: "So the meeting breaking up, without any other conclusion but the commending the success of it by prayer to the Lord, the governour brought the deputy onward of his way, and every man went to his own home." Winthrop the historian advises the reader, "See two pages after," and there he concludes: "Notwithstanding the heat of contention, which had been between the governour and deputy, yet they usually met about their affairs, and that without any appearance of any breach or discontent: and ever after kept peace and good correspondency together, in love and friendship." With a jealous, would-be martinet like Dudley as second in command, Winthrop was wise to introduce legislation clarifying and limiting the governor's authority. Such orders would protect his administration from roundhouse attacks like that of Dudley's in 1632. Perhaps more important, such boundaries would safeguard the stability of the colony when men less balanced gained the governorship. When Thomas Dudley was elected governor two years later, was he frustrated by the limitations of authority that his petty attacks on Winthrop had inspired?

At the private meeting of the assistants in May, after Dudley's attempted resignation and his criticisms of Winthrop had been aired, Winthrop prepared his fellow magistrates for a dramatic change in the political process.

"After dinner, the governour told them that he had heard, that the people intended, at the next general court, to desire, that the assistants might be chosen anew every year, and that the governour might be chosen by the whole court, and not by the assistants only." Upon hearing this, Dudley "grew into passion, and said, that then we should have no government, but there would be an interim, wherein every man might do what he pleased, &c. This was answered and cleared in the judgment of the rest of the assistants, but he continued stiff in his opinion, and protested he would then return back to England." Dudley's distemper notwithstanding, one week later the elections began to be held in this fashion. By yielding to the people's desire for annual elections with broader participation in the selection of their leaders, Winthrop and the others enhanced the stability of the colony.

Without referring to democracy, on 8 May 1632 Winthrop noted this important second step in the colony's political development and its conservative consequence: "Whereas it was (at our first coming) agreed, that the freemen should choose the assistants, and they the governour, the whole court agreed now, that the governour and assistants should all be new chosen every year by the general court, (the governour to be always chosen out of the assistants;) and accordingly the old governour, John Winthrop, was chosen; accordingly all the rest as before, and Mr. Humfrey and Mr. Coddington also, because they were daily expected." The immediate consequence of liberalizing the electoral process was the continuity of the incumbents. If it meant that less qualified men might be elected in future years, the change also meant that the people would be able to restore the stability of their government in the face of a genuine crisis. The lines between the governed and their governors were being redrawn, at least in theory, with less emphasis on inherited status or innate characteristics and more on popular control.

If the boundaries between the people and their leaders were becoming clearer in one sense, they became cloudier in others. Taxation for the common defense raised the question of the relations between Boston as the center and the other towns as the peripheries of the colony. This became an issue that simply would not go away. To establish a way of coping with this inevitably increasing tension, in early May "every town chose two men to be at the next court, to advise with the governour and assistants about the raising of a publick stock, so as to what they should agree upon should bind all." Ensuing years saw considerable tension between these more democratic deputies from the towns and the more aristocratic magistrates who represented the colony at large. Several generations later the cry "No taxation without representation" led to the dumping of British goods in Boston Harbor; in 1632 the development of a representative political system enabled work to begin on the construction of a fort "upon the Corn Hill at

Boston," with workers coming first from Charlestown, then Roxbury, then Dorchester, and so on in rotation. In less than a year the Boston fort was completed and a new one at Natascott begun in response to rumors of French designs upon New England. On 17 January 1632 Winthrop wrote of the Puritans' concern "for our safety, in regard the French were like to prove ill neighbors (being Papists)" with "divers priests and Jesuits among them." In response to a common enemy, the Puritans devised ways to live apart while working together for the common good.

While they worked to fortify strong boundaries between English Protestants and French Catholics, the Puritans were less certain about what kind of lines should be drawn between themselves and other Protestants in New England. As continuing immigration pushed the growing Puritan population outward, disputes arose over real estate and control of trade, within a general pattern of cooperation. Religious differences between Puritans and Pilgrims, so crucial in relation to the nature of their separation from the established church, seemed less significant when an ocean separated both groups from England. While respecting their differences, Puritans and Pilgrims learned early to share resources, to work cooperatively, and even to worship together. In October Winthrop went with John Wilson and Roger Williams to Plimouth, where "the governour of Plimouth, Mr. William Bradford, (a very discreet and grave man,) and Mr. Brewster, the elder, and some others, came forth and met them without the town, and conducted them to the governour's house, where they were very kindly entertained, and feasted every day at several houses." On the Lord's day, they worshiped together, with Roger Williams and the Pilgrim pastor speaking, followed by Bradford and Brewster and then by Winthrop and Wilson. FInally a deacon "put the congregation in mind of their duty of contribution; whereupon the governour and all the rest went down to the deacon's seat, and put into the box, and then returned." Distances requiring journeys of a day or two made their settlements sufficiently separate to preserve distinctive religious identities and sufficiently close to promote cooperation. Space between settlements made a doctrine of toleration unnecessary and allowed the Puritans to work out their own religious and political system without making a place for radical dissent. From within the Bay Colony, the distance between the towns seemed to provide sufficient freedom, while preserving order and agreement on important matters of belief. From outside, the Puritans' desire for uniformity and their lack of a policy of toleration soon made their establishment appear oppressive. In the earliest years, discouragement of significant dissent was a source of strength; before long, it became a crucial weakness in the Puritan design.

Within the Puritan settlement, the growth of the general population outpaced the supply of experienced leaders, threatening to confuse the already close relationship between church and state, or, more accurately, between elders and magistrates. In July 1632 "the congregation at Boston wrote to the elders and brethren of the churches of Plimouth, Salem, &c. for their advice in three questions: 1. Whether one person might be a civil magistrate and a ruling elder at the same time? 2. If not, then which should be laid down? 3. Whether there might be divers pastors in the same church?—The 1st was agreed by all negatively; the 2d doubtfully; the 3d doubtful also." The chief purpose of civil government, for the Puritans, was to preserve purity in the church. While the franchise had been significantly broadened, adult men who were not church members could not participate in elections, much less hold office. The civil magistrates also routinely sought advice from the elders on a broad range of issues. Nevertheless, the boundary between religion and politics divided the formal operations of church and government, even while connecting the two realms by assuring their continuing interaction.

The drawing of boundaries between themselves and the native inhabitants of the land, between leaders and the people, between the center and the periphery of their settlement, between themselves and other religious groups, and between church and civil government within their own society was essential to the Puritans' preservation of order in an environment whose openness surpassed all expectations. Care in defining and adjusting these boundaries helped the Puritans build lasting institutions, laying foundations for a society increasingly distinct from the one they had set out to reform. The effort the Puritans invested in establishing their own society reinforced the lines connecting and dividing them from England.

The religious independence the Puritans sought was sometimes gained more through appeals to England's economic interest than through theological argument or political intrigue. For example, in May 1633 three men who had been punished in Massachusetts for misdemeanors petitioned the king and council against the Puritans. Their timing seemed propitious, for religious sentiments were hardening in England, with increasing repression of Puritan clergy. In addition, they had support from Sir Ferdinando Gorges and Captain Mason, who had begun a plantation in Massachusetts and were seeking control over the entire government of New England. Nevertheless, the king said that "he would have them severely punished, who did abuse his governour and the plantation," and the Puritan defendants "were dismissed with a favourable order for their encouragement, being assured from some of the council, that his majesty did not intend to impose the ceremonies of the church of England upon us; for that it was considered, that it was the freedom from such things that made people come over to us; and it was credibly informed to the council, that this country would, in time, be very beneficial to England for masts, cordage, &c." The king and his counselors might allow a certain amount of religious independence in exchange for timber and hemp from New England, and while deeply religious, the Puritans were pragmatists. Winthrop and the other leaders employed whatever means proved effective in safeguarding the Puritan way of life.

While the king's interest in using the natural resources of the Bay Colony to equip the royal navy forestalled this direct challenge to Winthrop's government, the ecclesiastical suppression of Puritans in England continued unabated. Among the two hundred passengers brought to Massachusetts by the *Griffin* in September were ministers John Cotton, Thomas Hooker, and Samuel Stone, along with such men of good and great estate as William Peirce and John Haynes: "They gat out of England with much difficulty, all places being belaid to have taken Mr. Cotton and Mr. Hooker, who had been long sought for to have been brought into the high commission," but by boarding the ship secretly these future leaders of church and state came safely to New England. Thus when direct argument and diplomacy failed to protect their colony, the Puritans became adept at connivance and subterfuge. Fortunately their enemies were increasingly distracted by the tensions within England which had led Winthrop and his party to leave their native land. As pressures mounted in England, the Puritans in Massachusetts learned to play a waiting game. Communication across the Atlantic was slow at best, and Puritan pretense made it slower still. If exposure to its perils had made crossing the ocean a rite of passage for the early Puritans, now the Atlantic became a vast natural boundary protecting them from the dangerous vagaries of English politics. English Puritans could escape across it, and they did so in increasing numbers, but it presented a wonderful barricade to organized repression and control.

Operating more and more on their own with an increasingly large and diverse society to manage, the Puritans in Massachusetts began to develop standard practices, procedures, and routines that helped to stabilize the institutions they were creating. At a meeting of the court on 2 July 1633 Winthrop submitted his expenses, and "it was agreed, that the governour, John Winthrop, should have, towards his charges this year £150, and the money, which he had disbursed in publick businesses, as officers' wages, &c., being between two and three hundred pounds, should be forthwith paid." But the governor's finances proved easier to manage than the runaway prices for goods and services in an economy driven by immigration. Responding to "a general complaint," in November the court noted that "the scarcity of workmen had caused them to raise their wages to an excessive rate, so as a carpenter would have three shillings the day, a labourer two shillings and sixpence, &c.; and accordingly those who had commodities to sell advanced their prices sometime double to that they cost in England." With a desire for justice and a lingering medieval sense of an ordered social economy, the court tried, though ultimately in vain, to set fair wages and prices. Skilled workmen should make no more than two shillings per day, and laborers only eighteen pence, they believed, and "no commodity should be sold at above four pence in the shilling more than it cost for ready money in England." Such controls were intended to regulate the lives, as well as the finances, of the people: "The evils which were springing, &c. were, 1. Many spent much time idly, &c. because they could get as much in four days as would keep them a week. 2. They spent much in tobacco and strong waters, &c. which was a great waste to the commonwealth which, by reason of so many foreign commodities expended, could not have subsisted to this time, but that it was supplied by the cattle and corn, which were sold to new comers at very dear rates." But such regulations, however well intended, proved impossible to enforce as more and more immigrants poured into the burgeoning colony.

The integrity of the new society could be guarded in other ways, and "the ministers in the bay and Sagus did meet, once a fortnight, at one of their houses by course, where some question of moment was debated." In religious matters, which were ever the center of Puritan life and thought, the goal was to achieve consensus without appearing to impose uniformity. The Bible spoke plainly on many matters, and the truth about the remainder could be reached through reasoned argument by sincere, holy, learned men. In this way the integrity, coherence, and independence of the Puritan commonwealth could be sustained, but only so long as and to the extent that the freedom of the churches was not compromised. For some, naturally, freedom was the central concern. "Mr. Skelton, the pastor of Salem, and Mr. Williams, who was removed from Plimouth thither, (but not in any office, though he exercised by way of prophecy,) took some exception against it, as fearing it might grow in time to a presbytery or superintendency, to the prejudice of the churches' liberties." For others, such as Winthrop, order was the greater goal: "But this fear was without cause; for they were all clear in that point, that no church or person can have power over another church; neither did they in their meetings exercise any such jurisdiction." Their difference of judgment in this particular case highlights what became an ongoing disagreement between John Winthrop and Roger Williams as contrary advocates of religious liberty. Winthrop stood for the freedom of a society ordered and organized by religious truth, whereas Williams stood for increasingly extreme versions of individual religious freedom regardless of its social consequences. In the early years of the Massachusetts Bay Colony, Winthrop's version of freedom prevailed, so long as the Puritans did not drift into constructing an established church like the one they had left behind in England. If Roger Williams wanted a different form of religious freedom, then he was free to leave, and he was eventually required to do so.

With the arrival of John Cotton, whose learned and powerful preaching had stirred the Puritan faction in England, the church at Boston, where he became the teaching minister, complementing John Wilson's work as pastor and guardian of discipline, quickly became the largest, most influential church in the colony. "More were converted and added to that church, than to all the other churches in the bay," Winthrop notes on 5 December 1633, and "divers profane and notorious evil persons came and confessed their sins, and were comfortably received into the bosom of the church. Yea, the Lord gave witness to the exercise of prophecy, so as thereby some were converted, and others much edified. Also, the Lord pleased greatly to bless the practice of discipline, wherein he gave the pastor, Mr. Wilson, a singular gift, to the great benefit of the church." Not only were Cotton's and Wilson's offices as teacher and pastor carefully distinguished within this leading institution, but the Boston church also led the way in formalizing the financial arrangements in support of the ministry: "After much deliberation and serious advice, the Lord directed the teacher, Mr. Cotton, to make it clear by scripture, that the minister's maintenance, as well as all other charges of the church, should be defrayed out of a stock, or treasury, which was to be raised out of the weekly contribution; which accordingly was agreed upon." Thus were patterns established for regular support of the work done by the leaders of both church and state.

Not everything was harmonious, however. Roger Williams continued to raise questions that perplexed the other ministers, and in the political arena, the continuing jealousy between Winthrop and Dudley inspired conflicts that would be mirrored and magnified several years later within the churches. In November 1633 "some differences fell out still, now and then, between the governour and the deputy, which were soon healed." This time the trouble was over a court order regarding the completion of the fort at Boston. Despite the order and a "friendly" letter from Winthrop, Dudley refused to send his neighbors from Newtown to work on the fort until the towns of Salem and Sagus had sent in the money that was to be their contribution to the project. Fortunately, Haynes and Hooker were living with Dudley, and when they brought Winthrop "a letter from the deputy full of bitterness and resolution not to send till Salem, &c.," Winthrop was able to defer the matter until the next court and to return the letter "with this speech: I am not willing to keep such an occasion of provocation by me." In addition, Winthrop offered simply to give Dudley one of the fat hogs he needed, "as a testimony of his good will." If Dudley had scruples about accepting such a gift, Winthrop suggested that he share it with Haynes and Hooker, in response to this Dudley wrote, "'Your overcoming yourself hath overcome me. Mr. Haynes, Mr. Hooker, and myself, do most kindly accept your good will; but we desire, without offense, to refuse your offer, and that

I may only trade with you for two hogs'; and so very lovingly concluded." Historian Winthrop concludes the episode by noting: "The court being two days after, ordered, that Newtown should do their work as others had done, and then Salem, &c. should pay for three days at eighteen pence a man." The Puritans were developing institutions that could mediate petty jealousies and local disputes for the good of the colony as a whole.

As immigration continued and as the stability of Puritan institutions began to ensure the colony's success, the demand for land and trading rights increased. By October 1633 a Puritan trading ship, the *Blessing of the Bay*, had confronted the Dutch on Long Island, where the English and the Dutch both claimed the right to trade for beaver with the Indians. Likewise the Pilgrims encountered opposition when men from Plimouth built a trading house upriver from the Dutch in Connecticut, hoping to divert some of the ten thousand beaver skins the Dutch were getting annually from the Indians there. "Very courteous and respectful" letters were exchanged, with Dutch and English governors hoping that such disputes might be resolved between their respective sovereigns. As long as the stream of immigration brought new money into Massachusetts, the English could afford to wait. Several years later, when the English Civil War abruptly cut off the supply of immigrants, the Puritans and their neighbors would need to develop inter-colonial institutions to safeguard their access to these and other markets.

Such cooperation would soon be needed as well to protect the New Englanders from the Indians, from whom they were taking land while also trading for pelts. On 27 December 1633 the court at the Bay Colony considered a treatise that Roger Williams had sent to them as well as to the Pilgrim governor and council at Plimouth, in which, among other notions they found strange and erroneous, "he disputes their right to the lands they possessed here, and concluded that, claiming by the king's grant, they could have no title, nor otherwise, except they compounded with the natives." Rather than be censured, Williams recanted. "Mr. Williams also wrote to the governour, and also to him and the rest of the council, very submissively, professing his intent to have been only to have written for the private satisfaction of the governour, &c. of Plimouth, without any purpose to have stirred any further in it, if the governour here had not required a copy of him; withal offering his book, or any part of it, to be burnt. At the next court, he appeared penitently, and gave satisfaction of his intention and loyalty. So it was left, and nothing done in it." Nor were the Indians at this point making an issue of the English hunger for land, for a smallpox epidemic was devastating their tribes in Massachusetts. The Puritans tried to help, as Winthrop notes on 5 December 1633: "Among others, Mr. Maverick of Winesemett is worthy of a perpetual remembrance. Himself, his wife and servants, went daily to them, ministered to their necessities, and buried their dead, and took home many of their children. So did other of the neighbors. This infectious disease spread to Pascataquack, where all the Indians (except one or two) died." Nevertheless, an English disease seemed almost providentially to open the land in which the Puritans believed they had rights to settle. In a short time organized violence replaced disease and ministry, leading the Puritans and their English neighbors to develop patterns of intercolonial cooperation for their common defense.

Although actively engaged in his work as governor in these early years, Winthrop found time to write longer entries in his journal. While some entries simply record public events, the logbook format of the voyage had given way to a somewhat more flowing narrative. Winthrop begins to provide instructions for readers to see notes and entries in subsequent sections, and he leaves large blanks in the manuscript, indicating that he plans to return at a later date to complete certain narratives. Although the journal in these years is far from a uniform narrative, these blanks and directions to readers suggest that Winthrop was becoming more conscious of his work as a historian, or that he was beginning to see that work, and perhaps the history itself, in a new way. Some entries cover entire months, without the intrusion of daily dates, and at times he writes vignettes to express the meaning of events. In March 1633, for example, after describing the conversion experience of a fourteen-year-old son of one of the magistrates, he includes an episode which shows that he has been writing about the life of his own family: "Upon this occasion it is not impertinent (though no credit nor regard be to be had of dreams in these days) to report a dream, which the father of these children had at the same time, viz. that, coming into his chamber, he found his wife (she was a very gracious woman) in bed, and three or four of their children lying by her, with most sweet and smiling countenances, with crowns upon their heads and blue ribbons about their leaves. When he awaked, he told his wife his dream, and made this interpretation of it, that God would take of her children to make them fellow heirs with Christ in his kingdom." Whatever were Winthrop's abilities as an analyst of dreams, such a vignette indicates that his work as governor was being recorded by a historian with an increasingly self-conscious literary sensibility.

Winthrop's ability to write about his own actions, by seeing himself as a character in the history he was writing, may have been associated with his tendency to hold strong convictions and also to be open to change in the political arena. Such ambivalence equipped him well for leadership in a colony that was beginning to develop its own ways of doing things and also prepared him for exercising leadership even when he was not formally in charge of the colony's affairs. Rather early on he seemed to have understood that an organization's strength depends on an appropriate distribution of power. Nevertheless, he also had high standards regarding the qualifications of those among whom power should be shared. Thus, while he knew that the colony's continuing growth would soon require more representative government, he also knew that a swelling population did not necessarily indicate the presence of more men who were qualified to manage public affairs. However valid such political instincts may have been, articulating these ideas ironically put Winthrop himself in a precarious position.

Thus Winthrop notes dispassionately on 1 April 1634 that the freemen of the colony "deputed two of each town to meet and consider of such matters as they were to take order in" at the next meeting of the general court. But when these deputies met, they decided that their involvement in the making of laws gave them the right to question some of the governor's actions, and they wanted to see whether the original patent gave Winthrop the power he had in fact been exercising. Winthrop was no more ready to show them the patent than he was to let it be returned to the king's council in England, yet he recognized that the deputies were fundamentally right. He responded with classic political equivocation:

He told them, that, when the patent was granted, the number of freemen was supposed to be (as in like corporations) so few, as they might well join in making laws; but now they were grown to so great a body, as it was not possible for them to make or execute laws, but they must choose others for that purpose: and that howsoever it would be necessary hereafter to have a select company to intend that work, yet for the present they were not furnished with a sufficient number of men qualified for such a business, neither could the commonwealth bear the loss of time of so many as must intend it. Yet this they might do at present, viz they might, at the general court, make an order, that, once in the year, a certain number should be appointed (upon summons from the governor) to revise all laws, &c. and to reform what they found amiss therein; but not to make any new laws, but prefer their grievances to the court of assistants; and that no assessment should be laid upon the country without the consent of such a committee, nor any lands disposed.

This was a significant admission of the need for change, but it did not satisfy the deputies' desire for their share of power.

When the general court met on 14 May, the Reverend John Cotton took his freeman's oath as a newcomer to the colony and proceeded to preach a sermon to the effect that "a magistrate ought not to be turned into the condition of a private man without just cause" any more than the magistrates could take away the citizenship of a private man without a public trial. To grant such continuing tenure to the standing order was too much for even the other ministers to endorse. Knowing their own people, they referred Cotton's ideas "to further consideration," and the assembled freemen "chose a new governor, viz. Thomas Dudley, Esq. the former deputy; and Mr. Ludlow was chosen deputy; and John Haines, Esq. an assistant, and all the rest of the assistants chosen again." Thus, although Winthrop continued to be a member of the court as an assistant, he was out of the governor's office for the first time.

The people were feeling new power, and the changes in the political system that the deputies had discussed privately with Winthrop two weeks earlier were now put into effect: "At this court it was ordered, that four general courts should be kept every year, and that the whole body of the freemen should be present only at the court of election of magistrates, &c. and that, at the other three, every town should send their deputies, who should assist in making laws, disposing lands, &c." Winthrop's judgment was not unbalanced by his loss of office, though, for he observes: "Many good orders were made this court. It held three days, and all things were carried very peaceably, notwithstanding that some of the assistants were questioned by the freemen for some errours in their government, and some fines imposed, but remitted again before the court brake up. The court was kept in the meeting-house at Boston, and the new governour and the assistants were together entertained at the house of the old governour, as before." Losing his office did not diminish Winthrop's hospitality. He had been in power long enough to be known as "the old governour," and when not directly in power, he would continue to exercise leadership as the first citizen of the colony. As he observed in a letter to Sir Simonds D'Ewes, who had requested a full account of the colony's terrain and affairs, "I did hope vpon the discharge of my place, to have good leysure to that end, but our new Governor (my brother Dudly) dwelling out of the waye, I am still as full of Companye and business as before."[12] Such excuses aside, being out of office gave Winthrop a new perspective on the colony's affairs and more time to write its history.

Through their deputies the people were claiming a larger share in governance, but the separation of power did not come naturally to men whose worldview was still in some ways medieval. Whatever legitimacy the deputies might claim as representatives of the people, the assistants were still the magistrates, and these men of wealth and prestige were not about to relinquish a sense of authority that had come to seem almost a natural or hereditary right. Subsequent meetings of the court saw much dissension about whether the deputies had a right to the "negative voice," or veto, that the magistrates asserted was theirs alone. Power might be shared, but not equally, in the minds of the magistrates, and in March a deputy who denied their authority was barred from office for three years. The notion of a fully bicameral legislature was an idea whose day had not yet come.

Nevertheless, within weeks of Dudley's election, Winthrop wrote privately to the Puritans' friend and supporter Sir Nathaniel Rich that the colony, with upwards of four thousand people and newcomers arriving frequently, was thriving. Winthrop was evidently satisfied with the system he described: "Our Civill Government is mixt: the freemen choose the magistrats everye yeare (and for the present they have chosen Tho: Dudly esqr. Governour) and at 4 Courts in the yeare 3 out of each towne (there being 8 in all) doe assist the magistrats in making of lawes, imposing taxes, and disposing of lands: our Juries are chosen by the freemen of everye towne. Our Churches are governed by Pastors, Teachers ruling Elders and Deacons, yet the power lies in the wholl Congregation and not in the Presbityre further then for order and precedencye. For the natives, they are neere all dead of the small Poxe, so as the Lord hathe cleared our title to what we possess."[13] In his private correspondence as in his public journal, Winthrop was apparently pleased with the overall direction of the colony.

Changes, though, were not made without personal tensions and irritations. When called to account for his financial transactions as governor, Winthrop made it clear that his generosity while in an office that he had accepted but never sought was beyond recompense, and he asked that "as it stands vpon record that vpon the discharge of my office I was called to accompt, soe this my declaracion may be recorded also: least hereafter, when I shalbe forgotten, some bleamishe may lye vpon my posteritie when there shalbe noething to cleare it."[14] As historian, he made a point of noting each time that Governor Dudley was reimbursed for hospitality or other expenses that would have been covered by the former governor's personal generosity. But Winthrop was far from being the cranky critic of the present governor that Dudley had been. He knew that the colony faced far more important problems, both immediately in sustaining its relative autonomy from England and soon in preserving the integrity of its own Puritan identity.

In July 1634 Winthrop bravely asserted in private correspondence that, although Puritans in England still had to wrestle with the problem of conformity to an established church, "our case heere is otherwise: being come to clearer light and more Libertye, which we trust by the good hand of our God with vs, and the gratious indulgence of our Kinge, we may freely enjoye it."[15] Yet in fact their sovereign and his counselors became less and less indulgent of New England's liberties. That very month, when the Company's original governor, Matthew Cradock, sent the Puritans "a copy of the council's order, whereby we were required to send over our patent," the magistrates were devious: "Upon long consultation whether we should return answer or not, we agreed, and returned answer to Mr. Cradock, excusing that it could not be done but by a general court, which was to be holden in September next." Despite their penchant for direct action in response to adversity, the Puritans also knew the strategic value of delay.

A month later, Winthrop received a letter warning the Puritans "that a commission was granted for a general governor to be sent over, with many railing speeches against this plantation, and Mr. Winthrop in particular." On 18 September "there came over a copy of the commission granted to the two archbishops and ten others of the council, to regulate all plantations, and power given them, or any five of them, to call in all patents, to make laws, to raise tythes and portions for ministers, to remove and punish governours, and to hear and determine all causes, and inflict all punishments, even death itself." This design "to compel us, by force, to receive a new governour, and the discipline of the church of England, and the laws of the commission-ers,—occasioned the magistrates and deputies to hasten our fortifications, and to discover our minds each to other." Internal bickering gave way to cooperation in response to the common threat. On 19 January the ministers spoke for everyone: "If a general governour were sent, we ought not to accept him, but defend our lawful possessions, (if we are able;) otherwise to avoid or protract." If the Puritans were wise in completing their fortifica-tions while engaging in endless delays about returning their patent, certain factions within the colony did bear some of the responsibility for English animosity toward Massachusetts Bay.

Again the radicals in Salem had caused most of the trouble. It was first reported on 5 November that the ensign at Salem had been defaced by the removal of part of the red cross: "Much matter was made of this, as fearing it would be taken as an act of rebellion, or of like high nature, in defacing the king's colours; though the truth were, it was done upon this opinion, that the red cross was given to the king of England by the pope, as an ensign of victory, and so a superstitious thing, and a relique of antichrist." Three weeks later the assistants met, considered advice from some of the ministers, and decided to apologize "with as much wariness as we might, being doubt-ful of the lawful use of the cross in an ensign, though we were clear that fact, as concerning the manner, was very unlawful." Nor did it help to learn "that Mr. Williams of Salem had broken his promise to us, in teaching publickly against the king's patent, and our great sin in claiming rightly thereby to this country, &c. and for usual terming the churches of England antichristian." Hence "we granted summons to him for his appearance at the next court." Yet when the court met in March, something of a pattern began to emerge: "Mr Endecott was called to answer for defacing the cross in the ensign; but, because the court could not agree about the thing, whether the ensigns should be laid by, in regard that many refused to follow them, the whole cause was deferred till the next general court; and the commissioners for military affairs gave order, in the mean time, that all the ensigns should be laid aside." The vastness of the ocean, together with increasing distractions in England, made protraction a plausible policy for dealing with English anger, even when it was inspired, or at least augmented, by the Puritans themselves.

Endless delay was not a possible strategy, however, for coping with tensions with other plantations in New England or, indeed, with pressures mounting within the Bay Colony itself. On 9 July 1634 Governor Bradford, Edward Winslow, and Pastor Smith came from Plimouth to meet with Winthrop, Cotton, and Wilson in Boston to settle a messy dispute over trade at Kenebeck, where a Puritan trader had been killed. The Puritan negotia-tors agreed to recognize the priority of Plimouth's right to trade in that area, while the Pilgrim representatives acknowledged their responsibility for pre-venting such violence in the future. Bradford and Winthrop "wrote their letters into England to mediate their peace, and sent them by Mr. Winslow." Governors Bradford and Winthrop were not men to compromise on matters of belief. Because they also knew that every dispute was not a conflict of ultimate principles, however, they could find reasonable solutions.

Dealing directly with the matter at hand was likewise required to convince Thomas Hooker and his congregation in Newtown not to move to Connecticut. In early September the general court was locked in dispute, for while Hooker's people had run out of land in Newtown and were strongly drawn to "the fruitfulness and commodiousness of Connecticut," their fellow Puritans felt that "in point of conscience, they ought not to depart from us, being knit to us in one body, and bound by oath to seek the welfare of this commonwealth," and had even offered to accommodate them by enlarging Newtown at the expense of other towns in the Bay Colony. A majority of the deputies favored the move, but the magistrates, even though split among themselves, vetoed the deputies' action. The magistrates refused to yield their veto, "considering how dangerous it might be to the commonwealth, if they should not keep that strength to balance the greater number of the deputies." Three weeks later, after a day of humiliation and a sermon from John Cotton, "the affairs of the court went on cheerfully; and although all were not satisfied about the negative voice to be left to the magistrates, yet no man moved aught about it, and the congregation of Newtown came and accepted of such enlargement as had formerly been offered them by Boston and Watertown; and so the fear of their removal to Connecticut was removed." The pressure on land was unremitting, however, and always tangled with politics.

In December Winthrop was elected to a committee to divide Boston's remaining land, but he refused to serve because some of the other leading men had been left out. By secret ballot, the townsmen had elected primarily men "of the inferiour sort" because they feared "that the richer men would give the poorer sort no great proportions of land, but would rather leave a great part at liberty for new comers and for common, which Mr. Winthrop had oft persuaded them unto, as best for the town." John Cotton and others led the move for a new election, in which the leading men were indeed chosen. Winthrop the historian explains the thinking of the group that finally did the work: "The reason why some were not willing that the people should have more land in the bay than they might be likely to use in some reasonable time, was partly to prevent the neglect of trades, and other more necessary employments, and partly that there might be place to receive such as should come after; seeing it would be very prejudicial to the commonwealth, if men should be forced to go far off for land, while others had much, and could make no use of it, more than to please their eye with it." The long-term interest of the town required a balance between immediate and future needs and depended on the ability of men like Winthrop to keep the good of the community as a whole and its future in mind. Though they could still be reminded of such considerations, as the population continued to grow the people became increasingly restless with the traditional authorities to which they were expected to defer.

The ministers could be relied on to support the judgment of the leading men, and the political leaders did all they could to support the ministers and to shore up the religious foundations of their society. At the meeting of the general court on 18 September "were many laws made against tobacco, and immodest fashions, and costly apparel, &c." Such moralistic proscriptions, coupled with mandatory observance of the Sabbath and two lectures per week (reduced from the original four), helped to keep the burgeoning colony "knit together." But what might happen if the community's coherence were challenged directly from the religion that was supposed to be the center of its integrity? When men with less balanced judgment than Winthrop came to hold the highest offices, how would such a challenge be met? In the years immediately ahead the foundations so carefully laid would be severely shaken. Then all that Winthrop was learning by observing his community would be needed in order for balance and direction to be restored. The historian would be called upon to return as governor, but not until the religious center of the Puritan experiment had almost come apart.

3

A Time of Testing

MANY OF the events and experiences that John Winthrop recorded
during the middle years of his journal directly challenged the
central assumptions of Puritan life. Between 1635 and 1641 the
foundations of the fledgling colony were broadly and intensely
shaken. Whether in or out of the governor's office, Winthrop was close to
the center of the tempest. In addition, his private condition, at least finan-
cially, was unexpectedly and extensively troubled during these years. It is
quite natural, therefore, for Winthrop's journal to show how tensions in
various areas of life exacerbated one another. Historians invariably seize
upon one kind of problem to explain, or at least to characterize, the others.
But when they tell history as a story, as Winthrop did, the intermixed or even
jumbled nature of actual experience comes clear. The colonists knew religious controversy, Indian warfare, troubled relations with England, and the
dispersion of their own people to new towns and churches as pieces of a
puzzle that fit together in time but no longer matched their original pattern.
Some were completely caught up in one crisis or another, others tried to
force the pieces back together by violently reasserting the initial design,
some reveled in newfound freedom, and others saw the chance to take
personal advantage of the opportunities afforded by uncharted change. Like
everyone else, Winthrop occasionally lost his balance. Yet, given his temperament, his was often the voice of moderation. Unlike those who were fully
caught up in one issue or another, Winthrop had an overriding passion for
the ongoing preservation of the Puritan community. While fighting hard for
what he believed was right, Winthrop also kept on believing that apparently
unrelated or inexplicable incidents were events in a story with an overall
purpose. So he recorded it all.

70

Because her personal force and spiritual convictions challenged the religious beliefs and symbols at the center of the whole Puritan project, Anne Hutchinson played a central role in the drama of these middle years. Her intrepid questioning of religious rules symbolizes the tension between freedom and order that stretched through every aspect of Puritan life. She was more catalyst than cause, however, for others challenged Puritan beliefs more thoroughly than she, and even the woman Winthrop denounced as "this *American Jesabel*" was not responsible for the unsettling diffusion of the population or the growing trouble with and in England. Certainly she was a victim and not the cause of violence between Puritans and Indians. She played her part brilliantly in a drama directed by others, on a stage set by men such as Roger Williams, who was indeed centrally involved in all that occurred and with whom the story of these years, as faithfully recorded in Winthrop's journal, appropriately begins.

The magistrates called Williams to task on 30 April 1635, because "he had taught publickly, that a magistrate ought not to tender an oath to an unregenerate man, for that we thereby have communion with a wicked man in the worship of God, and cause him to take the name of God in vain." The high degree of religious purity that Williams demanded would have made even the routine business of public life impossible, so "he was heard before all the ministers, and very clearly confuted." However clear the confutation seemed to the ministers and magistrates, though, Roger Williams continued to think for himself and to lead others toward a further separation of religion from the messy world of politics. He believed, for example, that the magistrates should not punish anyone for breaking religious commandments except in cases that disturbed civil peace and that a righteous man should not pray together with anyone, even his own wife and children, if they were unregenerate. Hence Williams was summoned to a meeting of the general court in early July. Again his ideas were pronounced "erroneous, and very dangerous," and the church at Salem, where Williams had been called to work as a teacher, was cited for "a great contempt of authority." If his mind was unchanged by the next meeting of the court, the magistrates warned, the other churches should request that he be removed, for Williams's obstinate opinions might lead a church "into heresy, apostasy, or tyranny, and yet the civil magistrate could not intermeddle." Governor John Haynes, Deputy Governor Richard Bellingham, and the other magistrates, among whom were Winthrop and John Winthrop, Jr., knew how to apply pressure: they refused to consider Salem's request to annex some land at Marblehead Neck until Williams changed his thinking or Salem came to its senses and removed him from office.

Nevertheless, one month later "Mr. Williams, pastor of Salem, being sick and not able to speak, wrote to his church a protestation, that he could not communicate with the churches in the bay; neither would he communicate with them, except they would refuse communion with the rest; but the whole church was grieved herewith." In essence, Williams was too pure to share the sacrament of Communion with his own church if they did not join him in separating from the other Puritans in the Bay Colony. When the general court met in October, Williams maintained the opinions expressed in two letters, one "to the churches, complaining of the magistrates for injustice, extreme oppression, etc. and the other to his own church, to persuade them to renounce communion with all the churches in the bay, as full of antichristian pollution." Rejecting the offer of a month's respite to prepare for a final argument, Williams entered a formal disputation with Thomas Hooker, who, like everyone else, "could not reduce him from any of his errours. So, the next morning, the court sentenced him to depart out of our jurisdiction within six weeks." Returning to Salem, Williams "refused communication with his own church, who openly disclaimed his errours, and wrote an humble submission to the magistrates, acknowledging their fault in joining with Mr. Williams in that letter to the churches against them." Even for the radicals in Salem, Williams had simply gone too far.

The magistrates granted Williams liberty to remain until the spring on the condition that he stop converting people to his opinions, but silence was foreign to him. Fearing that he might start a rival settlement nearby, "from whence the infection would easily spread into these churches, (the people being, many of them, much taken with the apprehension of his godliness)," in January the magistrates issued a warrant for him to be shipped back to England. Someone warned him to flee, however, and the warmth of Williams's lifelong affection and respect for Winthrop suggests that he may have been the one who helped Williams elude the Puritans' grasp. Shortly after his departure, Williams aptly described the difference between the two leaders in a letter to Winthrop: "I therefore now thanckfully acknowledge your Wisedome and Gentlenes in receaving so lovingly my late rude and foolish Lines: You beare with Fooles gladly because you are wise."[1] Yet Williams was too passionate a truth-seeker to emulate the Puritan whose political skills he admired.

Roger Williams ultimately settled in Providence, where his quest for purity initially led him to observe Communion with no one other than his wife. Then, following one of those leaps or twists of intuition that characterized his thinking, he began to worship with everyone. Thus a great experiment in religious toleration began in Rhode Island, whence Williams issued broadsides against Puritan rigidity while corresponding regularly in confidence with Winthrop to share intelligence regarding the Indians. Now the way was clear for Williams's former flock in Salem to pursue their annexation of Marblehead. A challenge to the Puritan system had been issued, entertained, and removed. Yet if a precedent for dealing with dissent from within had been established, so too had theological dissent, along with its challenges to political order and social harmony, become a feature of life in Massachusetts Bay. As the Puritans began to thrive, their little commonwealth became unruly.

Fifteen shiploads of passengers and cattle arrived within a six-week period in the spring of 1635. In early June Winthrop noted what happened to the orderly, logical system the Puritans devised to regulate a burgeoning economy: "For preventing the loss of time, and drunkenness, which sometimes happened, by people's running to the ships, and the excessive prices of commodities, it was ordered, that one in each town should buy for all, &c. and should retain the same within twenty days at five per hundred, if any came to buy in that time. But this took no good effect; for most of the people would not buy, except they might buy for themselves; and the merchants appointed could not disburse so much money, &c.; and the seamen were much discontented, yet some of them brought their goods on shore and sold them there." Ministers and magistrates were no match for the merchants in a thriving colony.

The king and his counselors might threaten regularly to send "a general governor" to manage New England for the Crown, but the increasing turmoil of English politics prevented the implementation of such plans, so that what actually came across the ocean was a steady stream of new people, goods, and money. Tradesmen did not want their wages regulated by aristocratic magistrates, and merchants did not want anyone limiting their volume of business or the rates of interest they charged and paid. A free market was in the making, and those whose present livelihood and future profits depended on it were predisposed to side with anyone who championed freedom and challenged the ruling elite. They would soon be sympathetic to Anne Hutchinson's bold attempt to scuttle the religious establishment's regulation of morality, at least until too much disorder threatened to upset the social system altogether. Deregulation was good for business; anarchy was not.

In 1635 the people were ready for new political leaders, replacing one-term governor Thomas Dudley with John Haynes, electing Richard Bellingham as deputy governor, and, as Winthrop observed in May, "because the people would exercise their absolute power," leaving the former deputy governor out of office completely. The locally elected deputies, who represented particular towns, "had agreed on the election before they came," and they reflected the general population's desire for some constraints on the executive and judicial powers of the big men who served as magistrates: "The deputies having conceived great danger to our state, in regard that our magistrates, for want of positive laws, in many cases, might proceed according to their discretions, it was agreed, that some men should be appointed to frame a body or ground of laws, in resemblance to a Magna Charta, which, being allowed by some of the ministers, and the general court, should be received for fundamental laws." Formulating and adopting such a code was a long process; in the meantime, the people put their trust in new men.

In October 1635 "a young gentleman of excellent parts," Henry Vane, arrived, and he was admitted as a member of the Boston church the following month. Soon he was in the thick of things. On 18 January "Mr. Vane and Mr. Peter, finding some distraction in the commonwealth, arising from some difference in judgment, and withal some alienation of affection among the magistrates and some other persons of quality, and that hereby factions began to grow among the people, some adhering more to the old governour, Mr. Winthrop, and others to the late governour, Mr. Dudley,—the former carrying matters with more lenity, and the latter with more severity,—they procured a meeting," ostensibly to pacify the smoldering rivalry.

Winthrop told the group "that he knew not of any breach between his brother Dudley and himself, since they were reconciled long since" and asked "all the company, that, if they had seen any thing amiss in his government or otherwise, they would deal freely and faithfully with him, and for his part he promised to take it in good part, and would endeavour, by God's grace, to amend it." Likewise Dudley maintained "that for his part he came thither a mere patient, not with any intent to charge his brother Winthrop with any thing; for though there had been formerly some differences and breaches between them, yet they had been healed, and, for his part, he was not willing to renew them again; and so left it to others to utter their own complaints." Whatever factions might be forming, neither of the former governors was willing to reopen old wounds.

However workable the relationship between Winthrop and Dudley had become, Governor Haynes at least, while proclaiming his affection and good intentions, saw in their old rivalry an occasion for pressing his cause by criticizing some of Winthrop's indulgent decisions. While Winthrop thought "that his speeches and carriage had been part mistaken," he did profess "that it was his judgment, that, in the infancy of plantations, justice should be administered with more lenity than in a settled state, because people were then more apt to trangress, partly of ignorance of new laws and orders, partly through oppression of business and other straits; but, if it might be made clear to him, that it was an errour, he would be ready to take up a stricter course." The next morning the ministers brought everyone "to this conclusion, that strict discipline, both in criminal offences and in martial affairs, was more needful in plantations than in a settled state, as tending to the honour and safety of the gospel. Whereupon Mr. Winthrop acknowledged, that he was convinced that he had failed in over much lenity and remissness, and would endeavour (by God's assistance) to take a more strict course hereafter." Whatever this pledge cost Winthrop, its full price would be paid by Anne Hutchinson and her followers when the people brought

Winthrop back as governor to restore the order their new leaders had jeopardized.

Concluding their meeting, the magistrates agreed, in addition to "a renewal of love amongst them," to be more strict in matters of discipline, to "ripen their consultations beforehand, that their vote in publick might bear (as the voice of God)," to avoid discussing government business out of court, and to see that trivial matters were dealt with in the towns instead of being brought to the court. If arguments should break out in court, they resolved to speak about causes rather than persons, to express their differences modestly and respectfully or "to propound their difference by way of question," to move to table troublesome issues, to accept majority decisions graciously, to "be more familiar and open each to other," to "avoid all jealousies and suspicions, each seeking the honour of another, and all, of the court, not opening the nakedness of one another to private persons," to "honour the governour in submitting to him the main direction and ordering the business of the court," to punish any contempt against the court, and, in all things, to uphold the court's reputation among the people.

Winthrop's description of this meeting of magistrates and ministers portrays an elite divided against itself, fearful of losing respect from and control over the society, and pledging to shore up its authority by acting with unanimity and severity. Likewise, three months later, on 7 April 1636, "at a general court, it was ordered, that a certain number of the magistrates should be chosen for life." Whether this was an effort to stabilize the government by assuring some continuity in office for the leading men, or an attempt to attract English aristocrats to join the colony, or simply, as Winthrop and the other magistrates believed, an application of biblical teaching, the Council for Life turned out to be a short-lived institution. Winthrop and Dudley were chosen as life magistrates at a court of election in late May, along with the newly elected Henry Vane, who "by his place of governour, was president of this council for his year." Their powers and prerogatives were never clearly specified, though, and the council, clearly out of touch with the democratic sentiments and the pace of change in the Bay Colony, was disbanded after three years.

The authority of the ruling elite was further undermined as the growing population began inevitably, and to some disturbingly, to seek adequate space by moving outward into new towns and even new colonies. Thomas Hooker's people provided the most dramatic example. Less than two years after the magistrates had vetoed the move and despite the reapportionment of additional land from other towns in the Bay Colony, at the end of May 1636 "Mr. Hooker, pastor of the church of Newtown, and most of his congregation, went to Connecticut. His wife was carried in a horse litter; and they drove one hundred and sixty cattle, and fed of their milk by the way." Although Winthrop felt strongly that the Puritan people were bound to remain together in one community, on personal grounds he could no longer contest Hooker's move, for already the previous October on a ship from England "there came also John Winthrop, the younger, with commission from the Lord Say, Lord Brook, and divers other great persons in England, to begin a plantation at Connecticut, and to be governour there. They sent also men and ammunition, and £2000 in money, to begin a fortification at the mouth of the river." Within a month Winthrop's son's enterprise began to succeed, for "about sixty men, women, and little children, went by land towards Connecticut with their cows, horses, and swine, and, after a tedious and difficult journey, arrived safe there." With such leaders as Thomas Hooker and the younger John Winthrop, Connecticut would grow into a strong colony.

With their center of authority strained in several ways, the Puritans found themselves exposed to danger from displaced, disgruntled Indians as well as to an unforeseen, virtually simultaneous attack upon the very center of their religious identity. As the variety of events and the pace of change recorded in Winthrop's journal make clear, Anne Hutchinson's new spiritual ideas were doubly unsettling because they arrived just when so much of the Puritan project seemed to be coming apart. In particular, relations between the Puritans and the Indians had been strained to the point of war. A connection between the two dangers was expressed in a letter Winthrop received from John Higginson, who wondered "whether now the Lord begins not to send (as shepards vse to doe their dogs to fetch in their straggling sheep so he) the Indians vpon his servants, to make them cleaue more close togither, and prize each other, to prevent contentions of Brethren which may proue as hard to break as Castle barres, and stop their now beginning breaches before they be as the letting out of many waters that cannot be gathered in againe."[2] Despite recurrent fears of warfare, however, contact between Indians and Englishmen had been relatively tranquil during the early years of the Bay Colony. Conferences between Puritan magistrates and the sagamores of various local tribes enabled enlightened leaders from both cultures to seek equal justice in dealing with random incidents of thievery and violence. Even when Captain Stone, a Virginian trading along the New England coast, killed several Pequod Indians and was in turn killed by them and had his ship blown up, the Puritans simply wrote to the governor of Virginia and made subsequent trade with the Pequods dependent on the capture of the particular responsible parties.

There was always more trading than proselytizing, as Roger Williams complained to Winthrop: "I obserue our Country men haue allmost quite forgotten our great pretences to King and State and all the world concerning their soules."[3] In the early years the Puritans managed to avoid being drawn into intertribal fighting. They saw divine providence at work in the smallpox epidemic which decimated local tribes in 1633, doing what they could to assist survivors even while believing that the disease was God's way of clearing the land for their possession. But bad theology gave no protection from gruesome violence in 1636, and the Puritans, convinced of their moral superiority and right to the land, undertook thoroughgoing revenge. Warfare against the native Americans coincided almost exactly with the loosening of the center of Puritan political authority and with new challenges to their religious system. Several forms of fear combined into a general sense of crisis, as the Puritans sought to regain control by subduing both the savages outside and the intrepid questioners within their society.

A Puritan trading ship spotted a smaller Puritan craft overrun by Indians on 20 July 1636, and upon boarding the vessel after a brief skirmish, the sailors "found John Oldham under an old seine, stark naked, his head cleft to the brains, and his hand and legs cut as if they had been cutting them off, and yet warm." Oldham was "an old planter, and a member of Watertown congregation, who had been long out a-trading, having with him only two English boys, and two Indians of Naragansett." The boys were returned by two Narragansett sachems, who told the Puritans that Oldham had been punished by other members of their tribe for trading with their enemies, the Pequods. In late August a force of ninety Puritan volunteers, led by John Endecott as general, set out to "do justice upon the Indians for the death of Mr. Oldham" and to demand the murderers of Captain Stone and his men from the Pequods. Searching Block Island for the elusive Narragansetts, the Puritans killed only a few but laid to waste two large settlements and destroyed their crops; they then sailed to the mouth of the Connecticut River and worked similar havoc upon the Pequods. By mid-September the Puritan warriors "all came safe to Boston, which was a marvellous providence of God, that not a hair fell from the head of nay of them, nor any sick or feeble person among them." In October articles of peace were signed between the Puritans and the Narragansetts, leaving the Pequods as enemies of both.

The lengthy entry in John Winthrop's journal for 21 October 1636 records the conclusion of hostilities with the Narragansetts, mentions the burning of a house in Watertown and another in Salem, and describes two additional, apparently unrelated yet simultaneous upsetting events. The first incident evokes the terror aroused in Puritans by the Indians: "About the middle of this month, John Tilley, master of a bark, coming down the Connecticut River, went on shore in a canoe, three miles above the fort, to kill fowl; and having shot off his piece, many Indians arose out of the covert and took him, and killed one other, who was in the canoe. This Tilley was a very stout man, and of great understanding. They cut off his hands, and sent them before, and after cut off his feet. He lived three days after his hands were cut off; and themselves confessed, that he was a stout man, because he

cried not in his torture." The second incident introduces a character des-
tined to cause more trouble than the Pequods and Narragansetts combined:
"One Mrs. Hutchinson, a member of the church of Boston, a woman of a
ready wit and bold spirit, brought over with her two dangerous errours."
The radical substance and extreme consequences of her beliefs were especially dangerous in a society living with stories of savage torture and death,
one that had just completed its first military campaign against the Indians
and would soon undertake a considerably more violent crusade against the
Pequods.

The Puritans experienced these and similar events as one profoundly
troubling set of problems. In response, on 20 February 1636 "a general fast
was kept in all the churches. The occasion was, the miserable estate of the
churches in Germany; the calamities upon our native country, the bishops
making havock in the churches, putting down the faithful ministers, and
advanceing popish ceremonies and doctrines, the plague raging exceedingly,
and famine and sword threatening them; the dangers of those at Connecticut, and of ourselves also, by the Indians; and the dissensions in our
churches." The Puritans could do little but fast and pray for their fellow
Protestants in Germany and Puritans in England, but they could take up
arms against the Indians and do battle against the dissensions within their
own churches caused by Anne Hutchinson's ideas. Of these two, the fear-
some Pequods turned out to be the more tractable.

As a middleman in communications between the Puritans and these
formidable warriors, Roger Williams in 1637 advised Winthrop to be very
careful, "for though I would not feare a Jarr with them yet I would fend of
from being fowle, and deale with them wisely as with wolues endewed with
mens braines."[4] Hearing that the Pequod men had sent their women and
children to an island for safety, the Puritans first sent 40 men to join the
Narragansetts against them and then dispatched an additional 160 men,
along with magistrate Israel Stoughton and pastor John Wilson, to crush the
enemy. On 25 May Winthrop noted that the Puritan force trapped the
Pequods in their fort at Mistick, burned the fort, "and slew therein two chief
sachems, and one hundred and fifty fighting men, and about one hundred
and fifty old men, women, and children, with the loss of two English,
whereof but one was killed by the enemy." Although "divers of the Indian
friends were hurt by the English, because they had not some mark to
distinguish them from the Pequods, as some of them had," Winthrop
observed that "the general defeat of the Pequods at Mistick happened the
day after our general fast." By 15 June "there was a day of thanksgiving kept
in all the churches for the victory obtained against the Pequods, and for
other mercies." The disposal of eighty Pequod women and children "to
particular persons in the country" was noted on 6 July, and a week later
Winthrop recorded the results of a second campaign against the Pequods by
eighty Puritans led by Stoughton, estimating that "we had now slain and

taken, in all, about seven hundred." The Indian women and children were dispersed as slaves in Massachusetts and Connecticut, and some, sent to Bermuda, were turned over to the English on Providence Isle. By 5 August word came that other Indians had slain many Pequods, "and their heads brought to the English; so that now there had been slain and taken between eight and nine hundred. Whereupon letters were sent to Mr. Stoughton and the rest, to call them all home." All the soldiers were home by the end of the month, and "the Naragansetts sent us the hands of three Pequods,—one the chief of those who murdered Capt. Stone." So the violence had come full circle, and the extensive Puritan defeat of the Pequods was followed by a policy of peace and a return to the earlier pattern of random overt violence within a more general order of reciprocal kindness, justice, and trade. As far as the first generation of Puritans was concerned, they had subjugated the Indians, and their part of America was indeed New England.

Yet resolution of the internal dilemmas with which the Puritans had been wrestling while they fought the Indians required different skills and, if anything, even more fortitude. Anne Hutchinson's ideas were profoundly unsettling because they were, in a sense, logical extensions of basic Puritan beliefs. As such, the controversies they ignited challenged the authority of the standing order, both magistrates and ministers, to guide and control the colony. Winthrop knew Hutchinson's ideas were "dangerous errours," not intrinsic to the Puritanism of the Bay Colony but "brought over with her" from England, when he summarized them on 21 October 1636: "1. That the person of the Holy Ghost dwells in a justified person. 2. That no sanctification can help to evidence to us our justification." She believed, in other words, that in the process of conversion the spirit of God actually comes to live within the believer and, therefore, that the true Christian has been so thoroughly justified with God that he or she has no need for the elaborate process of self-scrutiny and more exertion known as sanctification.

Assurance of oneness with God frees the Christian from obeying rules and laws and from deferring to those who articulate, interpret, and enforce them. Since *nomos* means "law," Hutchinson and her followers were quickly, and derisively, labeled Antinomians. It is not hard to see why their beliefs were anathema to most of the magistrates and ministers. Yet Anne Hutchinson was extraordinarily adept at reasoned argument, to which the Puritans were committed as a means for resolving disputes, so it was not clear for a while how, or whether, the Puritan community might survive the challenge her thinking represented. Attendance swelled at the weekly meetings she held to examine and discuss the teaching and preaching of the ministers. Soon virtually everyone in the Bay Colony, and certainly its entire leadership, was involved in one way or another in the Antinomian crisis.

Seeking to quell the trouble Hutchinson's ideas were brewing in the Boston church, the other ministers conferred privately with the magistrates at a meeting of the general court in late October 1636. Here the Reverend

John Cotton, who had been Hutchinson's spiritual guide in old England, and the more radical John Wheelwright, her brother-in-law whose ministry had been silenced in England, agreed with their colleagues that sanctification did indeed provide worthwhile evidence of justification. Wheelwright and some others argued for the "indwelling" of the Holy Ghost during the experience of justification, but they stopped short of agreeing with the "personal union" of the believer with God that Hutchinson and her followers asserted. Throughout the Antinomian controversy, Cotton proved more nimble at sitting on the fence than did Wheelwright, who was among the first to feel the force of the nervous establishment. When Hutchinson and her followers attempted to have Wheelwright called as a teaching minister at Boston, Cotton equivocated adroitly, and Winthrop argued the congregation out of making the appointment but had to defend himself at length against the opinion of what had become an Antinomian majority in his own church.

In November Governor Vane indicated his agreement with John Cotton regarding the indwelling of the Holy Ghost and then took the next step, asserting that indeed a personal union exists between the believer and the spirit of God. In the fracas that ensued, peace was restored only when everyone agreed to avoid using the word *person* when referring to the Holy Spirit. Such tranquillity was too fragile for a hothead like Vane, however, and within a month he tried to resign from office, citing pressing business in England. When the other magistrates pleaded for stability in the face of the dangers the colony faced from the Indians and the French, Vane said his real reason for resigning was his involvement in the religious controversy, but the court would not allow him to resign on such grounds. So he again professed that the business regarding his estate in England was sufficient to justify his departure, and this time the court silently assented. But when preparations were completed for the election of his successor, Vane shifted ground again and indicated that he would remain in office out of respect for the members of the Boston church. Hence the court of election was not formally convened, and Vane remained in office. Hutchinson's ideas were disrupting the government as well as the churches, just when violence between Puritans and Indians was escalating toward full-scale warfare and just as anxiety was growing in response to competing French claims to the territory of the Bay Colony. With Winthrop out of office, the journal suggests, things went from bad to worse.

Charges and countercharges flew, and controversy increased to the point that religious dissension in the Bay Colony seemed to have brought the "Citty vpon a hill" down into the slough of troubles that vexed the world at large. A general fast in the churches failed to produce harmony, and Winthrop noted in the late winter of 1636 that "the differences in all the said points of religion increased more and more, and the ministers of both sides (there being only Mr. Cotton of one party) did publickly declare their judgments in some of them, so as all men's mouths were full of them." When John Cotton and John Wilson, both ministers of the Boston church, delivered conflicting interpretations of the troubles for the passengers on a ship departing for England to relay to the faithful among their countrymen, Winthrop observed: "Thus every occasion increased the contention, and caused great alienation of minds; and the members of Boston (frequenting the lectures of other ministers) did make much disturbance by publick questions, and objections to their doctrines, which did any way disagree from their opinions; and it began to be as common here to distinguish between men, by being under a covenant of grace or a covenant of works, as in other countries between Protestants and Papists." Winthrop thought that Anne Hutchinson's ideas were about to undo the coherence of the party he had led across the seas to further the true Reformation.

For some individuals, the strain of living in such a highly charged religious atmosphere proved unbearable. Thus on 6 February "a man of Weymouth (but not of the church) fell into some trouble of mind, and in the night cried out, 'Art thou come, Lord Jesus?' and with that leaped out of his bed in his shirt, and, breaking from his wife, leaped out at a high window into the snow, and ran about seven miles off, and, being traced in the snow, was found dead the next morning. They might perceive, that he had kneeled down to prayer in divers places." Fortunately, as Winthrop saw things, although arguments continued, most of the ministers, magistrates, and people—especially those outside of Boston—were less volatile.

At the next general court, which began in March, "when any matter about these new opinions was mentioned, the court was divided; yet the greater number far were sound." If religious turmoil made for political instability, the Puritans responded by clarifying the boundary between church and state: "The ministers, being called to give advice about the authority of the court in things concerning the churches, &c. did all agree of these two things: 1. That no member of the court ought to be publickly questioned by a church for any speech in the court, without the license of the court. The reason was, because the court may have sufficient reason that may excuse the sin, which yet may not be fit to acquaint the church with, being a secret of state. The second thing was, that, in all such heresies or errours of any church members as are manifest and dangerous to the state, the court may proceed without tarrying for the church; but if the opinions be doubtful, &c. they are first to refer them to the church." Consensus on these points opened the way for the court to deal directly with the Antinomians.

Summoned to court, Wheelwright was asked whether he meant what he had said in a sermon during the last fast, when he had vehemently stirred up the people by preaching that all ministers who believed that sanctification was evidence of justification were Antichrists. He affirmed his judgment and applied it to all who so believed, whereupon the elders of all the churches except Boston, being called into court, acknowledged that they did so believe and preach. "So, after much debate, the court adjudged him guilty of sedition, and also of contempt, for that the court had appointed the fast as a means of reconciliation of the differences, &c. and he purposely set himself to kindle and increase them." Sentencing was deferred until the next court. Governor Vane was so upset and the membership of the Boston church so contentious that the magistrates decided to move the next court from Boston to Newtown. Thus the stage was set across the river for restoring the order that Anne Hutchinson's ideas had undermined. Shaken to its foundations, the power structure was preparing to deal with the troublemaker herself.

At the court of election in May 1637, Governor Vane and others from Boston attempted to bring a petition to revoke Wheelwright's sentence, but the majority of the people wanted to proceed to the election of new magistrates before any other business was addressed. They returned Winthrop to the governor's office, chose Dudley as deputy governor, selected Endecott as the third member of the standing council, and elected Israel Stoughton and Richard Saltonstall as assistants. The old guard was back to deal with the disorder caused by the Boston zealots, "and Mr. Vane, Mr. Coddington, and Mr. Dummer (being all of that faction) were quite left out." Hard feelings remained deeply held; six sergeants, all Boston men, quit to avoid carrying the ceremonial weapons that honored the governor. But Winthrop and the others knew they were in command, for as they again postponed sentencing Wheelwright, "the intent of the court in deferring the sentence was, that, being thus provoked by their tumultuous course, and divers insolent speeches, which some of that party had uttered in the court, and having now power enough to have crushed them, their moderation and desire of reconciliation might appear to all." Yet reconciliation proved impossible. By July "the differences grew so much here, as tended fast to a separation; so as Mr. Vane, being, among others, invited by the governour to accompany the Lord Ley at dinner, not only refused to come, (alleging by letter that his conscience withheld him,) but also, at the same hour, he went over to Nottle's Island to dine with Mr. Maverick, and carried the Lord Ley with him." Vane's spiritual enthusiasm and dislike for moral rules established unusual common ground with Samuel Maverick's notorious libertinism. Within a month Vane made good his petulant threats and boarded a ship to return to England.

Once again Winthrop found himself walking a fine line of moderation, this time between the Antinomians and those who were eager to crush them. Fearful of unsound influences, the court prohibited anyone from lodging strangers longer than three weeks, reasoning that "though the execution of this law should turne to the damage of some of this household, yet better it is some member should suffer the evil they bring upon themselves, than that, by indulgence towards them, the whole familye of God in this countrey should be scattered, if not destroyed." Further defending the court order, Winthrop pointed out that "by our law, such as we hold not fitt to dwell among us are not denyed to dwell by us."[5] Yet the mainline Puritans refused to relinquish control, and the Antinomian radicals would not sacrifice the freedom in which they believed. The test came on 12 July, when "here came over a brother of Mrs. Hutchinson, and some other of Mr. Wheelwright's friends, whom the governour thought not fit to allow, as others, to sit down among us, without some trial of them. Therefore, to save others from the danger of the law in receiving of them, he allowed them for four months. This was taken very ill by those of the other party, and many hot speeches given forth about it, and about their removal, &c." Moderation was not the order of the day, and even Winthrop's authority as governor was not sufficient to heal the breach between these factions. Although the magistrates were no longer bound to "tarry for the churches" in resolving matters that threatened the security of the state, the division was so deep that whatever verdicts were finally handed down would need broad support if the colony were to move beyond the crisis.

A definitive end to the Indian wars—marked by the return of the soldiers who had been fighting the Pequods, the receipt of many Pequod heads and hands from Indians on Long Island and elsewhere, the voluntary submission of many sachems, and even the receipt of the hands of the chief who had murdered Captain Stone—enabled the Puritans to turn their attention more fully to restoring order within the Bay Colony. While being careful to avoid the nomenclature of Presbyterianism, in late August they proceeded in a manner that was becoming characteristic, convening at Newtown "the synod, called the assembly," of "all the teaching elders through the country, and some new come out of England, not yet called to any place here." Taking care not to name the parties but simply to focus on matters of doctrine, the assembled ministers reasoned their way toward the orthodoxy they believed the situation demanded. "There were some eighty opinions, some blasphemous, others erroneous, and all unsafe, condemned by the whole assembly; whereto near all the elders, and others sent by the churches, subscribed their names; but some few liked not subscription, though they consented to the condemning of them." Then five points were isolated on which Cotton and Wheelwright differed from all the other ministers; these were reduced by argument to three, and these remaining points were "put into such expressions as Mr. Cotton and they agreed, but Mr. Wheelwright did not." Cotton was finally off the fence, siding with his colleagues, and Wheelwright was left alone beyond the pale.

On the final day of the assembly some particularly pointed questions were debated and resolved. The first was especially ominous: "That though women might meet (some few together) to pray and edify one another; yet such a set assembly, (as was then in practice in Boston,) where sixty or more did meet every week, and one woman (in a prophetical way, by resolving questions of doctrine, and expounding scripture) took upon her the whole exercise, was agreed to be disorderly, and without rule." The other resolutions were more pacific, to the point that public questioning of ministers about their sermons should be done sparingly and without bitterness, that even though assemblies could deal with persons who were absent it would be better for the magistrates to compel them to be present, and that members should not seek to leave one church and join another over matters of opinion that were not fundamental to the faith. The entire business "had been carried on so peaceably, and concluded so comfortably in all love," that Winthrop's proposal for such assemblies to become annual affairs was met with general agreement, if not formal adoption. Either peace was at hand or the lines had been drawn that would enable the magistrates to establish it. Formal boundaries were clear between church and state, but their cooperation in restoring order was so extensive that "the diet of the assembly was provided at the country's charge, as also the fetching and sending back of those, which came from Connecticut." For good or ill, the Puritan establishment was firmly in place.

Its historian described how the establishment acted definitively in November 1637 to secure itself by removing the source of its troubles. A sense of inexorable justice pervades Winthrop's description of the magistrates' deliberations: "There was great hope, that the late general assembly would have had some good effect in pacifying the troubles and dissensions about matters of religion; but it fell out otherwise. For though Mr. Wheelwright and those of his party had been clearly confuted and confounded in the assembly, yet they persisted in their opinions, and were as busy in nourishing contentions (the principal of them) as before. Whereupon the general court, being assembled in the 2 of the 9th month, and finding, upon consultation, that two so opposite parties could not continue in the same body, without apparent hazard of ruin to the whole, agreed to send away some of the principal." The petition on behalf of Wheelwright that had been presented to the court by more than sixty of the Antinomian faction offered "a fair opportunity" for the court to act. Wheelwright and several others were disfranchised and banished, and Hutchinson was summoned and charged "with divers matters, as her keeping two publick lectures every week in her house, whereto sixty or eighty persons did usually resort, and for reproaching most of the ministers (viz. all except Mr. Cotton) for not preaching a covenant of free grace, and that they had not the seal of the Spirit, nor were able ministers of the New Testament; which were clearly proved against her, though she sought to shift it off." As recorded in Winthrop's journal, her trial seems straightforward: "After many speeches to and fro, at last she was so full as she could not contain, but vented her revelations; amongst which this was one, that she had it revealed to her, that she should come into New England, and should here be persecuted, and that God would ruin us and our posterity, and the whole state, for the same. So the court proceeded and banished her; but, because it was winter, they committed her to a private house, where she was well provided, and her own friends and the elders permitted to go to her, but none else." In completing their work, the court disfranchised the five or six remaining leaders of the group, removed from office those who held public positions, and disarmed all of the others who refused to acknowledge their error in signing the Wheelwright petition.

Readers of Winthrop's journal learn that "all the proceedings of this court against these persons were set down at large, with the reasons and other observations, and were sent into England to be published there, to the end that all our godly friends might not be discouraged from coming to us, &c." But in his journal Winthrop does not delay recording the flow of public events in which the governor found himself. Since he was a member of the Boston church, spiritual home of the strongest Antinomian contingent, the controversy swirled around him. John Wilson and John Cotton would not let their people call him to account, but the governor "himself, understanding their intent, thought fit to prevent such a publick disorder, and so took occasion to speak to the congregation," reminding them of the boundaries between religious concerns and affairs of state and asserting that in this matter he had simply followed his conscience in judging "that those brethren, &c. were so divided from the rest of the country in their judgment and practice, as it could not stand with the publick peace, that they should continue amongst us." Toward the end of January, John Cotton, "finding how he had been abused, and made (as himself said) their stalking horse," spent "most of his time, both publickly and privately, to discover" additional secret teachings of the Antinomians—such heresies as "that we are not bound to the law, not as a rule; that the Sabbath is but as other days; that the soul is mortal, till it be united to Christ, and then it is annihilated, and the body also, and a new given by Christ; and that there is no resurrection of the body"—in order to correct "and to reduce such as were gone astray." But no one, it seemed, could convince Anne Hutchinson herself to change her thinking.

The people of Roxbury, where Hutchinson had been staying since her trial, asked the Boston church in early March to try her for her errors. She was argued out of some but persisted in others, so that she and two of her sons were disciplined in their own church: her former mentor "Mr. Cotton pronounced the sentence of admonition with great solemnity, and with much zeal and destation of her errours and pride of spirit." Cotton and the Reverend John Davenport made progress as they continued to reason with her privately, and when she was brought before the church on 22 March she admitted many errors and affirmed God's justice in punishing her "as he had done, for her slighting his ordinances, both magistracy and ministry; and confessed, that what she had spoken against the magistrates at the court (by way of revelation) was rash and ungrounded; and desired the church to pray for her." She even claimed never to have held some of her previous beliefs, "and though it was proved by many testimonies, that she had been of that judgment, and so had persisted, and maintained it by argument against divers, yet she impudently persisted in her affirmation, to the astonishment of the assembly. So that, after much time and many arguments had been spent to bring her to see her sin, but all in vain, the church, with one consent, cast her out." When John Wilson delivered the sentence of excommunication, "her spirits, which seemed before to be somewhat dejected, revived again, and she gloried in her suffering, saying, that it was the greatest happiness, next to Christ, that ever befel her." Evidently she had been made willing to say that she had never held certain beliefs but could not be brought to deny the beliefs themselves. Catching her in a manifest lie, the members of her own church, her former brothers and sisters in spirit, cast her out. The people of Boston returned to the Puritan fold with their teacher, John Cotton, who had come back into line with John Wilson and the rest of the ministers in the Bay. Having nothing left to lose, Anne Hutchinson gloried in her freedom.

With the consensus of church and state, people and leaders, firmly in place, "after two or three days, the governour sent a warrant to Mrs. Hutchinson to depart this jurisdiction before the last of this month, according to the order of court." Denied permission to settle in Plimouth, Hutchinson removed herself, along with her husband and the remainder of her sect, to an island purchased from the Indians in Narragansett Bay. But her influence continued to haunt the Puritans. Excommunication and banishment did not suffice to prove their difference from her heresies. In the spring of 1638 she was suspected of being a witch, on the basis of her assistance as midwife at the delivery of a stillborn "monster" by Mary Dyer. On the advice of John Cotton, Anne Hutchinson had concealed the deformed birth. Nevertheless, in April "the governour, with advice of some other of the magistrates and of the elders of Boston, caused the said monster to be taken up" from its grave and examined, linking its monstrosities with the deformed beliefs of the midwife. That autumn Anne Hutchinson herself delivered an abnormal fetus, and on the basis of Governor Winthrop's correspondence with her physician, John Cotton preached twice about the precise ways its deformities signified the errors of her beliefs. Reality was all of one piece for the seventeenth-century mind, and the men who controlled the symbols that ordered public and private life stopped at nothing to secure their world by demonstrating the rationality of the Puritan beliefs.

Yet something had happened to the coherence of the Puritan community and to the unquestioned integrity of its fundamental beliefs that even the continuing governorship of Winthrop, who was reelected in 1638 and 1639, could not wholly restore. The leaders of the Antinomian faction had been pushed outside the explicit boundaries of the Bay Colony, but most of their followers, many of whom were merchants or tradespeople, remained. Their economic as well as religious interests led in the direction of more freedom and less regulation. The welfare, and soon indeed the very future, of the colony depended on their success. The magistrates and ministers worked together to protect the community's moral standards, yet sometimes innovation was unstoppable. In late September 1638, for example, Winthrop noted: "The court, taking into consideration the great disorder general through the country in costliness of apparel, and following new fashions, sent for the elders of the churches, and conferred with them about it, and laid it upon them, as belonging to them, to redress it, by urging it upon the consciences of their people, which they promised to do. But little was done about it; for divers of the elders' wives, &c. were in some measure partners of the general disorder." Apparently some forms of expression were easier to control than others.

As Governor William Bradford was discovering in Plimouth, too much emphasis on strict control might sometimes even engender wanton immorality. However variously particular cases might be explained, between 1638 and 1641 the Bay Colony was troubled by several cases of adultery, fornication, and bestiality that Winthrop found noteworthy. Sexual misconduct struck him as remarkably notorious in 1640 and 1641, years when Thomas Dudley and then Richard Bellingham were governors. Perhaps as a historian, Winthrop was more sensitive to disorder when other men were in power. And no doubt Winthrop's eyes were opened to deception when he discovered, as he noted in May 1640, that "his bailiff, whom he had trusted with managing his farm, had engaged him for £2500 without his privity." His fellow church members in Boston raised funds on his behalf, and the magistrates helped secure his estate by giving a large tract of land to Margaret Winthrop. Nevertheless, it took Winthrop two years, during which time money was scarce throughout New England, to repay the debts that bailiff Luxford's double-dealing had incurred. However grievous such personal matters were, though, the Bay Colony's problems in these years went well beyond instances of individual immorality. Indeed, upon the heels of their victory in the Pequod war and their resolution of the Antinomian crisis, the Puritans faced a broader, more far-reaching challenge, involving their relationship with England and raising unavoidable questions about the stability, success, and meaning of their entire errand.

Over the years Winthrop and his fellow magistrates had deftly sidestepped royal demands for the return of the Puritan patent, and the Crown's threat of imposing a "general governor" upon the whole of New England had never been accomplished. Likewise, the Puritans resisted pressure from their supporters in England to move the whole colony southward to a gentler climate and better trade routes. But political connivance, skillful argument, and even the vast Atlantic Ocean could not protect the Bay Colony from the unfortunate consequences of the rising success of the Puritans in England and the outbreak of civil war there. However heartened the Puritans in Massachusetts were regarding the political fortunes of their comrades in England, by June 1640 Winthrop was observing that "this year there came over great store of provisions, both out of England and Ireland, and but few passengers, (and those brought very little money,) which was occasioned by the store of money and quick markets, which the merchants found here the two or three years before, so as now all our money was drained from us, and cattle and all commodities grew very cheap, which enforced us at the next general court, in the 8th month, to make an order, that corn should pass in payments of new debts; Indian at 4s. the bushel; rye at 5s. and wheat at 6s.; and that, upon all executions for former debts, the creditor might take what goods he pleased, (or, if he had no goods, then his lands,) to be appraised by three men, one chosen by the creditor, one by the debtor, and one by the marshal." Virtually everyone was in debt. By October "the scarcity of money made a great change in all commerce. Merchants would sell no wares but for ready money, men could not pay their debts though they had enough, prices of lands and cattle fell soon to one half and less, yea to a third, and after one fourth part." A fishing ship arriving in December "brought us news of the Scots entering England, and the calling of a parliament, and the hope of a thorough reformation, &c. whereupon some among us began to think of returning back to England." Some in the Bay Colony sought to improve their lot by moving south and sold their estates at very low rates. "These things, together with the scarcity of money, caused a sudden and very great abatement of the prices of all our own commodities . . . whereby God taught us the vanity of all outward things." Prosperity in the Bay had depended on growth, driven by a steady stream of new immigrants with money to spend. Puritan success in England, which Winthrop and the others had come to Massachusetts to help bring about, apparently meant economic failure in New England.

Instead of returning home to contribute to the triumph of the saints, though, virtually all of Winthrop's Puritans stayed put, analyzed their situation honestly, and changed their economic course. By February 1640 "the general fear of want of foreign commodities, now our money was gone, and that things were like to go well in England, set us to work to provide shipping of our own." Hugh Peter led in building a ship of three hundred tons at Salem and another half that size at Boston. Economic self-reliance was matched by political independence, even from the Puritans' own party: "Upon the great liberty which the king had left the parliament to in England, some of our friends there wrote to us advice to send over some to solicit for us in the parliament, giving us hope that we might obtain much, &c. But consulting about it, we declined motion for this consideration, that if we should put ourselves under the protection of the parliament, we must then be subject to all such laws as they should make, or at least such as they might impose upon us; in which course though they should intend our good, yet it might prove very prejudicial to us." Soon immigration ceased, and by June 1641 it was clear that the Bay Colony was on its own: "The parliament of England setting upon a general reformation both of church and state, the earl of Strafford being beheaded, and the archbishop (our great enemy) and many others of the great officers and judges, bishops and others, imprisoned and called to account, this caused all men to stay in England in expectation of a new world, so as few coming to us, all foreign commodities grew scarce, and our own of no price." Massachusetts responded with characteristic Puritan vigor in the face of hardship: "These straits set our people to work to provide fish, clapboards, plank, &c. and to sow hemp and flax (which prospered very well) and to look out to the W. Indies for a trade for cotton." Establishing a printing house in late 1638 freed the Bay Colony in one way from cultural dependence on England. In their reaction to new political and economic realities, the Puritans continued to broaden their commitment to independence.

According to Winthrop's record, the governorship of Dudley in 1640 was undistinguished, and that of Bellingham in 1641 was disastrous. Competition between the locally representative deputies and the generally elected magistrates was sharp and unremitting, as Winthrop noted on 12 November 1641, to the extent that "Mr. Dudley, who being a very wise and just man, and one that would not be trodden under foot of any man, took occasion (alleging his age &c.) to tell the court that he was resolved to leave his place, and therefore desire them against the next court of elections to think of some other." Many entreated him to change his mind, "but he continued resolute." There was no such response when Bellingham followed suit: "Thereupon the governor also made a speech, as if he desired to leave his place of magistracy also, but he was fain to make his own answer, for no man desired him to keep, or to consider better of it." Given their distaste for the latitude of the magistrates' authority in the face of the broad changes the colony was experiencing, the deputies pressed their case for specifying the fundamental laws according to which the people would be governed. After years of debate, in 1641 the "Body of Liberties" composed by Nathaniel Ward "had been revised and altered by the court, and sent forth into every town to be further considered of, and now again in this court, they were revised, amended and presented, and so established for three years, by that experience to have them fully amended and established to be perpetual." With these laws in place, fears that continued election might lead Winthrop to overstep his authority abated, and the people called him back to the governorship in 1642 to lead the colony into its uncharted future. With his personal finances back in order, he was ready to resume official leadership. As he looked steadily forward, Winthrop relied on his experience of governance through consensus during the Antinomian crisis and on what he had learned about the direction of the colony by writing its history throughout these critical years.

Winthrop's writing became more flowing and episodic during these years of transition; the entries in his journal lengthened into summaries of major events and trends within the Bay Colony. In addition to keeping a record of interesting incidents of daily life, Winthrop began to group events according to their significance, lacing his analysis with comments directed at his readers and explicitly for their benefit. As he moved into and out of the governor's office, he became more deliberate as a historian, more self-conscious about his construction of the Puritan public narrative. "It is useful to observe, as we go along, such especial providences of God as were manifested for the good of these plantations," he noted on 15 October 1635. He left blanks in the narrative where additional material or analysis could be added, and the fact that some entries refer backward to previous events and occasionally even forward to future occurrences indicates that he was consciously editing and revising his writing. The Puritan project was becoming a story, with an overall significance greater than its particular facts and an intended audience far broader than the participants and their immediate contemporaries.

Such conventions are especially evident in Winthrop's treatment of the scandals during Bellingham's governorship in 1641. An entry in November opens with "Query, whether the following be fit to be published," and Winthrop proceeds to relate the unsavory details: "The governour, Mr. Bellingham, was married, (I would not mention such ordinary matters in our history, but by occasion of some remarkable accidents.) The young gentlewoman was ready to be contracted to a friend of his, who lodged at his house, and by his consent had proceeded so far with her, when on the sudden the governour treated with her, and obtained her for himself. He excused it by the strength of his affection, and that she was not absolutely promised to the other gentleman." As Winthrop points out, Bellingham's violations of Puritan standards of decency were exacerbated by the haste of his marriage and by his refusal to answer the prosecution when the matter was raised in court. Continuing this theme, the next entry in the journal, which stretches for many pages, records several other, even more offensive breaches of sexual morality, including adultery, rape, incest, and sexual abuse of children and concludes with the sad tale of the trial and execution of "one Hackett, a servant in Salem, about 18 or 20 years of age [who] was found in buggery with a cow, upon the Lord's day." These incidents set the stage for Winthrop's description of the "uncomfortable agitations and contentions" into which the court was thrown by Bellingham's petty jealousy of other magistrates—all of which Winthrop claims to be willing to relate solely because "history must tell the whole truth."

In this instance, of course, Winthrop's announcement of his convictions about the historian's responsibility may have been colored by a desire to dramatize the failures of the man whom he succeeded as governor. In a different context within the same long entry in the journal, Winthrop reveals another of his beliefs about the importance of history. In arguing against an exact specification of the penalties for all crimes and offenses and thereby in favor of reserving some scope for judicial discretion, Winthrop asserts that "God hath not confined all wisdom, &c. to any one generation, that they should set rules for all others to walk by." Whether such observations were expedient political commentary or ingredients of an implicit philosophy of history, they fit together with the more flowing, episodic nature of the journal's narrative to suggest that Winthrop had begun to see his work as historian as complementary to, and even as providing a context for, his work as governor. However bound he was to the exigencies of circumstance, the historian's commitment to tell the whole truth and his willingness to remain open to the future by admitting the limitations of any one generation helped equip him to lead the colony successfully into an uncharted future.

The importance of Winthrop's work as the historian of the Bay Colony was recognized by his contemporaries, according to Thomas Shepard, who sent a letter full of judicious encouragement in January 1639:

Sir, I doubt not but that yow haue the harts and prayers of many in the compiling of the History tho yow be left alone in it. As for those objections; 1 That some mens virtues cannot be commended with modesty because they are now liuing; I suppose the Historian may without any just offence giue them there due, especially in those cases where there vertues are exemplary to others, and the expressions modestly setting them out without swelling the socket where such lights are set up. 2 That some persons errours cannot be mentioned without prejudice to there places; I confesse tis some what, yet let the History make its progresse till it comes to such persons times and practises; and then vpon serious thoughts spent how to carry on that busines, I doubt not but god will manifest himselfe on way or another by that time, that there will not be much cause of sticking here what to doe; 3: That some things may prejudice vs in regard of the state of England if divulged; I know not what they be which can do so, more then what is known to all the woorld already; if there be any secret hid things which may be prouoking; it may be left to the judgement of others how far it will be fit to divulge them when the coppy is priuately examined.[6]

The historian must have found Shepard's concluding blessing particularly heartening: "Surely Sir the woorke is of god and many eyes and harts will be now expecting it with prayers; the good Lord guide and encourage yow in your way and recompense it abundantly to yow."[7] By this time Winthrop knew that his work had an audience who appreciated its significance.

91

In dealing with religious as well as political matters during these years, Winthrop's writing underwent developments which reveal the man's personal beliefs and suggest his view of the nature and purpose of the history he was writing. In the winter of 1636, "in the 49 yeare of my age just compleat" and at the height of the religious turmoil caused by Anne Hutchinson's teaching, Winthrop wrote a long description of his own spiritual development. In this separate narrative, titled "John Winthrop's Christian Experience," Winthrop reviews his life, finding that ever since his boyhood he has been involved in a process of conversion, moving backward and forward between sin and grace, up and down between exultation and melancholy. Throughout his mature years, "I have gone under continuall conflicts between the flesh and the spirit, and sometimes with Satan himself (which I have more discerned of late then I did formerly) many falls I have had, and have lyen long under some, yet never quite forsaken of the Lord." His experience was contrary to the instant and thoroughgoing oneness with the Spirit the Antinomians were preaching: "My usual falls have been through dead heartednesse, and presumptuousnesse, by which Satan hath taken advantage to wind mee into other sinnes. When the flesh prevayles the spirit withdrawes, and is sometimes so grieved as he seems not to acknowledge his owne work. Yet in my worst times hee hath been pleased to stirre, when hee would not speak, and would yet support mee that my fayth hath not fayled utterly."[8] Such had become the pattern of his life.

Hence Winthrop confesses that he was caught off guard by the new teachings, yet given his understanding of the religious life as a continuing struggle, even this incident is simply an episode in an ongoing process: "The Doctrine of free justification lately taught here took me in as drowsy a condition, as I had been in (to my remembrance) these twenty yeares, and brought mee as low (in my own apprehension) as if the whole work had been to begin anew. But when the voice of peace came I knew it to bee the same that I had been acquainted with before, though it did not speak so loud nor in that measure of joy that I had felt sometimes." He concludes the narrative by yielding the spotty nature of his spiritual life to Christ in prayer: "The Lord Jesus who (of his own free grace) hath washed my soul in the blood of the everlasting Covenant, wash away all those spotts also in his own good time. Amen, even so doe Lord Jesus."[9] Because of the Antinomians' denial of the enduring connection between the joys and the imperfections of the Christian life that was fundamental to his own spiritual experience, Winthrop was profoundly opposed to their opinions.

It is significant that he was moved to write an account of his religious life at the height of the crisis. By not including this account in his journal, Winthrop showed that as a historian his focus was on the colony's corporate life, even when public events such as the Antinomian crisis concerned intensely personal experiences. Yet along with this important distinction went an equally important connection between his personal and public narratives, for in both genres Winthrop portrayed life as a purposeful process of enduring struggle, rather than as a one-time contest between absolute good and evil. In both contexts, the insights that guided his writing were in concert with the moderation and fortitude that most characterized his political leadership.

At the conclusion of the Antinomian affair, Winthrop collected the relevant documents and proceedings and sent them to England to be published as *A Short Story of the Rise, reign, and ruin of the Antinomians, Familists, & Libertines.*[10] Given the years that passed between its initial composition and its eventual publication in 1644 in England under the intrusive editorship of Thomas Weld, it is very difficult to determine exactly which portions of the text itself and which of the sentiments it expresses were written by Winthrop. Because of the sweeping changes that occurred in English religious and political life between those years, the author's intentions cannot be assessed by way of the text's reception. Thus the *Short Story* can best be understood as ancillary to the story that Winthrop's history told, and as such it will be discussed in Part Two of this book. Indeed, Winthrop's decision to publish it separately indicates that he did not view the intricate theological arguments and the inner workings of church discipline that its documents trace as essential ingredients of the history he was recording in his journal. That is to say, for Winthrop, the Antinomian crisis was chiefly significant as an important episode in the ongoing story of the Puritans in New England. For him, the way the community resolved and moved beyond the crisis was more important than the force of Anne Hutchinson's arguments and her skill in making them. As historian and as governor, Winthrop came through these years of testing as one prepared to lead the colony in looking steadily forward. In either capacity, he might fail to deal with particular incidents with complete success. Yet because of his experience in both of his callings, Winthrop was well prepared to lead the Puritans in facing the large challenge of charting an independent future.

4

Looking Steadily Forward

T HE PURITANS chose John Winthrop as governor of the Massachusetts Bay Colony for five of the seven final years of his life and as
deputy governor twice. In leading the colony through the
challenges of these years, he helped set a course that would guide
New England long after the powerful figures of his own generation had
passed. The institutions these early Puritans established and the patterns of
life they shaped were living presences and then powerfully remembered
ideals in subsequent American life. Because ideas and beliefs were serious
business, not abstractions, for the Puritans, the values that later generations
looked to as the Puritan legacy were tested and contested in daily life. While
events across the seas seemed to isolate New England, the Puritans discovered that their lives depended on working out successful relationships with
others both like and quite different from themselves. As the final sections of
Winthrop's journal show, an ongoing Puritan identity was achieved through
conflicts between the strong men and colorful personalities of the 1640s.

Given the Civil War between Parliament and the king, some events were
clearly momentous. In other cases, apparently trivial or mundane events
would focus questions in ways that had lasting consequences. Thus at a
meeting of the general court in June 1642, one month after Winthrop
replaced Bellingham as governor, "there fell out a great business upon a very
small occasion." The facts of the case appeared simple enough. Back in 1636
"there was a stray sow in Boston, which was brought to Captain Keayne: he
had it cried divers times, and divers came to see it, but none made claim to it
for near a year. He kept it in his yard with a sow of his own. Afterwards one
Sherman's wife, having lost such a sow, laid claim to it, but came not to see

it, till Captain Keayne had killed his own sow. After being showed the stray sow, she gave out that he had killed her sow. The noise hereof being spread about the town, the matter was brought before the elders of the church as a case of offense; many witnesses were examined, and Captain Keayne was cleared." Yet because this apparently petty matter revealed deep-seated social tensions, a tidy resolution proved impossible.

Mrs. Sherman was not satisfied and was encouraged to press onward "by the instigation of one George Story, a young merchant of London, who kept in her house (her husband being then in England)." Mr. Story and Mrs. Sherman, it turns out, "had been brought before the governour upon complaint of Captain Keayne as living under suspicion," so they had an additional motive for pursuing the case. Even so, they were not successful. At a lower court in Boston "upon a full hearing, Captain Keayne was again cleared, and the jury gave him £3 for his cost, and he bringing his action against Story and her for reporting about that he had stolen her sow, recovered £20 of either of them." In response, George Story "searcheth town and country to find matter against Captain Keayne about this stray sow, and got one of his witnesses to come into Salem court and to confess there that he had forsworn himself; and upon this he petitions in Sherman's name, to this general court, to have the cause heard again, which was granted." At this point, the plot thickens, and an apparently trivial, personally vindictive case takes on wider significance.

Even when "the best part of seven days were spent in examining of witnesses debating of the cause," a conclusive judgment could not be reached, for the court was split down lines that divided the colony as a whole: "For there being nine magistrates and thirty deputies, no sentence could by law pass without the greater number of both, which neither plaintiff nor defendant had." Two magistrates and fifteen deputies sided with Mrs. Sherman, and seven magistrates and eight deputies stood with Captain Keayne, with the other seven deputies remaining doubtful. In essence, the more aristocratic magistrates sided with the well-to-do Captain Keayne, while the more democratic deputies backed poor Mrs. Sherman. Although characteristically judicious, Winthrop's assessment revealed his own bias. He saw contentiousness, earnestness, and prejudice on both sides, yet he found Keayne's witnesses somewhat more persuasive. Moreover, the captain had actual possession of the sow, whereas the most that Mrs. Sherman could establish was the probability that the sow was hers, and when all other things are equal, possession is preferable to possibility in point of law. In addition, on the one hand, it turned out that Captain Keayne had previously been censured in both church and court for being "a hard dealer in his course of trading." Although "he was very worthy of blame in that kind," on the other hand, "to give every man his due, he was very useful to the country both by his hospitality and otherwise." Small wonder, then, that Winthrop observed, "But one dead fly spoils much good ointment." Yet the maxims of the historian provided no refuge for the governor.

The failure of Story and Sherman's suit "gave occasion to many to speak unreverently of the court, especially of the magistrates," whose veto, or "negative voice," had saved Captain Keayne. People spoke of recalling these magistrates and taking the power of the veto away from the magistrates altogether. The governor and magistrates published "a declaration of the true state of the cause, that truth might not be condemned unknown," and before the court adjourned, Winthrop tried and failed to have the magistrates and deputies adopt "a declaration in nature of a pacification, whereby it might have appeared, that, howsoever the members of the court dissented in judgment, yet they were the same in affection, and had a charitable opinion of each other." The Puritans were working their way painfully toward a truly bicameral legislature and toward a clear separation of legislative, judicial, and executive powers within their government. But until a better system was devised, the differences undermining their present arrangements could not be papered over.

Therefore, it is not surprising to find Winthrop remarking a year later, in June 1643, that "the sow business" had not yet been "digested in the country." In the interim, the plaintiff and defendant remained at odds, with George Story and Mrs. Sherman doing their best to enlist support from additional deputies, church elders, and any magistrates whose opinions they could sway. By now it was clear that the people sympathized with Mrs. Sherman because she was poor and that her fine for slander, although never collected, was confused with the facts of the case in popular opinion. So some of the magistrates convinced Captain Keayne to restore the smaller fine that she had actually paid, thereby leaving the sentence unfulfilled and symbolically removing whatever harm the proceedings had caused. Evidently the principal parties were satisfied, but the larger political issues remained on the table. Since they could not be so conveniently resolved, Winthrop bought a little time with a discreet exercise of gubernatorial humility.

When some of the elders, who knew the sentiments in their churches and towns, advised Winthrop to remove the offense caused by a writing he had published regarding the case of the sow, "he easily consented to them so far as they had convinced him of his failing therein." The governor was willing to retract the manner of his expression but not the substance of his argument, and as historian, Winthrop made sure that "his speech was set down verbatim to avoid misrepresentation, as if he had retracted what he had wrote in the point of the case." Indeed, the magistrates and deputies together, as a group, were responsible for the judgment in the case, but the manner of expression was Winthrop's own, and he now affirmed that even "the great provocation by some of the adverse party" and the desire of some of the magistrates "to vindicate ourselves from that aspersion that was cast upon us" was "no sufficient warrant for me to break out into any distemper. I confess I was too prodigal of my brother's reputation: I might have obtained the cause I had in hand without casting such blemish upon others as I did." He acknowledged that his tone had been proud: "It is true a man may (as the case may be) appeal to the judgment of religion and reason, but, as I there carried it, I did arrogate too much to myself and ascribe too little to others." He concluded this little speech by stating his desire to reform: "I hope I shall be more wise and watchful hereafter." As governor, Winthrop was willing to secure tranquillity by apologizing for a style of writing that had proved offensive, though even then he was careful not to confess any more substantial errors of judgment. As historian, he deliberately recorded the event in a way that preserved the distinction between matter and manner. By showing his own readiness to respond to criticism for the good of the colony, Winthrop actually won on both counts. Winthrop was refining his style of writing, and being conscious of the role he was playing in the history he was writing may have made a political apology easier to perform.

Now that the sow affair itself had been resolved, the major question it raised, concerning the veto power of the magistrates, also required Winthrop's skills in both politics and writing. Encouraged by arguments among the magistrates, the deputies pressed for a speedy decision. The magistrates responded that since the present form of government "had been established upon serious consultation and consent of all the elders," it would be imprudent to change it without their considered advice. So the matter was deferred pending broader discussion, particularly by the elders, with historian Winthrop noting candidly that "it was the magistrates' only care to gain time, that so the people's heat might be abated, for then they knew they would hear reason, and that the advice of the elders might be interposed." One of the elders obligingly circulated an argument that removing the magistrates' veto would jettison the safeguards of a mixed government and move the colony dangerously toward a simple democracy.

Winthrop himself joined the fray with a defense of the negative vote, concluding a lengthy argument by observing "this longe approved maxime It is better for the Commonwealth that a mischeife be tollerated, then an Inconvenience indured, much more, foundations of Goverment over-throwne, as must needs be if this Neg: vo: be layd down." In a summary memorandum, he repeated that the present system had in fact worked well and should not be changed simply because of the possibility that the magistrates might abuse their power, and he concluded with three examples from common experience which all Puritans would understand: "The hande consisting of two parts: the 4 fingers and the thumbe, have each of them a negative power, so as the fingers cannot effecte any work without the thumbe, nor the thumbe without the fingers. A windmill may consist of divers wheeles and Rudders hath an vpper wheele or break which hath a neg: power to all the rest, otherwise the mill would make madd work in a tempest. In an Armye, they are the common soldiers vpon whom the whole work lyes, yet the Commanders have a neg: power over them as well as direction, otherwise they would soone be in Confusion."[1] For the time being, delaying tactics and Winthrop's arguments prevailed, "so as the deputies and the people also, having their heat moderated by time, and their judgments better informed by what they had learned about it, let the cause fall." In the following year the elders negotiated a lasting solution, establishing a workable bicameral legislature by more clearly separating the legislative, executive, and judicial powers of government.

At the end of October 1644, "the general court assembled again, and all the elders were sent for, to reconcile the differences between the magistrates and deputies." The two groups still jostled for power, but the elders proved themselves capable of answering questions in a way that limited strife and produced a system in which ongoing tensions would be constructive. The elders affirmed that on the basis of the patent and by their election by the people the magistrates were the standing council of the commonwealth, with executive power to govern according to laws passed by the general court. If action was required in situations where no particular laws applied, then the magistrates were "to be guided by the word of God, till the general court give particular rules in such cases." Legislative power remained in the general court, where both magistrates and deputies had veto power; therefore, passage of laws to guide and control the executive required cooperation and consent between the two bodies.

Subject to the laws of the commonwealth, the administration of justice was in the hands of the magistrates also, but their judgments could be appealed to the general court, and a magistrate whose adjudication was found to be defective or delinquent could be removed by the general court. As justices, magistrates could assess the circumstances of a crime and pronounce a lesser but not a greater sentence than the law prescribed, and the elders felt that the laws should be as explicit as possible in regulating crimes and penalties. The elders also agreed with the deputies that as the legislative body of the commonwealth, the general court could commission officers to discharge certain business as particular occasions required, without circumscribing or conflicting with the general executive authority of the magistrates. "Finally," they said, "it is our humble request, that in case any difference grow in the general court, between magistrates and deputies, either in these, or any like weighty cases, which cannot be presently issued with mutual peace, that both parties will be pleased to defer the same to further deliberation for the honour of God and of the court." The magistrates and deputies together approved all of the resolutions formulated by the elders. "Still fixed upon their own opinions, " a few men dissented, leading Winthrop to observe, "So hard a matter it is, to draw men (even wise and godly) from the love of the fruit of their own inventions." But in the main there was agreement. Though a purportedly stolen sow had instigated this chain of events, other and more significant circumstances had joined in moving the Puritans toward a more stable system to govern internal and guide external affairs.

News traveled slowly across the Atlantic, but the Puritans in Massachusetts followed the military campaigns and political intrigues of the English Civil War with close interest, and they continued to suffer its effects as immigration was at a standstill, money scarce, and English goods in short supply. If the Bay Colony was to survive, the Puritans would have to become more self-sufficient and to trade with others for what England no longer provided. "Our supplies from England failing much," Winthrop noted on 12 June 1643, "men began to look about them, and fell to a manufacture of cotton, whereof we had store from Barbados, and of hemp and flax, wherein Rowley, to their great commendation, exceeded all other towns." John Winthrop, Jr., led an ambitious project to establish an ironworks in New England. Since commerce with England was haphazard at best, the Puritans built their own ships and began to trade in earnest with other colonies and countries. Crucial as such efforts were for the Puritan economy, they led to murky foreign relations and required Winthrop and the other leaders to take risks for which they were not well prepared. One case in particular seemed full of danger and intrigue.

While the Puritans were sorting out their political system within the Bay Colony, they attracted the attention of two French noblemen with competing claims to the governorship of French possessions north of New England. The rivalry between Charles de Saint Etienne de la Tour and Charles de Menon, Sieur d'Aulnay de Charnise, known to the Puritans simply as La Tour and D'Aulnay, spilled southward along the Maine coast and sometimes into Boston Harbor itself. As French papists and pirates, both were clearly enemies in Puritan eyes. Yet neutrality was not an option, and at the outset La Tour was more friendly and forthcoming. On 6 October 1642 one of La Tour's lieutenants sailed into Massachusetts Bay with fourteen men: "They brought letters from La Tour to the governour, full of compliments, and desire of assistance from us against Monsieur D'Aulnay. They staid here about a week, and were kindly entertained, and though they were papists, yet they came to our church meeting; and the lieutenant seemed to be much affected to find things as he did, and professed he never saw so good order in any place. One of the elders gave him a French testament with notes, which he kindly accepted, and promised to read it." One month later the lines were clearly drawn: "Some of our merchants sents a pinnace to trade with La Tour in St. John's river. He welcomed them very kindly, and wrote to our governour letters very gratulatory for his lieutenant's entertainment, &c. and withal a relation of the state of the controversy between himself and Monsieur D'Aulnay. In their return they met with D'Aulnay at Pemaquid, who wrote also to our governour, and sent him a printed copy of the arrest against La Tour, and threatened us, that if any of our vessels came to La Tour, he would make prize of them." Governor Winthrop was in a tight spot, for if the Puritans were to pursue the increased trade their economy required, they would have to side with one of these otherwise undesirable allies.

In June 1643 just as "the sow business" was finally being resolved, "Mr. La Tour arrived here in a ship of 140 tons and 140 persons," unannounced and, fortunately, seeking aid from the Puritans rather than coming to do them harm. This band of strangers frightened the first person they met, Captain Gibbons's wife, who "hastened to get from them, and landed at the governour's garden. La Tour landed presently after her, and there found the governour and his wife, and two of his sons, and his son's wife," all unguarded. Winthrop listened to La Tour's plea for military assistance and "answered that he could say nothing to it till he had conferred with other of the magistrates." Mrs. Gibbons was carried home in Winthrop's boat, and the governor's party sailed into Boston aboard La Tour's ship, arousing considerable alarm.

Since La Tour passed the unmanned, uncompleted fort on Castle Island with the governor in his power, it was good that the Frenchman came in friendship, "for if La Tour had been ill minded towards us, he had such a opportunity as we hope neither he nor any other shall ever have the like again." Indeed, "he might have gone and spoiled Boston," Winthrop observed, "but his neglecting this opportunity gave us assurance of his true meaning." Winthrop conferred quickly with "such of the magistrates as were at hand, and some of the deputies." La Tour's commission, "which was farily engrossed in parchment, under the hand and seal of the Vice Admiral of France," was convincing, and the Puritan leaders decided not to aid La Tour outright but to allow him to hire men and ships from Boston. A few days later, when the French troops were permitted to exercise on shore, they practiced a charge, and "some alarm was excited among women and children, and perhaps a little suspicion among full grown men." Even with La Tour's courtesy in sharing entertainment with the Puritans and attending their church meetings, rumors flew, and the magistrates, deputies, and elders were summoned to debate whether and to what extent good Christians might aid "idolaters" and, if they did, whether it was safe to back La Tour against D'Aulnay. That they had the discussion at all shows how far the Puritans had journeyed since leaving England to further the true Reformation.

Those who sided with Winthrop in favor of helping La Tour went even further. If a biblical reference seemed to lead in the other direction, they argued, it should not be taken too literally but interpreted in context, "not simply according to the words of that one sentence taken apart from the rest." Furthermore, when opponents asserted that "papists are not to be trusted, seeing it is one of their tenets that they are not to keep promise with heretics," Winthrop's supporters replied that "in this case we rely not upon their faith but their interest, it being for their advantage to hold in with us, we may safely trust them; besides we shall not need to hazard ourselves upon their fidelity, having sufficient strength to secure ourselves." Finally, when every possibility seems tainted, "we may and must trust God with our safety so long as we serve his providence in the use of such means as he affords us." After all, Jesus used the example of the good Samaritan who helped a Jew, "though as opposite in religion as protestants and papists." Therefore, "we are exhorted to be like our Heavenly Father in doing good to the just and unjust, that is to all, as occasion is offered, even such as he causeth the sun to shine upon, and the rain to fall upon, though excommunicated persons, blasphemers and persecutors, yet if they be in distress, we are to do them good, and therefore to relieve them." If the necessity of trade had liberalized Winthrop's principles of interpretation, he could still cite the Scriptures with the best of the Puritans, even when he led them in new directions.

The principles upon which Winthrop based his argument guided the Puritans well as they developed a mercantile economy in the years ahead, but their immediate application proved faulty, though not disastrous. As the two Frenchmen squabbled and fought during the 1640s, La Tour turned out to be weaker, less reliable, and more of a pirate than D'Aulnay. Fortunately for the Puritans, D'Aulnay was more practical and did not hold a grudge. Throughout the affair Winthrop stayed in touch with both parties and tried to play them off against each other. By July 1643 he was repenting "three errours the governour &c. committed in managing this business." He regretted the hastiness of his support for La Tour, his failure to consult the elders adequately, and his omission of prayer at the outset of deliberations. There were "occasions" but not excuses for these mistakes, but Winthrop as historian was forthright in his self-assessment: "But this fault hath been many times found in the governour to be oversudden in his resolutions, for although the course were both warrantable and safe, yet it had beseemed men of wisdom and gravity to have proceeded with more deliberation and further advice."

While Winthrop had other occasions to heed his own advice during these years, his first serious venture into foreign affairs ended well enough. Some bad feelings remained, for La Tour and his wife left several Boston merchants deeply in debt. More important, despite a nasty outburst during his decisive defeat of La Tour in 1645, D'Aulnay soon forgave the Puritans for backing his rival. Within a year La Tour had become a vicious pirate, and articles of peace were signed between the Puritans and D'Aulnay. On 20

September 1646 the new allies resolved their conflicting claims, and the injuries and damages D'Aulnay's men had suffered at the hands of the Puritans who fought with La Tour required only a small present: "Accordingly we sent Monsieur D'Aulney by his commissioners a very fair new sedan, (worth forty or fifty pounds where it was made, but of no use to us,) sent by the viceroy of Mexico to a lady his sister, and taken in the West Indies by Captain Cromwell, and by him given to our governour." An ornate and useless chair sealed the bargain between the French warlord and the Purtitans, who were indeed becoming traders.

Faced with threats from marauding Frenchmen, competition for trade from the Dutch, and continuing occasional violence from the Indians, the Puritans recognized the need for cooperation among the English settlements spread throughout New England. As they developed a more stable system of government within Massachusetts Bay, the Puritans also worked toward a way of coordinating foreign relations, commerce, and a common defense with other New Englanders. Despite a rousing sermon from Ezekiel Rogers against the danger of continuing to elect the same governor, at the court of elections in May 1643 the Puritans reelected Winthrop, who led their delegation in negotiating with commissioners from Plimouth, Connecticut, and New Haven: "These coming to consultation encountered some difficulties, but being all desirous of union and studious of peace, they readily yielded each to other in such things as tended to common utility, &c. so as in some two or three meetings they lovingly accorded on these ensuing articles" of confederation, which were soon ratified by their respective general courts.

The United Colonies of New England came into existence to assist the individual colonies in coping with immediate problems, at a time when they were experiencing an increasing desire to act independently of their mother country. "At this court of elections there arose a scruple about the oath which the governour and the rest of the magistrates were to take, viz. about the first part of it: 'You shall bear true faith and allegiance to our sovereign Lord King Charles,' seeing he had violated the privileges of parliament, and made war upon them, and thereby had lost much of his kingdom and many of his subjects; whereupon it was thought fit to omit that part of it for the present." While remaining separate colonies, their larger loyalty was now to their fellow Americans.

Winthrop's evolving understanding of the purpose of the entire Puritan project and a new sense of the future audience of the history he was writing are expressed eloquently in the preamble and initial sections of the Articles of Confederation that he helped to draft and duly recorded in his journal:

WHEREAS we all come into these parts of America with one and the same end and aim, namely, to advance the kingdom of our Lord Jesus Christ, and to enjoy the liberties of the gospel in purity with peace: and whereas by our settling, by the wise providence of God, we are further dispersed upon the seacoasts and rivers than was at first intended, so that we cannot, according to our desire, with convenience communicate in one government and jurisdiction: and whereas we live encompassed with people of several nations and strange languages, which hereafter may prove injurious to us or our posterity; and for as much as the natives have formerly committed sundry insolences and outrages upon several plantations of the English, and have of late combined themselves against us, and seeing by reason of the sad distractions in England, (which they have heard of,) and by which they know we are hindered both from that humble way of seeking advice, and reaping those comfortable fruits of protection, which at other times we might well expect; we therefore do conceive it our bounded duty, without delay, to enter into a present consociation amongst ourselves for mutual help and strength in all future concernment, that, as in nation and religion, so in other respects, we be and continue one, according to the tenor and true meaning of the ensuing articles—1. Wherefore it is fully agreed and concluded between the parties above named, and they jointly and severally do, by these presents, agree and conclude that they all be, and henceforth be called by the name of the United Colonies of New England. 2. These united colonies, for themselves and their posterities, do jointly and severally hereby enter into a firm and perpetual league of friendship and amity, for offence and defence, mutual advice and succour upon all just occasions, both for preserving and propagating the truth and liberties of the gospel, and for their own mutual safety and welfare.

The obligations and operations of the United Colonies, as laid out in the ensuing ten articles, established a basis of cooperation that was an early prelude to the American federal system of governance.

Recognition of the new organization came quickly. On 22 July 1643 "a Dutch sloop arrived with letters in Latin, signed by the secretary there in the name and by the command of the governour and senate, directed to the governour and senate of the U.C. of New England, wherein 1st, he congratulates our late confederation, then he complains of unsufferable wrongs done to their people upon Connecticut," desiring "to know by a categorical answer, whether we will aid or desert them, (meaning Hartford,) that so they may know their friends from their enemies, &c." By September the commisioners of the United Colonies were dealing with religious fanatic Samuel Gorton's troublemaking between English settlers and Indians at Providence, denying the Dutch claims against Hartford and New Haven, "nor might we desert either of our confederates in a righteous cause," and demanding satisfaction for injuries and damages perpetuated along the Delaware River by the Swedish governor, who "demeaned himself as if he had neither christian nor moral conscience." In addition to bolstering the colonies in the conflicts with foreigners that their expanding trade inevitably engendered, the United Colonies also adjudicated competing claims to land and resources between the English colonies themselves.

Two decades earlier the religious differences between the Separatists who settled Plimouth and the nonseparating Puritans who settled the Bay Colony had seemed enormously important. Now the frictions between Massachusetts and Plimouth were over real estate, rather than theology and church governance, and their disputes concerned whether it was fair for the Bay Colony to bear the greatest portion of the costs of the United Colonies while having the same number of representatives as the other colonies. Their experiences in New England had not been identical, to be sure, but the several English colonies worked together to develop a fledgling federal system for cooperating against common enemies, nurturing trade, and managing whatever conflicts remained. Thomas Hooker, who had earlier led his people out of Massachusetts, was so delighted with the new confederation that he wrote to Winthrop to praise the governor's "christian readines" and his "candid, and cordiall cariage in a matter of so great consequence: Laboring by your spetiall prudence to settle a foundation of safety and prosperity in succeeding ages: A work which will be found not only for your comfort, but for your crowne at the great day of your account. Its the greatest good, that can befall a man in this world, to be an instrument vnder God to do a great deale of good: To be the repayrer of the breach, was of ould counted matter of highest prayse and acceptace with God and man: much more to be a meanes not only to mayntayne peace and truth in your dayes, but to leave both, as a Legacy to those that come after, vntill the coming of the Sonne of God in the clouds." Hoping to assist as Winthrop and the others were "laying the first stone of the foundation of this combynation of peace," Hooker encouraged the governor: "Goe on therefore (worthy Sir) and be ever enlarged in such worthy services, and the God of truth and peace will ever be with you."[2] In keeping with his leading role in the new system, Winthrop toward the end of his life was portraying the events he recorded not simply as the story of the Puritans or even as the affairs of Massachusetts but as the history of New England.

Likewise, as the Puritans developed better political systems within and between their colonies, most discovered that their bonds with New England had become stronger than their ties to the old England they had set out to reform. On 6 September 1642 "there came letters from divers Lords of the upper house, and some 30 of the house of commons, and others from the ministers there, who stood for the independency of the churches, to Mr. Cotton of Boston, Mr. Hooker of Hartford, and Mr. Davenport of New Haven, to call them, or some of them, if all could not, to England, to assist in the synod there appointed, to consider and advise about the settling of church government." Their responses were telling:

Mr. Hooker liked not the business, nor thought it any sufficient call for them to go 3,000 miles to agree with three men (meaning those three ministers who were for independency, and did solicit in the parliament, &c.) Mr. Davenport thought other-wise of it, so as the church there set apart a day to seek the Lord in it, and thereupon came to this conclusion, that seeing the church had no other officer but himself, therefore they might not spare him. Mr. Cotton apprehended strongly a call of God in it, though he were very averse to a sea voyage, and the more because his ordinary topic in Acts 13, led him to deliver that doctrine of the interest all churches have in each other's members for mutual helpfulness, &c. But soon after came other letters out of England, upon the breach between the king and parliament, from one of the former Lords, and from Mr. Welde and Mr. Peter, to advise them to stay till they heard further; so this care came to an end.

But not everyone had such fortitude.

Later that same month Winthrop noted that "the sudden fall of land and cattle, and the scarcity of foreign commodities, and money, &c. with the thin access of people from England, put many into an unsettled frame of spirit, so as they concluded there would be no subsisting here, and accord-ingly they began to hasten away, some to the West Indies, others to the Dutch, at Long Island, &. (for the governour there invited them by fair offers,) and others back for England." Winthrop points out that these people were unsavory characters, and he portrays the troubles they encoun-tered as just retribution for their weakness. His impassioned commentary calls directly upon the reader to affirm the covenant that sustains the ongo-ing Puritan community:

Others who went to other places, upon like grounds, succeeded no better. They fled for fear of want, and many of them fell into it, even to extremity, as if they had hastened into the misery which they feared and fled from, besides the depriving themselves of the ordinances and church fellowship, and those civil liberties which they enjoyed here; whereas, such as staid in their places, kept their peace and ease, and enjoyed still the blessing of the ordinances, and never tasted of those troubles and miseries, which they heard to have befallen those who departed. Much disputa-tion there was about liberty of removing for outward advantages, and all ways were sought for an open door to get out at; but it is to be feared many crept out at a broken wall. For such as come together in a wilderness, where are nothing but wild beasts and beastlike men, and there confederate together in civil and church estate, whereby they do, implicitly at least, bind themselves to support each other, and all of them that society, whether civil or sacred, whereof they are members, how they can break from this without free consent, is hard to find, so as may satisfy a tender or good conscience in time of trial. Ask thy conscience, if thou wouldst have plucked up thy stakes, and brought thy family 3000 miles, if thou hadst expected that all, or most, would have forsaken thee there. Ask again, what liberty thou hast towards others, which thou likest not to allow others towards thyself; for if one may go, another may, and so the greater part, and so church and commonwealth may be left destitute in a wilderness, exposed to misery and reproach, and all for thy ease and pleasure, whereas these all, being now thy brethren, as near to thee as the Israelites were to Moses, it were much safer for thee, after his example, to choose rather to

suffer affliction with thy brrethren, than to enlarge thy ease and pleasure by furthering the occasion of their ruin.

With his strong sense of responsibility to the community, Winthrop believed
that liberty did not mean freedom to abandon one's commitments for mere
personal advantage.

Winthrop was more understanding on 14 May 1645, when "the scarcity
of good ministers in England, and want of employment for our new gradu-
ates here, occasioned some of them to look abroad." Similarly, he considered it honorable that "Mr. Israel Stoughton, one of the magistrates, having
been in England about merchandize, went for England again the last winter,
with divers other of our best military men, and entered into the parliament's
service." He also notes with satisfaction that "these did good service, and
were well approved, but Mr. Stoughton falling sick and dying at Lincoln, the
rest all returned to their wives and families. But three of them went to
England again about the end of this year, but came back again and settled
themselves here, all but the surgeon." When the time came to make his own
decision, on 4 November 1646, Winthrop was mindful of his duties but
clear about his preferences. The court had decided to send one magistrate
and one elder to England to guard the cause of New England.

The governour and Mr. Norton, teacher of the church in Ipswich, were named, and
in a manner agreed upon; but upon second thoughts it was let fall, chiefly for these
two reasons, 1. it was feared, in regard that Mr. Peter had written to the governour to
come over and assist in the parliament's cause &c. that if he were there, he would be
called into the parliament, and so detained, 2. many were upon the wing, and his
departure would occasion more new thoughts and apprehensions &c. 3. it was
feared what changes his absence might produce &c. The governour was very averse
to a voyage into England, yet he declared himself ready to accept the service, if he
should be called to it, though he were then fifty-nine years of age, wanting one
month; but he was very glad when he saw the mind of the Lord to be otherwise.

Winthrop would have undertaken whatever service came with his office, but
his deepest commitments were no longer to the Puritan cause in New
England but to New England itself.

The steadiness of Winthrop's authority and his understanding of the
covenant that held the community together and would sustain it in the
future had been tested and, if anything, strengthened and confirmed in a
sensational trial in the preceding years. As in many political controversies,
the trouble began when people saw a discrepancy between the behavior of
public officials and the theory upon which their government was supposed
to rest. Like everyone who shared the background of medieval Christianity,
the Puritans believed that the authority of their government ultimately
rested on God's will. As good Calvinists, they knew that such divinely
sanctioned authority was invested in the offices of their government, rather

than in the particular individuals who were elected to serve in them. When squabbling between elected officials turned into self-serving arguments about power and authority, Winthrop often relied on the ministers to calm the tempest by reminding wayward magistrates to accept one another's human frailties and failings as they worked together to serve God. For example, in late October 1644, during an especially nasty debate about the powers of magistrates and deputies, Winthrop observed that

indeed it occasioned much grief to all the elders, and gave great offence through the country; and such as were acquainted with other states in the world, and had not well known the persons, would have concluded such a faction here as hath been usual in the council of England and other states, who walk by politic principles only. But these gentlemen were such as feared God, and endeavored to walk by the rules of his word in all their proceedings, so as it might be conceived in charity, that they walked according to their judgments and conscience, and where they went aside, it was merely for want of light, or their eyes were held through some temptation for a time, that they could not make use of the light they had, for in all these differences and agitations about them, they continued in brotherly love, and in the exercise of all friendly offices each to other, as occasion required.

Or so it was supposed to be among men who were not mere politicians. But no one would cast events in such a charitable context when Winthrop himself came under fire.

In 1644 Winthrop was deputy governor while Endecott was governor, and in 1645 Winthrop continued as deputy while Dudley was governor and Endecott became the sergeant major general. During this time Winthrop became embroiled on behalf of the magistrates in a dispute regarding the town of Hingham's choice of the captain of their militia. After presenting Anthony Emes to the magistrates as their choice, the townspeople changed their minds and sent forward the name of Bozoun Allen. The magistrates, respecting Emes, sent the backers of the two men home to cool off, charging them not to engage in military activities until the court made its decision. Allen's supporters forced the issue by appointing a training day for the troops and then refusing to follow the orders of Emes, who was still at least nominally in charge. What right did the magistrates have to override the wishes of the local citizens, the townspeople asked, especially when their deputies supported Allen? They voted on the spot for Allen, who proceeded to exercise the militia. Tensions between the magistrates and deputies flared, and at the next meeting of the general court the deputies granted the townspeople's petition to hear their cause. When the petitioners singled out the deputy governor as the target of their dissatisfaction, the infuriated magistrates pointed out that nothing criminal was charged, since the deputy governor had acted in accordance with the order of the court. But if the deputies wanted a hearing, the magistrates said, they would have one. Wanting to clear his name from the slanders circulating through the colony,

Winthrop agreed to the public hearing. Yet despite their passions, neither side was prepared for the spectacle in court.

Political bristling between the deputies and magistrates was nothing new, but formal charges against John Winthrop caused a stir throughout the Bay Colony. A crowd saw the trial commence, and Winthrop's behavior shocked them all: "The day appointed being come, the court assembled in the meeting house at Boston. Divers of the elders were present, and a great assembly of people. The deputy governour, coming in with the rest of the magistrates, placed himself beneath within the bar, and so sate uncovered. Some question there was in court about his being in that place (for many both of the court and the assembly were grieved at it.) But the deputy telling them, that, being criminally accused, he might not sit as a judge in that cause, and if he were upon the bench, it would be a great disadvantage to him, for he could not take that liberty to plead the cause, which he ought to be allowed at the bar, upon this the court was satisfied." With head uncovered, sitting in the place of the accused instead of with the judges, Winthrop waived his right to procedural appeals. The petitioners charged him with overstepping the bounds of his office by issuing warrants for the constable to bring those who disturbed the peace in Hingham to court, summoning others, and refusing to say who the witnesses against them would be. Winthrop pointed out that he was merely following the orders of the court, the laws of the land, and the normal conventions of judicial procedure. But the particulars of the case were not the real issues.

Soon the divisions within the court were no longer between Winthrop and the petitioners from Hingham but between the officers of the court themselves: "Two of the magistrates and many of the deputies were of the opinion that the magistrates exercised too much power, and that the people's liberty was thereby in danger; and other of the deputies (being about half) and all the rest of the magistrates were of a different judgment, and that authority was overmuch slighted, which, if not timely remedied, would endanger the commonwealth, and bring us to a mere democracy." With such a rift and Winthrop himself on trial, no holds were barred: "By occasion of this difference, there was not so orderly carriage at the hearing, as was meet, each side striving unseasonably to enforce the evidence, and declaring their judgments thereupon, which should have been reserved to a more private debate, (as after it was,) so as the best part of two days was spent in this publick agitation and examination of witnesses, &c." Although both sides soon agreed that Winthrop should be acquitted and that the petition against him was false and scandalous, weeks of wrangling ensured over whether the petitioners should be censured and fined by the court. When the magistrates threatened to call in the elders for advice, the deputies agreed to send the matter to arbitration. The petitioners were made to pay the court costs, and small fines were levied against the principal agitators, including Hingham's two deputies, one of whom was would-be militia captain Allen. The court found "the deputy governour to be legally and publickly acquit of all that was laid to his charge." When the sentence was finally read and Winthrop resumed his place on the bench, "he desired leave for a little speech" about the heart of the matter.

With his hat back on, Winthrop mentioned his satisfaction in being acquitted and then recalled the court and people to a proper understanding of what they should expect from each other in the years ahead:

The great questions that have troubled the country, are about the authority of the magistrates and the liberty of the people. It is yourselves who have called us to this office, and being called by you, we have our authority from God, in way of an ordinance, such as hath the image of God eminently stamped upon it, the contempt and violation whereof hath been vindicated with examples of divine vengeance. I entreat you to consider, that when you choose magistrates, you take them from among yourselves, men subject to like passions as you are. Therefore when you see infirmities in us, you should reflect on your own, and that would make you bear the more with us, and not be severe censurers of the failings of your magistrates, when you have continual experience of the like infirmities in yourselves and others. We account him a good servant, who breaks not his covenant. The covenant between you and us is the oath you have taken of us, which is to this purpose, that we shall govern you and judge your causes by the rules of God's laws and our own, according to our best skill.

On the one hand, the people should bear with those errors and failures that a magistrate, being human, will make from time to time from lack of skill. On the other hand, "if he fail in faithfulness, which by his oath he is bound unto, that he must answer for." Such was the Puritan understanding of authority and accountability.

For Winthrop, the proper view of authority was crucially linked with a right understanding of freedom. So he continued: "For the other point concerning liberty, I observe a great mistake in the country about that. There is a twofold liberty, natural (I mean as our nature is now corrupt) and civil or federal." Man shares with all other creatures the natural liberty "to do as he lists; it is a liberty to evil as well as to good. This liberty is incompatible and inconsistent with authority, and cannot endure the least restraint of the most just authority." Such freedom from restraint is all that some men understand of freedom, and it is the great enemy of every social order. In contrast, Winthrop says, "the other kind of liberty I call civil or federal, it may also be termed moral, in reference to the covenant between God and man, in the moral law, and the politic covenants and constitutions, amongst men themselves. This liberty is the proper end and object of authority, and cannot subsist without it; and it is a liberty to that only which is good, just and honest. This liberty you are to stand for, with the hazard (not only of your goods, but) of your lives, if need be." Such liberty is to be protected by authority, "wherein, if we fail at any time, we hope we shall be willing (by God's assistance) to hearken to good advice from any of you, or in any other way of God; so shall your liberties be preserved, in upholding the honour and power of authority amongst you." The people's failure to understand their own freedom led them to suspect the authority of their magistrates, and their suspicions, whetted by deputies who understood neither, led Winthrop to write a treatise about arbitrary government. The essence of his argument was delivered in his "little speech" to the court. When liberty is understood as one's ability to contribute to accomplishing what is good and right, instead of as the individual's freedom from any restraint whatsoever, the connection between liberty and authority becomes one of cooperation rather than of conflict. Despite continuing bickering and jockeying for power, the people must have agreed with Winthrop's vision of authority and liberty, for they elected him as governor in every remaining year of his life. The Hingham affair settled some important issues, or at least defined the proper terms for living purposefully through the inevitable tensions of social and political life. Winthrop's vision of the connection between authority and liberty defined a Puritan ideal in subsequent American life.

In Winthrop's day, however, not everyone was privileged to participate in that ideal. Yet the colony's involvement in foreign affairs began to open its system of governance to new men. The Company, soon upon arrival in Massachusetts, had been dramatically transformed into a commonwealth by the extension of voting rights to all male church members, known as free-men. A decade later the franchise was similarly broadened. The first step came by way of the Bay Colony's membership in the United Colonies of New England. Winthrop's first journal entry for 1644 records the impact of the Civil War. Parliament appointed a commission "for regulating the West Indies and all other English plantations in America," but the king counter-manded the appointment. The governor of Virginia "withstood the parliament's commissioners, and drew most of the other magistrates to take oath upon the sacrament to maintain the king's authority, &c. so that the whole country was like to rise in parties, some for the king, and others for the parliament." Massachusetts responded quite differently: "A proposition was made this court for all the English within the united colonies to enter into a civil agreement for the maintenance of religion and our civil liberties, and for yielding some more of the freeman's privileges to such as were no church members that should join in this government. But nothing was concluded, but referred to next court, and in the mean time, that letters should be written to the other colonies to advise with them about it. Nothing was effected for want of opportunity of meeting." If it was not yet possible to coordinate such a change throughout New England, pressure to broaden the base of government was mounting within the Bay Colony.

With the resolution of the Hingham affair and Winthrop's election as governor in May 1646, the court acted to alter the way the colony's commissioners to the United Colonies were chosen: "The magistrates and deputies had formerly chosen the commissioners, but the freemen, looking at them as general officers, would now choose them themselves, and the rather because some of the deputies had formerly been chosen to that office, which gave offence to our confederates and to many among ourselves." This court received a more radical proposal as well, in the form of a petition and remonstrance to the court—and if it failed there, to parliament—to change the system so that freeborn English subjects who would not submit to the church covenant would no longer be "deprived of all power and interest in civil affairs." Dr. Robert Child, a freethinking scientific colleague of John Winthrop, Jr., brought the petition on behalf of several colonists, with the aim of extending the franchise, breaking the grip of the churches on the political process, putting New England more directly under the control of Parliament, and generally promoting toleration. Although the petitioners "pressed to have present answer," the magistrates stalled: "The court being then near at an end, and the matter being very weighty, they referred the further consideration thereof to the next session." While Winthrop personally was deeply opposed to Child's proposals, a mediating position was also put forward: "And whereas a law was drawn up, and ready to pass, for allowing non-freemen equal power with the freemen in all town affairs, and to some freemen of such estate &c. their votes in the election of magistrates, it was thought fit to defer this also to the next session." The wealthy among the unchurched might be allowed to vote in general elections, and it was probably time to permit all male citizens to participate fully in local matters.

Dr. Child, the opposite of Winthrop in character as well as thinking, was not one to tolerate moderation and delay. Yet the Puritans had come to prize their independence too highly to admit control, even by Parliament. Hence when Child renewed his case in court, he and his cohort were censured and fined for sedition and contempt. When they attempted to go to England, their trunks were searched, petitions charging the Puritan ministers and magistrates with high treason were seized, and Child and his fellow travelers were arrested and detained until the ship had sailed. When he finally reached England, Child was too late. The Puritans had ably and persuasively defended themselves from charges of arbitrary government, Parliament had declared its support for the broad authority of the Massachusetts court, and Child's passionate remonstrance came to naught in old as well as New England. Bending a little, Winthrop's government permitted nonchurchmen to vote on local matters, but any broader changes were sealed away with Child's petitions. Substantial majorities in subsequent elections indicated that most of the Puritans were pleased with Winthrop's defense of their political system.

A formal definition of religious orthodoxy was all that remained for the Puritan way of life to be firmly planted for future generations. Toward this end, a synod met in Cambridge in August 1648, with Winthrop noting on 15

August that "the synod went on comfortably, and intended only the framing of a confession of faith &c. and a form of church discipline (not entertaining any other business.).". England's recent Westminster Confession was the model from which the Puritans worked to formulate their own statement of belief and proper church order. "For the first, they wholly agreed with that which the assembly in England had lately set forth. For the other, viz. for discipline, they drew it by itself, according to the general practice of our churches. So they ended in fourteen days." In matters of faith and belief, the Puritans were in accord with the victorious Protestants in England. Rejecting the Presbyterian pattern that had been adopted in the old country, however, the Puritans formally established the primacy and independence of the local congregation that had been a central reason, and for some the only reason, for their settlement of New England. The "Cambridge platform" constructed by this synod remained the foundation of Puritan religious life for over a century and continued, even after the American Revolution, to define one of the dominant strands in the fabric of American church history. That it was articulated in fourteen days and agreed upon so "comfortably" further demonstrates the steadiness with which the Puritans had come to face the future.

Not everyone fit into the Puritan mold, of course, and some events defied explanation according to Puritan categories. Examining how the Puritans dealt with strangers and strangeness helps to illumine the cohesiveness that was at once the strength and the weakness of the Puritan way in New England and further reveals the character of their principal governor and historian. Relations between Puritans and Indians in the 1640s were marked by sporadic, localized violence as well as by acts of individual kindness, while New Englanders and other Europeans traded with various tribes and settled on their lands. By facilitating communication among New Englanders regarding Indian sentiments and activities, the United Colonies organization strengthened their common defense. By reducing fears and rumors, the cooperative system lessened the likelihood of individual colonies going to war against the Indians and therefore helped to preserve an uneasy peace. John Eliot's translation of the Bible and missionary work offered a beacon of hope, but real peace was impossible while New Englanders harbored the ambivalence expressed in Winthrop's commentary regarding a violent storm on 5 July 1643: "There arose a sudden gust at N.W. so violent for half an hour as it blew down multitudes of trees. It lifted up their meeting house at Newbury, the people being in it. It darkened the air with dust, yet through God's mercy it did no hurt, but only killed one Indian with the fall of a tree." Such an eerie foreshadowing of Mark Twain's examination, over two centuries later, of Euro-American ambivalence about the humanity of black slaves indicates that an inability or unwillingness to admit genuine otherness was an enduring element in the Puritan cultural legacy.

The closure to otherness that forms the dark side of the cohesive Puritan community had doubly tragic consequences later that year when Indians killed Anne Hutchinson and sixteen of her family and followers who were living among the Dutch. The benefits and the price of peace were clearly linked in Winthrop's observation on 5 February 1643: "We now began to conceive hope that the Lord's time was at hand for opening a door of light and grace to those Indians, and some fruit appeared of our kind dealing with Pumham and Sacononoco, protecting them against the Narragansett, and righting them against Gorton, &c who had taken away their land: for this example gave encouragement to all these Indians to come in and submit to our government, in expectation of like protection and benefit." To purchase peace, Indians paid tribute in wampum to the Puritans, who watched accounts and bristled at late payments while worrying that the Indians were obtaining guns and powder from the French and the Dutch. Violence among the Indians was worrisome, but the Puritan system of colonial and inter-colonial governance made the 1640s a decade of relative security for New England. The Puritans' denial of the full humanity of the Indians would be repaid in blood during King Philip's War a generation later, and again and again in subsequent centuries of American history. As he led the Puritans toward stability, Winthrop seemed unaware of the terrible dilemma their achievement preserved.

If the boundary between Puritans and Indians remained tragically clear, New Englanders were finding it harder to keep other strangers at bay. The loss of some colonists, such as soldier John Underhill, who played the Puritans for all they were worth, extracting promises and salary increases by threatening to leave, and then went over to the Dutch, was more than balanced by others who wanted to join, or rejoin, the successful Bay Colony. In 1643 and 1644 Winthrop helped the former Antinomian minister John Wheelwright negotiate a return that respected both the guidelines of Puritan orthodoxy and the dictates of Wheelwright's tender conscience. Along with a charter for his settlement at Providence, Roger Williams obtained from Parliament the right to pass freely through the Puritan community. Some turned out to be better Puritans at a distance; Winthrop noted on 25 July 1645 of Henry Vane, the petulant young governor during the early stages of the Antinomian affair who had returned to England: "Though he might have taken occasion against us for some dishonour which he apprehended to have been unjustly put upon him here, yet both now and at other times he showed himself a true friend to New England, and a man of noble and generous mind." The simple passage of time wore down others, such as Thomas Morton, once a spirited critic, who on 9 September 1644 was set at liberty after being fined for treason: "He was a charge to the country, for he had nothing, and we thought not fit to inflict corporal punishment upon him, being old and crazy, but thought better to fine him and give him his liberty, as if it had been to procure his fine, but indeed to leave him opportunity to go out of the jurisdiction, as he did soon after, and he went to Acomenticus, and living there poor and despised, he died within two years after." Of course not everyone was so tractable.

Even less sound than Roger Williams in belief, Samuel Gorton and his followers, living south of Providence, were so abusive to English settlers and Indians alike that in September 1643 a party of Puritans went to capture them. After a skirmish in which no one was hurt, the Puritans brought them to Boston, where they were imprisoned. But these heretics could not be reasoned with, for, as Winthrop noted in frustration on 13 October, "they were all illiterate men, the ablest of them could not write true English, yet they would take upon them the interpretation of the most difficult places of scripture, and wrest them any way to serve their own turns." As enemies of church and state, charged with blasphemy, seven of them were dispersed to separate towns, made to work and wear leg irons, and commanded to speak of religion only with magistrates and elders. But they were more trouble then they were worth: "At the next court they were all sent away, because we found that they did corrupt some of our people, especially the women, by their heresies." The Puritans had to settle for confiscating enough of their cattle to defray the costs of their capture and lengthy trial. When freed and banished, the Gortonists caused more trouble, obtaining an order from England in 1646 to allow them to settle freely in the Bay Colony. Governor Winthrop referred the matter to the commissioners of the United Colonies, who advised him to respect Parliament's wishes, to let Gorton go his way, and to repossess his land if he caused trouble in the future. Winthrop and the Massachusetts court protested to Parliament that they must be allowed to manage their own affairs. In June 1648 Gorton returned from England with a letter from the earl of Warwick asking liberty for Gorton to pass through the Bay Colony on his way home. The Puritans let him pass, considering that "it being only at the Earl's request (no command,) it could be no prejudice to our liberty, and our commissioner being still attending the parliament, it might much have disadvantaged our cause and his expedition, if the Earl should have heard that we had denied him so small a request." Hearing that things in England were going the Puritans' way, Gorton's followers made peace with the magistrates, as the intense small flame of their heresy spluttered out.

In July 1644 the magistrates ordered that Anabaptists, whose numbers were increasing, should be banished. Their order was opposed by many merchants, who tended to favor freedom and toleration, as they had during the Antinomian crisis a decade before. Late in October 1645 Winthrop wrote: "At the general court held at Boston the first of this month there was a petition preferred by divers merchants and others about two laws, the one forbidding the entertaining of any strangers above three weeks, except such as should be allowed by two magistrates &c. (this was made in Mrs.

Hutchinson's time;) the other for banishing anabaptists, made the last year."
The merchants complained that the churches in England, offended by these
laws, were denying Communion to Massachusetts Puritans who returned
there. Many of the magistrates were prepared to suspend the execution of
the laws, but the elders prevailed in their defense in the face of the rapid
increase of Anabaptists in old and New England alike. On this basis, a
certain captain Partridge, recently arrived from England, where he had
served in Parliament, was banished. Despite his openness to reason and his
apparent progress toward true belief, Partridge was forced to depart with his
family at the onset of winter. They went to Rhode Island, and Winthrop
recorded the event and his own opinion of it: "This strictness was offensive
to many, though approved of by others. But sure the rule of hospitality to
strangers, and of seeking to pluck out of the fire such as there may be hope
of to be reduced out of errour and the snare of the devil, do seem to require
more moderation and indulgence of human infirmity where there appears
not obstinacy against the clear truth." Even when supported by the merchants, Winthrop's leniency was no match for the ministers' zeal in protecting orthodox belief and preserving their status. The following June "a
petition was presented to the court under many hands for the continuance
of the two laws against anabaptists and other hereticks, which was done in
reference to a petition presented at the former court concerning the same
laws." The system was in place, and the elders knew how to protect their
position in it. Intolerance to otherness, within and without, was a central
weakness within the strength of Puritan institutions.

In addition to their manner of dealing with strangers, the ways the
Puritans responded to behavior and events that they found strange also
suggest both the power and the inadequacy of their thinking. Winthrop was
sad but not surprised to observe continuing evidence of fornication and
adultery among the Puritans, and he concurred in the condemnation of
sexual immorality and in the execution of men and women who violated the
bonds of marriage. His comment on 4 June 1646 regarding a man who was
executed for corrupting many of the youth of Guilford by masturbation and
for insinuating "seeds of atheism" reveals the connection in Puritan thinking
between social relationships and the natural order of creation: "And indeed
it was horrendum facinus, and he a monster in human shape, exceeding all
human rules and examples that ever had been heard of, and it tended to the
frustrating of the ordinance of marriage and the hindering the generation of
mankind." Because sexual, marital, social, political, and religious experiences were linked together in the Puritan world, particular experiences of
abnormal behavior were doubly dangerous, for disorder was not contained
in any single area of life.

The natural, godly order of human relationships might also be lost in
ways that were not immoral but certainly seemed unfortunate, as Winthrop
noted on 13 April 1645:

115

Mr. Hopkins, the governour of Hartford upon Connecticut, came to Boston, and brought his wife with him, (a godly young woman, and of special parts,) who was fallen into a sad infirmity, the loss of her understanding and reason, which had been growing upon her divers years, by occasion of her giving herself wholly to reading and writing, and had written many books. Her husband, being very loving and tender of her, was loath to grieve her; but he saw his errour, when it was too late. For if she had attended her household affairs, and such things as belong to women, and not gone out of her way and calling to meddle in such things as are proper for men, whose minds are stronger &c. she had kept her wits, and might have improved upon them usefully and honourably in the place God had set her. He brought her to Boston, and left her with her brother, one Mr. Yale, a merchant, to try what means might be had here for her. But no help could be had.

Preserving traditional roles and relationships sustained an ordered society, Puritans believed, and individuals who departed from them suffered consequences that seemed natural. Because Governor Hopkins failed to exercise his authority as her husband, Mrs. Hopkins lost her liberty to be an obedient wife; distracted from her true calling, she fell into mere natural freedom and lost her senses. Sometimes the price of the order upon which the Puritans believed their survival as a community depended was simply too high.

Occasional departures from the normal order of things also occurred in the natural world, and Winthrop's response to such events confirms the tolerance for ambiguity that leavened his actions as governor and his judgments as historian. He did not, however, question the accepted Puritan view of God's governance of both nature and history; indeed, faith in divine providence was a crucial ingredient in Winthrop's courage. But he did not suppose that people always understood God's purposes, and so he was intrigued with but not troubled by unexplained events. For example, when a calf was born in Ipswich in December 1645 "with one head, and three mouths, three noses, and six eyes," Winthrop could only say that "what these prodigies portended the Lord only knows, which in his due time he will manifest." He did not question that something was "portended," but he did not always leap to point out the lesson.

Likewise, when a venereal disease spread through Boston the next March, Winthrop noted the fortunate conjunction of divine providence and human science: "But (see the good providence of God) at that very season there came by accident a young surgeon out of the West Indies, who had had experience of the right way of the cure of that disease." The disease spread among people who had visited a woman after childbirth who "had a sore breast, where upon divers neighbors resorting to her, some of them drew her breast, and others suffered their children to draw her, and others let her child suck them." The mystery was how the woman acquired the disease in the first place, for "the magistrates examined the husband and wife, but could find no dishonesty in either, nor any probable occasion of how they should take it by any other, (and the husband was found to be free of it)." As a careful historian, Winthrop recorded what most people thought and then gave his own less certain conclusion: "So as it was concluded by some, that the woman was infected by the mixture of so many spirits of men and women as drew her breast, (for thence it began). But this is a question to be decided by physicians." As this incident shows, the Puritans were certainly not prudish about their bodies. While many of them relied on "spiritual" interpretations of unexplained physical events, Winthrop preferred to wait for future insight from the physicians. Every event the historian recorded did not require precise explanation.

Of course, Winthrop was not always ambivalent. When unusual events could be interpreted in ways that applied and confirmed scriptural teachings, Winthrop's record agreed with the orthodox views of the elders. While Mr. Allen of Dedham was preaching to the synod on 15 August 1648, for example,

it fell out, about the midst of his sermon, there came a snake into the seat, where many of the elders sate behind the preacher. It came in at the door where people stood thick upon the stairs. Divers of the elders shifted from it, but Mr. Thomson, one of the elders of Braintree, (a man of much faith,) trode upon the head of it, and so held it with his foot and staff with a small pair of grains, until it was killed. This being so remarkable, and nothing falling out but by divine providence, it is out of doubt, the Lord discovered somewhat of his mind in it. The serpent is the devil; the synod, the representative of the churches of Christ in New England. The devil had formerly and lately attempted their disturbance and dissolution; but their faith in the seed of the woman overcame him and crushed his head.

And in the heat of the moment, particularly when the political and religious stakes were high, science became the obedient servant of theology, as when Winthrop and Cotton read omens from Anne Hutchinson's "monstrous birth." Thus, depending on the nature of his involvement, Winthrop was capable of various interpretations of different events. When faced with a direct challenge, his mind was set; when confronted with uncertainty, his mind remained sufficiently open, at least, to admit the possibility of more adequate explanations in the future.

Seventeenth-century science provided scant protection from an epidemic that swept through New England in the summer of 1647, though in June Winthrop noted "a special providence of God" in the fact that fewer than a hundred people died in Massachusetts and Connecticut. Yet the sickness was "more sensible and grievous" for causing the death of Hartford's minister, Thomas Hooker, "who, for piety, prudence, wisdom, zeal, learning and what else might make him serviceable in the place and time he lived in, might be compared with men of greatest note; and he shall need no other praise:

117

the fruits of his labours in both Englands shall preserve an honourable and happy remembrance of him forever." Whatever antagonism may have existed between Winthrop and Hooker, or, as is more likely, between Hooker and John Cotton, over Hooker's decisions to lead his people to Connecticut in the 1630s was long past in New England's quickly evolving history. Winthrop now thought more of New England than simply of Boston or even Massachusetts, and Hooker was clearly one of the New England saints.

Another whom God's remarkable providence did not spare was Margaret Winthrop: "In this sickness the governour's wife, daughter of Sir John Tindal, Knight, left this world for a better, being about fifty-six years of age: a woman of singular virtue, prudence, modesty, and piety, and especially beloved and honored of all the country." The Winthrops' steadfast love had been tenderly expressed in every letter they exchanged, suggesting that in their relationship Winthrop knew the full value of the reciprocal love and commitment that was his ideal model for broader social and even political life. He honored the significance of such relatedness, as well as his ongoing commitment to living in the present rather than the past or the future, by marrying again before his next election as governor in the spring of 1648. Martha Coytmore, a widow from Charlestown, became Winthrop's fourth wife and bore him a son before the governor himself died of a fever in the spring of 1649. He had lived just over sixty-one years and at his death was accorded both the deep respect he acknowledged for Hooker and the broad affection he exhibited for Margaret. He had been the Puritans' first and most constant governor, as well as the primary historian of early New England—truly a singular man whose achievements made a place for the enduring Puritan contribution to American life.

As Winthrop recounted his role in the events that firmly established the Puritan institutions, attitudes, and beliefs that would guide New England in the years ahead, his writing became more flowing, with events often grouped together according to their significance rather than by strict chronology. Like his authority as governor, his control over the narrative of his journal was lenient but sure. He believed that the happenings he observed were events in a story, perhaps just beginning and sometimes misdirected, but still full of promise. While candid self-assessment outweighed any tendency toward narrow self-justification, Winthrop recollected and recorded Puritan history with the confidence of one who had faith in the ultimate direction and overall purposes of the enterprise. In every sense of the word, Winthrop made history. His view of the world was in some important and useful ways different from our own, yet we have no direct, immediate access to the past. If we are to tap that resource, at once remote from and connected intimately to contemporary American life, we must try to understand the story that others have told of Winthrop's role in the history he made.

Part Two

THE STORY AS HISTORY

5

The Perils of the Text

JOHN WINTHROP learned to see and to write history as a story, but it is impossible for us simply to read his story straight. His actions as governor have so overshadowed his work as a historian, and his character and accomplishments have been so thoroughly incorporated into the pantheon of early New England, that we cannot find direct access to the history he made. Winthrop stood foremost among the first generation of American Puritans; hence whatever judgment one makes regarding the social institutions and the cultural tradition these people established stands between John Winthrop and us. The Puritans have been venerated, castigated, forgotten, resuscitated, misunderstood, reinterpreted, and quoted or misquoted by generations of American historians, social critics, and political orators. Because so many images of Puritanism are part of American cultural history, the only sure path to understanding the story of Winthrop's history is through coming to terms with the subsequent history of his story. Thus we move from reading history as a story to examining the story as history.

The history of misreadings of Winthrop's journal is matched—curiously, if not symbolically, as the Puritans might have believed—by the perils of the text itself. Winthrop wrote his history in three notebooks. The third volume was misplaced in 1755 and discovered sixty years later in the tower of Boston's Old South Church. Upon its recovery, this notebook, like the others, was given by the Winthrop family to the Massachusetts Historical Society, whereupon a new edition of the journal was undertaken. During this process, the second volume was accidentally destroyed by a fire in the office of the society's librarian. "Over the years many people have endeavored to read, transcribe, and edit Winthrop's notebooks," observes historian Richard S. Dunn, the most recent scholar to work on a new edition of Winthrop's work. However, "this set of texts is surely the most baffling of all major early American documents to decipher or to edit. The handwriting in the two surviving volumes is notoriously hard to read, the ink is faded, the paper is often stained, worn, or torn, and the text is studded with marginalia, insertions, cancellations, and underscorings. Since the middle volume (containing 52 percent of Winthrop's text) is lost, the reader has to use a modernized transcription for this section, published by James Savage in 1825–26, that obliterates many of the nuances in the original manuscript. It is safe to say that no one will ever publish a satisfactory edition of this remarkable document."/ By correlating the varying lengths of Winthrop's entries in the notebooks with the increasing passage of time between them, Dunn concludes that by the 1640s "increasingly he wrote for several consecutive pages on the same topic, so that his narrative became less segmented and more continuous: in short, more of a history."¹ But Dunn notes that an interpretation of Winthrop's transition from record keeper to historian cannot be based on precise textual analysis, since the original copy of the entire second volume, containing most of the text and covering such crucial episodes as the Antinomian crisis, no longer exists. Hence Dunn's painstaking work with the text has to rely largely on the work done by Savage, a man of prodigious and volatile energy, as we shall see, and one with his own agenda to follow.

Dunn's conclusion about Winthrop and his notebooks is insightful and also suggests something of his own frustration: "Thanks to his narrative, it is very easy to recognize the lasting significance of events in early Massachusetts and very difficult to remain neutral on the subject of Winthrop's own leadership. For some, he is one of the great figures in American history. For others, he is the kind of man you love to hate."² The new edition of the text which Dunn's essay announced has yet to appear; even its eventual publication, however, will not provide an unambiguous image of Winthrop. No text could, for interpretation and action were inextricably linked in Winthrop's life and work. As if to underscore the impossibility, Winthrop's text itself is irretrievably tied to the history of its own production.

Convinced that Winthrop's journal "must always have an interest not only for New England but for America in general, and indeed for the world at large," in 1908 James Kendall Hosmer published *Winthrop's Journal, "History of New England," 1630–1649* in a series devoted to original narratives of early American history. A member of the Massachusetts Historical Society and the Colonial Society of Massachusetts, as well as the author of *A Short History of Anglo-Saxon Freedom,* Hosmer believed that "a stock so persistent, so virile, so widely eminent, claims attention in every period of its course, and naturally a special interest attaches to its earliest American memorials." Since Hosmer frankly "adopted without change the transcript of the text made by Savage," his editorial remarks are of interest chiefly for his discussion of the "young and zealous" James Savage, "a man most accurate and indefatigable," whose edition of Winthrop's journal in 1825–26 "took its place at once in the minds of men as the foundation of Massachusetts history, and the importance of the services of Savage was universally recognized: he became henceforth a man of mark." Observing that Savage "had peculiarities of character making him personally racy and interesting, but impairing the excellence of his commentary," Hosmer notes that Savage's "successor in the presidency of the Massachusetts Historical Society, Mr. Charles Francis Adams, aptly compares him to Dr. Samuel Johnson. Like Johnson, Savage while most laborious, scrupulously honest, and always resolute and unshrinking, was testy, prejudiced and opinionated." In Hosmer's view, "while possessed thus by the spirit of the county antiquary rather than by the broad temper of the proper historian, his hates and loves, equally undiscriminating, are curiously, often amusingly manifest"; hence Savage's extensive annotation of Winthrop's text "has much interest as a 'human document,' pleasantly tart from the individuality of a quaintly provincial but sincere and vigorous mind."[3] Evidently unaware of the ways his Anglo-Saxon prejudices narrowed his own focus, Hosmer appeals to "the broad temper of the proper historian," highlighting the more argumentative nature of his predecessor. But so long as their editing is accurate, historians whose convictions are readily apparent may ultimately prove more reliable, and certainly more interesting, than those whose prejudices are blandly unconscious. James Savage, upon whose work so much of our knowledge of Winthrop necessarily depends, had reason to be as passionate about Winthrop as Winthrop was about New England.

Along with following Savage as president of the Massachusetts Historical Society, Charles Francis Adams found himself involved in sorting out Savage's complex connection to Winthrop. Adams was interested in the Antinomian crisis, and understanding this critical episode in the Bay Colony's history required explaining Savage's peculiar passion about Winthrop, for Savage had become embroiled in controversy regarding the *Short Story* Winthrop wrote about the Anne Hutchinson affair. After recording the judgments of the general court against Hutchinson and her followers, Winthrop noted in his journal on 1 November 1637 that "all the proceedings of this court against these persons were set down at large, with the reasons and other observations, and were sent into England to be published there, to the end that all our godly friends might not be discouraged from coming to us, &c." Adams points out that "the harsh and intolerant policy pursued from the beginning in Massachusetts towards all intruders and dissentients had excited no little comment in England, and led to hostile proceedings, causing remonstrances from the friends of the enterprise." Hence "in thus writing down and sending to England an account of these proceedings," Adams says, Winthrop "wished, in his paternal care for the infant colony, to anticipate and forestall hostile criticism."[4] Winthrop's title made these intentions clear: *A Short Story of the Rise, reign, and ruin of the Antinomians, Familists, & Libertines, that infected the Churches of New England: And how they were confuted by the Assembly of Ministers there: As also of the Magistrates proceedings in Court against them. Together with Gods strange and remarkable judgements from Heaven upon some of the chief fomenters of these Opinions; And the Lamentable death of Mrs. Hutchinson: Very fit for these times; here being the same errours amongst us, and acted by the same spirit.* Yet although the title page notes that the work was "published at the instant request of sundry, by one that was an eye and eare-witnesse of the carriage of matters there," its final words are "London, Printed for *Ralph Smith* at the signe of the Bible in *Cornhill* near the *Royall Exchange*. 1644." Originally sent to England in 1637, the work was not published until 1644. Between these years a great deal happened that was important for English history, and this passage of time became significant, much later, for James Savage.

By 1644 Anne Hutchinson and most of her family had been massacred by Indians in New York. John Wheelwright, banished as one of the principal Antinomians, had been welcomed back into the Massachusetts Bay Colony, where the Hutchinson affair had long been replaced in the public mind by more immediate issues such as the final division of the legislature into two independent houses, the confederation of the United Colonies of New England, and volatile relations with the Narragansetts, the Dutch, and the feuding Frenchmen, La Tour and D'Aulnay. In old England, King Charles had left London, the Civil War was under way, and friends of the Bay Colony controlled Parliament. Indeed, by July 1643 the Westminster Assembly had launched a great debate over religious toleration, and Winthrop's *Short Story* was published the next year, in Adams's words, as "one of the pamphlet missiles which the participants in that battle freely hurled at each other."[5] The trajectory of this missile, though, proved most ironic.

With Anglicanism in retreat with the king, a new order of relations between church and state became possible in England. On one side of the debate was a party whose members were generally called Independents. Two of the chief spokesmen for this coalition on behalf of religious freedom and toleration were Roger Williams, in England attempting to secure a clear charter for Rhode Island, and Sir Henry Vane, the former governor of the Bay Colony who had left Massachusetts during the Antinomian crisis. On the other side were the Presbyterians, seeking a national church of their own design and pointing out that "the New England Way" had not led to paradise. As Adams explains, "at this juncture Winthrop's narrative, after resting six years in oblivion, went to the printer. It supplied the Presbyterian leaders with exactly the ammunition they wanted. In it was set forth not only the breaking down of the Toleration principle in the very land of its birth, but that breaking down had taken place under the magistracy of him who was now in England the Parliamentary mouthpiece of the Independents. Both Williams and Vane were to be confounded by an answer out of their own mouths."[6] It was apparently the Reverend Thomas Weld, an ardent supporter of John Wilson and John Winthrop now back in England to represent and obtain financial support for the Bay Colony, who brought the pamphlet forward as a weapon against his old enemy, the arch-Antinomian Vane. Although written originally to vindicate the New England Way, when published in the contentious political atmosphere of England in 1644, the booklet served the Presbyterian effort, in the words of a contemporary, "to tie Toleration round the neck of Independency, stuff the two struggling monsters into one sack, and sink them to the bottom of the sea."[7] Thus the writing of an ardent Congregationalist helped advance the Presbyterian cause by undercutting the efforts of Vane, whom Winthrop came to recognize as a friend and loyal supporter of the Puritan cause.

As historian David D. Hall notes, Winthrop's *Short Story,* "the official history of the Antinomian Controversy," is "essentially a collection of documents."[8] These are linked together by Winthrop's narration, more leisurely in pace and more reflexive in tone but otherwise little different from the account of the events in his journal, and the text concludes the story of "this *American Jesabel*" with a dramatic rendering of "her entrance, her progresse, her downfall." The booklet went through several editions, with Weld adding a brief introduction, some sharply worded prefatory matter, and a short postscript covering events subsequent to 1637. Adams aptly notes that while the body of the *Short Story,* apart from Weld's additions, is "an outspoken and earnest presentation in defence of one side of a political struggle, written at the time and with a view to prejudge the case in the minds of those for whom it was prepared, a careful reading reveals in it little that is vituperative, and nothing that can properly be called scurrilous. Indeed, tested by the standards of the time, if it is in any way unusual, it is in its moderation."[9] Weld simply sharpened Winthrop's ax and handed it to the English Presbyterians, who used it for their own purposes. Curiously enough, the text continued to cut in more than one direction when it was taken up by James Savage two centuries later.

If Savage's editorial tempest was less important than the Antinomian crisis or the politics of religion during the English Civil War, it nevertheless revealed something of great significance to him, suggesting why his devotion to editing Winthrop's journal was such a complicated passion. Indeed, without the intensely personal connection between Savage and Winthrop that an otherwise comical dispute between Massachusetts historians highlights, the immensely difficult work of transcribing, annotating, and publishing the journal might never have been done. In the early 1850s James Savage began to argue with increasing bitterness that Thomas Weld, not John Winthrop, was responsible for virtually the whole of the *Short Story* and hence to imply that Winthrop's opposition to the Antinomians had been a matter more of political necessity than of deep spiritual conviction. Yet Savage's arguments were as convoluted as they were circumstantial. Together with his strong will and hot temper, Savage's prejudice against Weld, and by implication his veneration of Winthrop, became, in Adams's words, "a byword and a jest among his associates."[10] The roots of such impetuous tenacity, appropriately, were historical. Charles Francis Adams explains:

Among the names of the men of Boston, "chief stirrers," as Winthrop expresses it, "in these [Antinomian] contentions," and for that reason ordered by the General Court of November, 1637, to be disarmed, was Thomas Savage, who had recently married Faith, the daughter of William and Anne Hutchinson. And at the church trial of the mother of his young wife in March, 1638, this Thomas Savage did himself infinite credit by rising and courageously protesting against the admonition about to be bestowed; and, as a result of so doing, he had the honor of being himself admonished together with her he so manfully sought to protect. James Savage traced his lineal descent in the fifth generation from Thomas and Faith (Hutchinson) Savage. He was, therefore, one of the offspring of Anne Hutchinson, to whom indeed in a characteristic note to Winthrop he refers as "his great, great, great, great grandmother." Conscious of a bias due to this remote relationship by descent, Savage throughout his notes to Winthrop endeavored to hold himself under strict control while dealing with events of the Antinomian controversy, and he succeeded in so doing to a, for him, considerable extent; but the *Short Story* he looked upon as a discreditable literary production, the scurrilous product of a mind at once narrow, vindictive, virulent, and malignant.[11]

Trapped within history by history, James Savage was caught between a sense of genealogical propriety and a stronger, more meaningful sense of cultural inheritance.

Despite his lineal descent from Anne Hutchinson, Savage regarded Winthrop "with a warmth of admiration almost devout," in Adams's words, looking "upon the first Boston governor as the incomparable Father of Massachusetts." Writing the exhaustive notes in his editions of Winthrop's journal may have been James Savage's way of working out this complex inheritance. Savage's extensive notes, Adams writes, afford "a not unpleasant contrast with the text,—the latter calm, self-restrained and inclined to the prosaic; the former intense, outspoken, replete with pith, individuality, learning and prejudice. These notes are, and will always remain, delightful as well as instructive reading; and to the student of New England history it is almost as difficult to think of Winthrop apart from Savage as it is for one learned in the English common law to separate Littleton from Coke."[12] Indeed, given the fiery loss—in Savage's library—of the notebook containing over half of the original manuscript, there is no way back to a pristine Winthrop "behind" Savage. Just as Savage was trapped within history by history, so Winthrop's history is irretrievably enmeshed in Savage's complex inheritance.

To characterize James Savage as a compulsively industrious New Englander is almost an understatement. Son of a Boston merchant who went insane after the young boy's mother died, Savage was raised by a maternal uncle, educated in private schools, and, despite involvement in at least one serious prank, graduated from Harvard College as valedictorian of the class of 1803. By the time he began to work on the Winthrop notebooks, Savage had studied law and passed the bar, started one of the nation's first savings banks, served on the committee that implemented the law he had supported to provide public elementary schools, and been a member of the Massachusetts constitutional convention of 1820. During his life he served as both a representative and a senator in the state legislature, edited one of the nation's earliest literary periodicals, helped to found the Boston Athenaeum, and served for fifteen years on the Board of Overseers of Harvard University. But the real center of his life was his work as a historian. He served the Massachusetts Historical Society in many capacities, including as president from 1841 to 1855, and published several books and collections of documents, most notably, in addition to Winthrop's journal, a four-volume *Genealogical Dictionary of the First Settlers of New England.*

Surveying such a life helps one appreciate Savage's statement, when the lost third notebook of Winthrop was discovered, that "the difficulty of transcribing it for the press seemed to appal several of the most competent members" of the Massachusetts Historical society, yet "the task appeared inviting to me." Likewise, he remarks that, "called abroad in 1822, I so carefully disposed of my copy of the third volume, as to leave it in a forgotten place, which afforded me the gratification of making a new one, begun 8 December 1823, and finished 30 March 1824." The high value that Savage assigned to primary texts, honoring the founders of New England far more than their often too respectful descendants, resounds in his criticism of Cotton Mather's failure to read Winthrop's actual writings when he wrote his "life": "Nor can I forgive the slight use of these invaluable documents, which is evinced by Mather, the unhappy author of Magnalia Christi Americana, who, in the hurry of composing that endless work, seems to have preferred useless quotations of worthless books, two or three centuries older, or popular and corrupt traditions, to the full matter and precise statement of facts, dates, principles and motives, furnished by authentick history."[13] Yet for Winthrop himself, Savage had respect that amounted to the awe reserved for the founders of a tribe, the great ones who establish traditions, whose works preserve the historical origins of a new world.

Thus on the title page of the 1825 and the 1853 editions of Winthrop's journal, across from a copy of Winthrop's portrait, Savage reveals his own purpose by quoting the Roman historian Sallust: "Often have I heard that

Quintus Maximus and Publius Scipio, as well as the most renowned men of our state, were accustomed to say that when they contemplated the images of their ancestors, their minds were most vehemently inspired toward courage." In the face of the various images of Winthrop that have been been constructed to inspire courage throughout American history, one has to wish that there were at least a remaining original text, through which one could, with however much or little sophistication, gain access to the beginnings of an important dimension of American culture by reading "the man himself." But Savage makes it clear that no such privileged access exists. How ironic that the Puritan movement, which came to life as a protest against the deadening influence of tradition on the life of the spirit, is itself locked in a tradition it helped so largely to make. Yet learning to live within such contradictions was what made it possible for Winthrop to make and to write history.

If the work of Winthrop as a historian is recoverable only insofar as it was edited and interpreted by later historians, we can establish and sustain connection with the story he told only through the history of its interpretation. Once the necessity of interpretation is recognized, the history of his story becomes a link, perhaps the only sure one, with the actual man who made and wrote history. For however much Winthrop's character was assailed during the political infighting of the Bay Colony's early years, almost immediately upon his death the real man was translated into a myth. Percival Lowell's "A Funeral Elegie on the Death of the Memorable and Truly Honourable John Winthrop Esq." decreed:

> With Lines of gold in Marble stone
> > With pens of steel engrave his name
> O let the Muses every one
> > In prose and Verse extol his Fame,
> Exceeding far those ancient Sages
> That ruled *Greeks* in former Ages.[14]

After comparing the departed governor favorably with the great leaders of ancient Israel and Greece, this ancestor of better poets moved his hero beyond the mortal realm:

> Such gifts of grace from God had he,
> That more than man he seem'd to be.
> But now hee's gone and clad in clay,
> Grim Death hath taken him away.
> Death like a murth'ring Jesuite
> Hath rob'd us of our hearts delight.[15]

Such flowery sentiments are far removed from the earthly Winthrop, who could write of himself in a letter to Thomas Hooker, "Truly Sir you have my naked thoughts of this matter, so farre as the Lord letteth me see mine owne heart, which I find very deceitful when it is at best."[16] Winthrop's honesty about the ongoing self-deception even within the hearts of the saints, himself included, made his story of the Bay Colony a history of men and women of mixed motives, a community of sinning saints. The perils of his text itself and the difficulty of our access to it seem oddly in keeping with the story he wrote, suggesting the distinctive character of Winthrop's way of making history in early New England.

6

Ways of Making History in Early New England

WINTHROP'S JOURNAL was not only about Puritans; it was a Puritan history. This quality, so quickly lost by those who wrote about the early Puritans, comes clearly into focus when Winthrop's history is compared with the other great history of first-generation New England. Like the Puritans' Winthrop, the Pilgrims' William Bradford was both governor and historian, and the two men interacted as leaders of communities as close as Boston and Plimouth. For all their day-to-day cooperation, though, the theological differences between the Puritans and Separatists had important consequences for the ways the two men understood and wrote history.

William Bradford's *Of Plimouth Plantation, 1620–1647* chronicles the endurance of a small group of English Protestants who shared many of the Puritans' beliefs about the degeneracy of their native land and its established church. Instead of hoping to reform the Church of England, though, Bradford's Pilgrims decided that purity of belief and practice could be achieved only through "removal to some other place."[1] Believing that true Reformation required separation, they sought religious freedom first in Holland, where their relative ease of acceptance exposed the group, especially the children, to the unforeseen danger of assimilation. So they separated again, this time going all the way to New England, a decade ahead of the Puritans, and settling in Plimouth.

Governor Bradford's history of the people he led is a year-by-year account of the ongoing tribulations they faced—from the sharp financial dealings of their backers, from the Indians, from starvation, from smallpox, and from tensions within their own community between those who were truly committed to the general undertaking and those whose primary motivations sprang from self-interest. The main theme of Separatist history is spelled out early and informs Bradford's entire account: the trials and temptations confronting this small band of believers were unrelenting, "but they knew they were pilgrims, and looked not much on those things, but lift up their eyes to the heavens, their dearest country, and quieted their spirits."[2] If the Puritans tried to live in the world without being of the world, then the Pilgrims sought to avoid being of the world by living apart from it. Unlike the Antinomians, the Pilgrims did not seek to be free from the rules that guide the soldier of faith in combat with the world, yet neither were they so bold as to expect to triumph in this life. Hence Bradford's history has an elegaic tone. Instead of hope for progress, the lives of Pilgrim saints display the courage of perseverance.

Although he was not a perfectionist, Bradford tended to distinguish between good and bad people; Winthrop, conversely, characteristically saw a mixture of good and bad within everyone. An interesting point of comparison comes in the early 1640s, when both historians had to deal with outbreaks of what their communities considered immoral and unnatural sexual acts. Both were committed to relating such unpleasant events; as Winthrop put it on 12 November 1641, "history must tell the whole truth," or, in Bradford's words, "the truth of history requires it."[3] Yet their different interpretations of similar events suggest a crucial distinction between the Puritan and Separatist views of human nature and, consequently, between their respective ways of making history.

In his journal entry for that same day in 1641, Winthrop enables his readers to witness the fate of William Hackett, a young servant in Salem who "was found in buggery with a cow, upon the Lord's day." Although "he was noted always to have been a very stupid, idle, and ill-disposed boy, and would never regard the means of instruction, either in the church or family," the Puritans worked with him, "labouring by the word of God to convince him of his sin, and the present danger of his soul," until finally "it pleased the Lord so to bless his own ordinances, that his hard heart melted." There was no question of escaping punishment, but his execution was postponed a week to allow more time for spiritual progress. Yet even upon the ladder prepared to be hanged, he had not fully repented: "But the cow (with which he had committed that abomination) being brought forth and slain before him, he brake out into a loud and doleful complaint against himself" and was led in prayer by John Wilson and the other elders in attendance. Winthrop's observation upon the lad's execution is noteworthy: "There is no doubt to be made but the Lord hath received his soul to his mercy; and he was pleased to lift up the light of his countenance so far towards him, as to keep him from despair, and to hold him close to his grace in a seeking condition; but he was not pleased to afford him that measure of peace and comfort as he might be able to hold out to others, lest sinful men, in the love of their lusts, should set mercy and repentance at too low a rate, and so miss of it when they vainly expect it." With their complex view of human nature, the Puritans were capable of applying to a single individual both aspects of Paul's New Testament claim, "For the wages of sin is death; but the gift of God is eternal life through Christ Jesus our Lord."[4] Their neighbors in Plimouth, in contrast, were inclined to separate Paul's clauses between the sinners and the saints.

In 1642 "the truth of history" required William Bradford to record how Thomas Granger was "detected of buggery, and indicted for the same, with a mare, a cow, two goats, five sheep, two calves and a turkey." While careful to "forbear particulars" regarding the young servant's "lewd practice towards the mare," Bradford does point out that "whereas some of the sheep could not be so well known by his description of them, others with them were brought before him and he declared which were they and which were not." But there is no mention of concern for the boy's soul. Instead, Bradford simply notes that Granger freely confessed the facts: "And accordingly he was cast by the jury and condemned, and after executed about the 8th of September, 1642. A very sad spectacle it was. For first the mare and the rest of the lesser cattle were killed before his face, according to the law, Leviticus XX.15; and then he himself was executed. The cattle were all cast into a great and large pit that was digged of purpose for them, and no use made of any part of them." Pilgrim authorities determined that "the knowledge and practice of such wickedness" was acquired "in old England," and Bradford points to a cautionary moral: "By which it appears how one wicked person may infect many, and what care all ought to have what servants they bring into their families."[5] If Winthrop's narrative about Hackett expresses the characteristic Puritan concern with the struggle between sin and grace in each individual's life, then Bradford's account of Granger's fate articulates a typical Separatist desire to weed out wicked people who may have crept into the community of the saints.

Beyond its immediate moral offensiveness, Granger's buggery raised important concerns about the meaning of history for Bradford, who worried that such incidents might lead future generations to question the integrity of their origins. Without doubting the propriety of the Pilgrim proceedings, Bradford faced the larger issue squarely: "But it may be demanded how it came to pass that so many wicked persons and profane people should so quickly come over into this land and mix themselves amongst them? Seeing it was religious men that began the work and they came for religion's sake? I confess this may be marveled at, at least in time to come, when the reasons thereof should not be known; and the more because here was so many hardships and wants met withal. I shall therefore endeavour to give some answer hereunto." Explanation outdistances narration for Bradford; the posterity he envisages will look to history for a source of inspiring moral examples rather than for the early chapters of a continuing story. Winthrop's story outgrows the framework of his original design, whereas Bradford's events are controlled by the meanings they illustrate and the questions they answer.

Bradford's answers are soundly Separatist. First, "it is ever to be remembered that where the Lord begins to sow good seed, there the envious man will endeavor to sow tares." Second, building and planting in a wilderness required so much work that the supply of good servants was exhausted; therefore, "many untoward servants" were brought over, served out their times of indenture, began their own families, and increased. Third, "and a main reason hereof," the traders who transported godly persons were simply good businessmen who "to make up their freight and advance their profit, cared not who the persons were, so they had money to pay them. And by this means the country became pestered with many unworthy persons who, being come over, crept into one place or other." And fourth, some good people in England were simply getting rid of their problems: "So also there were sent by their friends, some under hope that they would be made better, others that they might be eased of such burthens, and they kept from shame at home, that would necessarily follow their dissolute courses." Bradford's conclusion sounds a distinctly Separatist note of despair: "And thus, by one means or other, in 20 years' time it is a question whether the greater part be not grown the worser?" Because Bradford portrayed the conflict between good and evil by drawing a line between good people and bad people, rather than by examining the moral battleground within every human soul, the cards always seemed to be stacked against the Separatists, even in a relatively free and open new land.

Bradford's basic orientation did not change when he moved from explaining the wickedness of such an otherwise insignificant servant as Thomas Granger to expounding the lifelong goodness of a true servant of God such as the Reverend William Brewster, a faithful elder of "this poor persecuted church above 36 years in England, Holland and in this wilderness" and one of the eldest of the Pilgrim saints.[6] Elder Brewster exemplifies perseverance, for "notwithstanding the many troubles and sorrows he passed through, the Lord upheld him to a great age." Before cataloguing Brewster's virtues, Bradford makes his meaning clear: "I would now demand of any, what he was the worse for any former sufferings? What do I say, worse? Nay, sure he was the better, and they now added to his honour." Separatist virtues seem to emerge not simply in response to large challenges but chiefly through suffering. Endurance, rather than triumph, is the Pilgrim's goal.

Elder Brewster's intelligence and learning, his honesty and discretion, and his humility and faith earned him trust and affection throughout his life, especially in his role as a teaching minister in Plimouth. Rather than any particular accomplishments, though, what Bradford finds most noteworthy about Brewster is his life's demonstration of the longevity of the Pilgrim Fathers: "I cannot but here take occasion not only to mention but greatly to admire the marvelous providence of God! That notwithstanding the many changes and hardships that these people went through, and the many enemies they had and difficulties they met withal, that so many of them should live to very old age! It was not only this reverend man's condition (for one swallow makes no summer as they say) but many more of them did the like, some dying about and before this time and many still living, who attained to sixty years of age, and to sixty-five, divers to seventy and above, and some near eighty as he did. It must needs be more than ordinary and above natural reason, that so it should be." Given the "crosses, troubles, fears, wants and sorrows" they experienced, Bradford asks rhetorically, "What was it then that upheld them? It was God's visitation that preserved their spirits." Whatever ability and courage might accomplish, Bradford believed, the strength of saintly endurance required more than even Brewster's admirable character and virtues.

Once again, instead of telling a story, Bradford draws the lesson from the life: "God, it seems, would have all men to behold and observe such mercies and works of His providence as these are towards His people, that they in like cases might be encouraged to depend upon God in their trials, and also to bless His name when they see His goodness towards others." The lesson is one, Bradford acknowledges, that everyone will not appreciate: "It is not by good and dainty fare, by peace and rest and heart's ease in enjoying the contentments and good things of this world only that preserves health and prolongs life; God in such examples would have the world see and behold that He can do it without them; and if the world will shut their eyes and take no notice thereof, yet He would have His people to see and consider it." In Bradford's view, lack of widespread recognition does not diminish the truth. Indeed, for the Separatist, spiritual power and worldly failure seem to go hand in hand.

By 1644 even many of the faithful were lured to richer farmland and better harbors than Plimouth afforded, so that the staying image of Bradford's history is elegaic: "And thus was this poor church left, like an ancient mother grown old and forsaken of her children, though not in their affections yet in regard of their bodily presence and personal helpfulness; her ancient members being most of them worn away by death, and these of later time being like children translated into other families, and she like a widow left only to trust in God. Thus, she that had made many rich became herself poor."[7] After recounting the successful prevention of war with the Indians by the commissioners of the United Colonies, Bradford's history ends by bemoaning the loss of Separatist stalwart Edward Winslow, who upon returning to England to battle New England's adversaries had become involved in the Civil War that was bringing the Reformation back to life. William Bradford in Plimouth seemed to feel that the Pilgrim project had ended. If the Puritans had been on an errand and had transformed its meaning into an ongoing enterprise, the Pilgrims were already—and in a sense always—looking backward rather than ahead.

In 1650 William Bradford turned away from writing the history of Plimouth and began to study Hebrew, seeking a personal connection with more ancient origins:

> Though I am growne aged, yet I have had a longing
> desire to see, with my owne eyes, something of that most
> ancient language, and holy tongue, in which the Law
> and Oracles of God were write; and in which God
> and angels spake to the holy patriarks of old
> time; and what names were given to things
> from the creation. And though I cannot
> attaine to much herein, yet I am refresh-
> ed to have seen some glipse hereof;
> (as Moyses saw the land of Ca-
> nan a farr off. My aime and
> desire is, to see how the words
> and phrases lye in the
> holy texte; and to
> discerne somewhat
> of the same,
> for my owne
> contente.[8]

Unlike John Winthrop, whose involvement in the story he was writing continued until sickness took his life, William Bradford had finished his effort to guide his plantation by recalling its connection to an inspiring past. Bradford's decision suggests telling differences between the kinds of history that he and Winthrop wrote and between the ways they understood their work as historians, in keeping with their moral and religious points of view.

Contemporary historian Peter Gay suggests that English Protestants were heirs both of medieval and of Renaissance attitudes toward history: "Medieval historians, in sum, for all their biographies, all their chronicles, all their universal histories, were in their hearts unhistorical—Renaissance historians, whether they found in history a cyclical movement, or progress, or chaos, justified the course of history by, and within, the course of history."[9] Their medieval Christian heritage held that human history was meaningful by virtue of its connection to divine history, whereas Renaissance humanism taught that human history was justified, to the extent that it had meaning at all, in and on its own terms. As forthright participants in the reformation, English Protestants balanced these contradictory views of history, with Puri-

135

tans and Separatists agreeing that the Reformation in England was moving too slowly, if indeed at all, under the dead hand of an established church. An unstable mixture of medieval and Renaissance ideas about history was part of the cultural baggage on board the *Mayflower* and the *Arbella,* as Bradford and Winthrop led their people to New England for the sake of the Reformation.

Because the Puritans and Separatists believed they were advancing the Reformation by migrating to New England, they shared many spiritual concerns, social commitments, and political convictions. People who set out to further and possibly to perfect the Protestant movement believed that change was possible, that history did not simply repeat itself. But separatism and Puritanism represented antithetical strains within the broad heritage of the Reformation, and in the hands of Bradford and Winthrop these tendencies were developed into two views of history that have ever since been in conflict. While they often cooperated as governors, as historians Bradford and Winthrop were the first voices in an ongoing cultural debate that has been—and continues to be—profoundly important for American life. Two contradictory attitudes about the nature of American society and the purpose of American foreign policy are rooted in the Separatist and Puritan ways of making history in early New England.

Bradford justified the Pilgrim migration by looking back to the New Testament, the first years of Christianity, and the marytrs of the early Reformation for models to encourage the Separatist saints to endure the trials they faced. Inspired by the heroes of the faith chronicled in John Foxe's influential *Book of Martyrs,* the Pilgrims sought to redeem the present by reclaiming the true Christian past. Worried about his people's fortitude, suspicious of conspiracies against them, and looking backward for models, Bradford wrote a history that is nostalgic in tone, as fearful of the Pilgrims' declension as it is full of belief in the rightness of their cause. A sense of history was important for Bradford because it linked the temptations of the present to the age-old ceaseless struggle of the saints. He did not expect his people to tame the wilderness or to transform the Church of England. He wanted them, more simply, to live as witnesses to the true faith.

If assimilation had threatened their cause in Holland, the isolation of Plimouth was more promising. For the Pilgrim community to succeed, it had to remain separate from the wickedness of the wider world. Hence as his people dispersed for richer farmland and better commerce, as their need for a common defense drew Plimouth into cooperative agreements with other colonies in New England, and as the English Civil War pulled good men like Winslow into new conflicts across the seas, Bradford lost the sense of involvement in a meaningful historical process. He wrote more about the longevity of the original Pilgrim saints than about new energies and future challenges. The purpose of writing history, for Bradford, was to illumine a darkening world by testifying to the purity and courage of saints who struggled valiantly against the world, even in defeat.

Conversely, Winthrop wrote of Puritans who struggled for meaning within, rather than against, the world. Because they believed so strongly in a God beyond history, the Puritans threw themselves passionately into history, in order to bring this world into conformity with the next. Although Winthrop clearly set forth his design for the Puritan project in his "Modell of Christian Charity" sermon on board the *Arbella,* his history of New England tells the story of events as they happened, rather than attempting to organize Puritan experience along the lines of a predetermined plan. As they worked to establish themselves and to build a society in accordance with their various, often conflicting interests, Winthrop's characters, himself included, were not pure saints. Indeed, the security of their community was actually threatened less by external enemies, though they had plenty, than by insiders who believed that their personal union with the Holy Spirit freed them from obeying the rules of moral behavior. These Antinomians were the people the Puritans wanted to keep out of the Bay Colony, because Anne Hutchinson and her sort of people did not understand the necessity of moral rules. People need religious authority, social order, and moral laws, the Puritans believed, not so much to separate the bad people from the good people as, more fundamentally, to enable people, all of whom are mixtures of good and bad, to make some spiritual progress while living together. Winthrop's sense of the meaning of history as it is lived and written reflects these Puritan differences from the Separatists.

In contrast to Bradford, who looked backward for models to use in his effort to render the present significant, Winthrop observed present experience in order to record the events of an ongoing story. The Puritan mind was full of biblical models, to be sure, but instead of the Pilgrims' adoption of Christian martyrs, the heroes of "God's New Israel" were the patriarchs of the Old Testament who led a chosen people into the promised land. In his work as governor, Winthrop defended the order that he believed a continuing community required, bowing to the pressure for some changes and leading the way in others. His political balance sustained the Puritan project as a whole, helping to keep a sense of movement alive. Unlike the Pilgrims, who bore witness to the truth of the gospel in a seemingly solitary, almost antihistorical way, Winthrop's Puritans were laying the foundations of a new society. Their New England would chart its own course when a civil war in their homeland halted immigration, disrupted trade, and made it clear that the eyes of the world were not riveted on their "Citty vpon a hill." Winthrop kept writing history not so much for an English audience as for whoever would want to know about the early years of New England.

The justification of Puritan history was coming to be within history itself. The history of New England itself began to assume some of the

137

religious import for the sake of which it had originally begun. Given their realistic assessment of human nature, the Puritans knew that ongoing reform—of themselves and their society and thereby of the world—would be required if their project was to fulfill its promise. They learned to use the precariousness of their undertaking—whether the challenge came from Antinomians or Indians, marauding Frenchmen or adversaries in England— as a way of affirming the rightness of their enterprise, as their descendants would learn to use moral declension as a rhetoric of confirmation. If Bradford wrote history to help himself and his readers understand and endure the present through reference to the past, then Winthrop wrote in order to record the continuing reformation of the present into the future. Frequently in conflict with each other, Separatist and Puritan views of history long outlived Bradford and Winthrop to influence succeeding generations of Americans and their historians. In their own distinctive ways, both views charged history with religious importance. The way these alternatives focused the debate about America's role in history became one of New England's foremost contributions, for good or ill, to the history of American civilization.

As the more "medieval" of the two, the Separatist historian tends to interpret events by way of reference to particular moments in the past when exemplary acts revealed connections between the human and the divine. Likewise, Bradford's work as a historian is justified insofar as it remains true to God's plan. The honesty of his calling therefore requires him to say when the events he is recording fail to sustain the significance which the great models from the past have embodied. The Separatist's inherent dualism, seen in his desire to draw a firm line between good people and wicked people, inclines him toward a historyless cast of mind and makes him a foe of tradition as such. Everyone who responds to ambiguity and confusion by wanting to isolate the few good people from the mass of bad people and to find a place uncorrupted by the vicissitudes of history knows something of the Separatist dream. Yet even such an adventure, as Bradford discovered, begins to have its own history, from which there is finally no escape. The Separatist may then respond stoically, as Bradford did, resigning himself to events beyond his control and preserving a personal sense of meaning by abandoning history in favor of meditation upon those great moments from the past—in Bradford's case, at the very beginning of history itself—when truth was indeed said and done. Or with similar motivations, he may respond by trying to expell the bad people who have infiltrated the group, hoping to reclaim his people's original purity by securing borders that will prevent contact with a contaminated world.

When Pilgrim spirituality ebbed, the Separatist response to history remained. As the ultimate importance originally experienced through exemplary models from the past came to be invested instead in the identity of the present group, the Separatist view of history found cultural and political expression, often with religious overtones, in the ideology of American isolationism. Separatist political leaders have tried to protect America from involvement with an impure world, and Separatist historians have interpreted American history as a series of conflicts between darkness and light, in a myriad of forms. Separatist cultural criticism preserves Bradford's nostalgia, though often without recourse to the ancient models that sustained his religious faith. Whatever their professions, subsequent generations of Separatists have felt like Pilgrims, often without knowing exactly why. In contrast, Bradford's people "knew they were pilgrims." While salutary in some ways, the inevitable loss of a shared religious faith did not necessarily make American society more humane.

In keeping with the Renaissance humanism that Puritan leaders imbibed while acquiring university educations in divinity and law, the Puritan historian tends to find the meaning of events within his own history. Winthrop has a sense that history is the field in which a divine plan is being worked out. Rather than interpreting present experience in light of particular models in the past, the Puritan historian is alert for the ways current events, and the connections between them, may themselves have symbolic significance. The Puritan's belief that all people are mixtures of good and evil, seen in his insistence that even the justified saints need to pursue the hard path toward sanctification, inclines him to take history seriously. While there is no traditionless faith for the Puritan, he tends to believe that, human nature being what it is, even the English Protestant tradition can slip from its true purpose and will require occasional, perhaps continuing reformation and renewal. Everyone who, feeling surrounded by problems and failures, decides to stay on board and to work for change from within the system, convinced that some improvement is preferable to a fruitless search for perfection, experiences something of the Puritan temper. Yet even such a temperament, Winthrop learned, is apt to rise toward heedless enthusiasm or to fall into niggling precisionism. Since they take their own history so religiously, Puritans are always susceptible to flights of Antinomian fancy or to seizures of moralistic authoritarianism. The tendency of latter-day Puritans to move in one of these directions or the other recapitulates the tensions within the Bay Colony that Winthrop described.

Winthrop's commitment to writing history grew from his religious convictions about human nature, providing the governor a crucial additional perspective on his own involvement in history and strengthening his basic character, which historian Edmund S. Morgan has described so well: "John Winthrop, while trying to live as God required, learned that he must live *in* the world, face its temptations, and share its guilt; and Winthrop helped to prevent the government of Massachusetts from seeking a greater perfection in this world than God required or allowed. Winthrop had less control, and less understanding, of the church than the state. And the church, by any standards, had to be more pure than the state. . . . But the visible church, like the man himself, must remain *in* the world and must not only bring its members closer to God but must also help to redeem the rest of the world."[10] At his best, the Puritan historian applies Winthrop's sense of balance, self-criticism, and need for renewal not only to the people whose history he records but also to his own work as a historian. At his worst, whether in an Antinomian or precisionist mode, he thoroughly identifies the Puritan thrust toward renewal with the life of his group itself and assumes that his righteous people are called to reform the rest of the world.

The Puritan view of history was not lost when Puritan piety waned. Although the children of the founders designed a "Half-Way Covenant" to permit their offspring to retain church membership, subsequent generations soon lost the sense of balance that kept the original Puritans moving forward within the verges of a common path. As the errand into the wilderness took on its own meaning, Winthrop's Puritan view of history turned into a less explicitly religious tradition of reform, sometimes of America itself and sometimes, through the new nation's intervention, of the world. While some Puritan political leaders have crusaded for a congeries of social reforms, others, seeing less need for internal improvement, have tried with varying success to enlist America in campaigns to reform the world, usually according to their own image of American purity. Puritan historians have read and written American history as consensual themes of renewal. Puritan cultural critics have bemoaned America's moral decline as a way of renewing the nation's commitment to improve itself and the world, though often without recourse to the religious faith that sustained Winthrop's vision of "a Citty vpon a hill." Countless Americans have supported reform platforms and voted for reform tickets, purchased and tried out an apparently endless variety of self-improvement programs, often stirred deeply by vague motivations. In contrast, Winthrop's Puritans examined themselves scrupulously, reasoning carefully about the covenant they owned with God. While few contemporary Americans would choose to live within the ruled confines of the Massachusetts Bay Colony, many continue to respond, for better or worse, to the call for reform that characterizes the Puritan view of history.

There's nothing like a war to sharpen the debate between latter-day Puritans and Separatists and to make one wish for leaders with Winthrop's balanced involvement in and understanding of history. A clear view of Winthrop, heightened by consideration of what he shared with and where he differed from his colleague Bradford, might clarify current debates, if only by reminding present-day Americans that the Puritan and Separatist views of history were present, already in tension, in the earliest years of one of the traditions that most influentially informs American culture. Yet it is difficult to hear Winthrop's voice, for subsequent interpreters of America muted his image as they transformed the early historians of Pilgrim and Puritan saints into saints themselves. The telling differences between Bradford and Winthrop were silenced, as they were enshrined foremost among the founding fathers of New England. The inaugural hagiography was composed in a virtually insurmountable fashion by a third-generation descendant of premier Puritans, the complicated genius Cotton Mather.

Since his name was derived from two eminent grandfathers, John Cotton and Richard Mather, it is not surprising that Increase Mather's firstborn son felt driven to rekindle the fading embers of the Puritan faith. The New England in which the boy grew up was moving socially, politically, and commercially away from its Puritan foundations, and Cotton Mather devoted himself to restoring the spiritual vitality and shared moral commitments without which, he believed, thoroughgoing degeneration would ensue. Mather poured his energy into this task with an obsession that warranted historian Vernon Parrington's characterization: "Intensely emotional, high-strung and nervous, he was oversexed and overwrought, subject to ecstatic exaltations and, especially during his celibate years, given to seeing visions."[11] However one accounts for or copes with Mather's personal peculiarity, if indeed one can, it is clear that writing history was one of the chief weapons he fashioned in the struggle to revitalize an entire society and that the way Mather wrote history had lasting consequences. If Mather failed to revamp New England, by enshrining the early Puritans in an aura of perfection he articulated a sense of guilt sufficient to keep their memory alive. His audience was chastened rather than transformed; a slightly guilty conscience kept their noses to the grindstone of change. Subsequent historians shared Mather's praise for the founding fathers of New England. Without his freight of guilt, these early leaders were appealed to as the inspiring ancestors of a new civilization.

"I write the Wonders of the Christian Religion, flying from the depravations of Europe, to the American Strand," announced Mather at the outset of his great work, *Magnalia Christi Americana; or, The Ecclesiastical History of New England.* Because the churches of New England were patterned on the earliest years of Christianity, Mather asserts, they were heirs of an ongoing Reformation, with its greatest moments still ahead. His recipe for revitalization is simple: "In short, the *first* Age was the *golden* Age: to return unto *that,* will make a man a Protestant, and, I may add, a Puritan." But if Mather seems to be summoning his contemporaries actually to achieve what earlier generations had so heroically attempted, he quickly reveals that the future of the Reformation is less social than cultural. The full import of the Reformation, it turns out, is involved with Mather's own work as a historian, for "whether New-England may *live* any where else or no, it must *live* in our History!"[12] Pages of self-congratulatory comparisons with ancient historians great and small, however, bring Mather finally to acknowledge that the greatness of his own work will inhere more in the elegance and insight of his writing than in its effect upon his readers.

Indeed, bearing witness to the Puritan founders may primarily provoke negative reactions: "All good men will not be satisfied with every thing that is here set before them. In my own country, besides a considerable number of loose and vain inhabitants risen up, to whom the Congregational Church-discipline, which cannot live well where the power of godliness dyes, is become distasteful for the purity of it; there is also a number of eminently godly persons, who are for a larger way, and unto these my Church-History will give distaste, by the things which it may hapen to utter in favour of that Church-discipline on some few occasions; and the discoveries which I may happen to make of my apprehensions, that *Scripture,* and *reason,* and *antiquity* is for it; and that it is not far from a glorious resurrection." As if that were not enough rejection to expect, "on the other side, there are some among us who very strictly profess the Congregational Church-discipline, but at the same time they have an unhappy narrowness of soul, by which they confine their value and kindness too much unto their own party: and unto those my Church-History will be offensive, because my regard unto our own declared principles does not hinder me from giving the right hand of fellowship unto the valuable servants of the Lord Jesus Christ, who find not our Church-discipline as yet agreeable unto their present understandings and illuminations. If it be thus in my own country, it cannot be otherwise in that whereto I send this account of my own."[13] The Christian tradition had appropriated Isaiah's prophecy that the Suffering Servant would be "despised and rejected of men"; now Mather anticipated a similar response to his own calling. Mather wrote history to continue the Reformation, not expecting that reform would actually occur but in order to carve out an enduring place for himself as a true Puritan. His ambivalences were thoroughgoing and profound, for while undercutting the direct import of writing history, he invested the historian, himself, with immense significance.

By translating history into the biography of saints, Mather sanctified his own vocation. In the process, history became sermonic, more Separatist than Puritan in temper. Turned into icons, leaders such as Bradford and Winthrop might be venerated by the faithful or debunked by iconoclasts but would rarely be read as historians. Held up as "the shields of the churches," the governors and magistrates of New England were "perpetuated by the essay of Cotton Mather," with a pointed epigram:

> The glories of that elder age,
> Lustrous and pure, shall never wane,
> While hero, martyr, ruler, sage,
> Its living monuments remain.[14]

Despite ceaseless allusions to classical writers regarding his role as historian, and more in keeping with the tradition he was attempting to reclaim, Mather cast Bradford and Winthrop as Old Testament patriarchs. On the one hand, it was not difficult to find the proper niche for Bradford: "The leader of a people in a wilderness had need be a Moses; and if a Moses had not led the people of Plymouth Colony, when this worthy person was their governour, the people had never with so much unanimity and importunity still called him to lead them."[15] On the other hand, the Puritan governor elicited so many patriarchal allusions that Mather virtually constructed for Winthrop a chapel of his own.

Indeed, Winthrop's virtues surpassed those of leaders from the classical tradition that Mather quoted so fulsomely to dignify his own work as a historian:

Let Greece boast of her patient Lycurgus, the lawgiver, by whom diligence, temperance, fortitude and wit were made the fashions of a therefore long-lasting and renowned commonwealth: let Rome tell of her devout Numa, the lawgiver, by whom the most famous commonwealth saw peace triumphing over extinguished war and cruel plunders; and murders giving place to the more mollifying exercises of his religion. Our New-England shall tell and boast of her Winthrop, a lawgiver as patient as Lycurgus, but not admitting any of his criminal disorders; as devout as Numa, but not liable to any of *his* heathenish madnesses; a governour in whom the excellencies of Christianity made a most improving addition unto the virtues, wherein even without *those* he would have made a *parallel* for the great men of Greece, or of Rome, which the pen of a Plutarch has eternized.[16]

Mather sustained his own image as the Plutarch of a new republic by Romanizing the combined Old Testament model and New World order that he took Winthrop to represent. As "Nehemias Americanus," Mather's Winthrop promised to lead Christianity, in its American Puritan version, beyond ancient glories to found a new civilization.

For Mather, the Winthrop family heritage made the governor's justice, wisdom, and courage "the more illustrious, by emblazoning them with the constant liberality and hospitality of a gentleman. This made him the *terror* of the wicked, and the *delight* of the sober, the *envy* of the many, but the *hope* of those who had any hopeful design in hand for the common good of the nation and the interests of religion." It was natural for such an eminent person to be "chosen for the Moses" of the Puritan undertaking, and "nothing but a *Mosaic spirit* could have carried him through the temptations, to which either his farewell to his own land, or his travel in a strange land, must needs expose a gentleman of his education."[17] Moreover, since he not only led his people across the sea but also governed their settling in the new land, Winthrop was more than Moses to Mather.

Given the Puritans' desire to reform England by reconstituting the church according to its original, true design, Winthrop recalled the biblical Nehemiah, who led his people in rebuilding the walls of Jerusalem after a period of exile. Yet Winthrop's designation as "Americanus" is also significant, for Puritans did their rebuilding in a new place. Thus Mather's characterization of Winthrop as Nehemias Americanus aptly expresses the ambivalence of the Puritan undertaking as a whole. In some ways, it was a looking backward to origins and a reformulation of ongoing institutions; simultaneously, in other ways, it was a new undertaking in a new land. Winthrop was a successful leader, Mather suggests, because the unique combination of his virtues was apposite to the complex demands of the Puritan project.

Like Nehemiah, Winthrop knew how to endure petty infighting between the discontented and the overzealous in his own party, and he also knew when to be liberal with his goods and generous in overlooking faults: "But whilst he thus did, as our New-English Nehemiah, the part of a *ruler* in managing the public affairs of our American Jerusalem, . . . he made himself still an exacter *parallel* unto that governour of Israel, by doing the part of a neighbor among the distressed people of the new plantation." Winthrop's combined ability to husband frugally and to dispense bountifully evoked another patriarch in Mather's biblical imagination: "Indeed, for a while the governour was the Joseph, unto whom the whole body of the people repaired when their corn failed them; and he continued relieving them with his open-handed bounties, as long as he had any stock to do it with." The story of the arrival of a ship loaded with provisions at the very moment when Winthrop was "distributing the last handful of the meal in the barrel unto a poor man distressed by the 'wolf at the door'" elicits a worldly-wise aphorism from Mather: "Yea, the governour sometimes made his own *private purse* to be the *publick*: not by *sucking* into it, but by *squeezing* out of it."[18] The following parable, together with Mather's pointed commentary, illustrates Winthrop's saintly leadership:

In an hard and long winter, when wood was very scarce at Boston, a man gave him a private information that a needy person in the neighbourhood stole wood sometimes from *his* pile; whereupon the governour in a seeming anger did reply, "Does he so? I'll take a course with him; go, call that man to me; I'll warrant you I'll cure him of stealing." When the man came, the governour considering that if he had stolen, it was more out of necessity than disposition, said unto him, "Friend, it is a severe winter, and I doubt you are but meanly provided for wood; wherefore I would have you supply your self at my wood-pile till this cold season be over." And he then merrily asked his friends, "Whether he had not effectually cured this man of stealing his wood?" One would have imagined that so good a man could have had no enemies, if we had not a daily and woful experience to convince us that goodness it self will make enemies.[19]

Such vignettes kept Winthrop's memory alive in folktales as well as in the more "official" chronicle Mather composed.

In Mather's view, "there hardly ever was a more sensible *mixture* of those two things, *resolution* and *condescention,* than in this good man," and "it was not long before a compensation was made for these things by the *doubled respects* which were from all parts paid unto him." Such a "*mixture* of distant qualities" produced exactly the kind of leader the complex Puritan adventure required, demonstrating the particular way in which the achievements of God's New Israel surpassed the greatest accomplishments of classical antiquity: "In fine, the victories of an Alexander, an Hannibal, or a Caesar over *other men,* were not so glorious as the victories of this great man over *himself,* which also at last proved victories over other men." Foremost among the founders of New England, Winthrop stands in a way for the renewed triumph of the entire Old Testament tradition, as Mather's eulogy declares: "*Such* a governour, after he had been more than ten several times by the people chosen their governour, was New-England now to lose; who having, like Jacob, first left his council and blessing with his children gathered about his bed-side; and, like David, 'served his generation by the will of God,' he 'gave up the ghost,' and fell asleep on March 26, 1649. Having, like the dying Emperour Valentinian, this above all his other *victories* for his triumphs, *His overcoming of himself.*" Cleverly affirming his own role as the historian of the true faith, Mather adapts "the words of Josephus about Nehemiah, the governour of Israel," for Winthrop's epitaph: "He was by nature a man, at once benevolent and just: most zealous for the honour of his countrymen; and to them he left an imperishable monument—the walls of New England."[20] The irony is that in trying to write a history that would keep Winthrop alive as a model for future generations, Mather encapsulated the exemplary governor within the walls of history.

As Mather's hero becomes more saintly, at once more admirable and also more removed from common life, the power of the historian is irrevocably increased. Mather's heightened self-consciousness of his own role as historian overwhelmed his subjects, transforming flesh-and-blood men such as Bradford and Winthrop into exemplary figures in the service of Mather's vocation as the Josephus of the Puritan faith and the Plutarch of a New World civilization. Mather's eagerness to wear both hats coincides with the merging of religious and civic virtues in his iconography of early New England. Future interpreters of America would look back to the founders through Mather's eyes, responding to new cultural crises by invoking the memory of a time when piety and politics were at one.

Regardless of its historical accuracy and its author's unusual personality, Mather's *Magnalia Christi Americana* had monumental consequences for succeeding generations of historians and other keepers of the American dream. In probing the national ideal that informs *Uncle Tom's Cabin,* for example, literary historian and critic Edmund Wilson cites a revealing passage from the autobiography of Harriet Beecher Stowe: "There was one of my father's books that proved a mine of wealth to me. It was a happy hour when he brought home and set up in his bookcase Cotton Mather's *Magnalia,* in a new edition of two volumes. What wonderful stories those! Stories, too, about my own country. Stories that made me feel the very ground I trod on to be consecrated by some special dealings of God's providence." As for countless other Americans, for Stowe such feelings were intertwined with her emotional response to a reading of the Declaration of Independence: "I was as ready as any of them to pledge my life, fortune, and sacred honor for such a cause. The heroic element was strong in men, having come down by ordinary generation from a long line of Puritan ancestry, and just now it made me long to do something, I knew not what: to fight for my country, or to make some declaration on my own account."[21] To suggest how naturally Mather's inheritance provides religious roots for the ideology of the American Way of Life, Wilson cites an episode from Stowe's work *Poganuc People*:

After the singing came Dr. Cushing's prayer—which was a recounting of God's mercies to New England from the beginning, and of her deliverances from her enemies, and of petitions for the glorious future of the United States of America— that they might be chosen vessels, commissioned to bear the light of liberty and religion through all the earth and to bring in the great millennial day, when wars should cease and the whole world, released from the thraldom of evil, should rejoice in the sight of the Lord. The millennium was ever the star of hope in the eyes of the New England clergy; their faces were set eastward, towards the dawn of that day, and the cheerfulness of those anticipations illuminated the hard tenets of their theology with a rosy glow. They were children of the morning.[22]

Mather had turned Bradford and Winthrop into saints whose names resounded in the litany of cultural nationalism.

In keeping with Mather's intentions, the saints were invoked to recall a present generation from its forgetfulness in order to restore its confidence in the future. As American society became increasingly diverse, reference to the faith of the founders became less specific. Distinctions between Pilgrims and Puritans, once so important, were muted. If Mather looked to the past in order to reclaim the Puritan spirit, his cultural descendants did so on behalf of Protestantism more broadly, then for the sake of Christianity, and finally to revive religiousness in general, to bolster moral commitments, or simply to affirm some shared sense of civic purpose. Whether Bradford and Winthrop were praised as saints or, later, debunked as authoritarians, Mather's iconography was remarkably durable. For they were not read as men who wrote the histories in which their acts as governors were recorded. Consequently, the telling differences between Separatist and Puritan views of history were not remembered, and the critical perspectives each of the two men brought to bear upon history itself went unobserved. In the process, American history itself, read as the progress of American civilization, was invested with an authority that was for Bradford and Winthrop, in their respective ways, beyond history.

When later Americans clashed over essentially Separatist or Puritan versions of their past, present, and future, therefore, their arguments were the more dangerous insofar as their foundations, and the differences between them, were forgotten. Two related but distinct sorts of difficulties were engendered by this lack of awareness. On the one hand, subsequent generations of Americans experienced clashes between the Separatist desire for cultural and political isolation and the Puritan drive toward moral and political reform. The battle between isolation and reformation was played out between political parties in response to questions of American involvement in international conflicts, and a more personal struggle between Separatist and Puritan tendencies divided the hearts of individual citizens. On the other hand, since the distinctive histories of the two visions were forgotten, the ongoing dilemma was often superficially resolved. When the differences were glossed over, it could be asserted that American beginnings were actually as pristine as the Pilgrims had wished and also that Americans were impelled to press forward like Puritans to reform the world—in the image of their own deceptively innocent origins. Confusing the ideologies of these early voyagers to New England could become, in the political culture of a major world power, a recipe for domination and international disaster. Whether the outcome was experienced as a conflict between or as an amalgamation of Separatist and Puritan views of history, the consequences of forgetfulness might be benign or malicious, but they could not be understood and directed toward constructive ends. Without an appreciation of what they inherited from this part of their history, Americans were at its mercy.

As the civilization New England helped to inaugurate became increasingly complex, Mather's saints lost their voices. Without their contributions, the debate about the meaning of America and its role in the world became more strident and less profound. Given the inescapably international character of contemporary economic and political affairs, national problems and world events are inextricably intertwined for the United States. Hence, despite its understandable allure in periods of crisis, the Separatist tendency, manifested in the rhetoric of isolationism, remains an illusion, indeed unreachably in the past. If Bradford's voice is essentially contrapuntal, however, Winthrop's vision of principled involvement in the world, informed by his Puritan understanding of human nature and shaped by his commitment to history as an ongoing process, remains vitally important. For Winthrop's voice to be of better service in the future than his icon has been in the past, we must learn to read the history of his story as a significant episode in early New England and as part of the continuing Puritan strain in American culture.

7

The Governor and
the Historians

"OTHER MEN are lenses through which we read our own minds," wrote Ralph Waldo Emerson. "He is great who is what he is from nature, and who never reminds us of others. But he must be related to us, and our life receive from him some promise of explanation." John Winthrop has offered such a promise to the imaginations of historians who hve examined the early years of New England. Seeking their own connection with—or freedom from—the past, historians have portrayed Winthrop as the quintessential American Puritan and also, at the same time, as one whose character transcended his times. Such ambiguity, Emerson believed, is inspired by all truly "representative men." On the one hand, "men resemble their contemporaries even more than their progenitors." Yet because "the great . . . are saviors from these federal errors, and defend us from our contemporaries," Emerson also exclaimed: "What indemnification is one great man for populations of pigmies!"[1] Historians who admire the Puritans naturally find much to praise in the man they so often chose as governor. For those whose assessment of the Puritans is finally more negative, Winthrop often seems nevertheless to represent what was best about the Puritan project, what the Puritans somehow might have been. In either case, as "the Puritan Governor," Winthrop promises to unlock the meaning of early New England. Our interpretation of his life and work, therefore, must take into account the image of Winthrop that emerges from the variety of views of Puritanism in America.

Like many nineteenth-century Americans, George Bancroft viewed American civilization in the light cast backward and forward by the United States Constitution. His ten-volume *History of the United States,* a monumental achievement that was arguably the most influential history written in America during the 1800s, portrays the years leading toward design and adoption of the federal government as an era that "has within itself perfect unity and completeness." Bancroft's love for Jacksonian democracy was bolstered by certain rather generalized convictions from the Puritan era. For example, since "the fortunes of a nation are not under the control of blind destiny," he believed that the historian's task is "to follow the steps by which a favoring Providence, calling our institutions into being, has conducted the country to its present happiness and glory." Hence, while his appreciation of the Puritans was considerably less pointed than the sermonic veneration produced by Cotton Mather, Bancroft continued to extol the leaders of New England: "The early history of Massachusetts is the history of a class of men as remarkable for their qualities and influence as any by which the human race has been diversified."[2] He simply included men like Bradford and Winthrop among a broader group of founding fathers.

Bancroft relied on Winthrop as a resource for assessing the whole Puritan undertaking, and his interpretation of the impetus for the Puritans' emigration, for instance, reads straight from the early lists of reasons and arguments that Winthrop circulated to recruit potential New Englanders. Recognizing the central role that Winthrop played throughout the Puritan era, Bancroft portrays the governor as a saintly moderate who led the way toward a more liberal American future:

It was principally the calm decision of Winthrop which sustained the courage of his companions. In him a yielding gentleness of temper and a never failing desire for unity and harmony were secured against weakness by deep but tranquil enthusiasm. His nature was touched by the sweetest sympathies of affection for wife, children, and associates; cheerful in serving others and suffering with them, liberal without reluctance, helpful without reproaching, in him God so exercised his grace that he discerned his own image and resemblance in his fellow-man and cared for his neighbor like himself. He was of a sociable nature; so that "to love and be beloved was his soul's paradise," and works of mercy were the habit of his life. Parting from affluence in England, he unrepiningly went to meet impoverishment and premature age for the welfare of Massachusetts. His lenient benevolence tempered the bigotry of his companions, without impairing their resoluteness. An honest royalist, averse to pure democracy, yet firm in his regard for existing popular liberties; in his native parish, a conformist, yet wishing for "gospel purity"; in America, mildly aristocratic, advocating a government of "the least part," yet desiring that part to be "the wiser of the best"; disinterested, brave, and conscientious—his character marks the transition of the reformation into virtual republicanism. The sentiment of loyalty, which it was still intended to cherish, gradually yielded to the unobstructed spirit of civil freedom.[3]

In Bancroft's hands, the rough edges of seventeenth-century Puritan politics, to say nothing of the conversionist core of Puritan religious experience and the hard reasoning of Puritan theology, are smoothed away in this image of Winthrop as a forefather of the American republic.

After losing the tolerant leadership of John Winthrop and John Winthrop, Jr., the Puritans, Bancroft acknowledges, became more harsh, as evidenced in their cruelty toward the Quakers: "By degrees the spirit of the establishment began to subvert the fundamental principles of independency. . . . The union of church and state was fast corrupting both. . . . The uncompromising Congregationalists of Massachusetts indulged the passions of their English persecutors." Nevertheless, Bancroft's overall assessment of the movement fits more charitably into his general sense of the progress of American civilization: "If from the outside peculiarities we look to the genius of the sect itself, Puritanism had two cardinal principles: Faith in the absolute sovereignty of God, whose will is perfect right; and the equality of all who believe that his will is to be done. It was Religion struggling in, with, and for the People; a war against tyranny and superstition."[4] By the time Bancroft was writing, denominationalism had developed as the distinctive pattern of religious organization in the new nation, and Bancroft was evidently pleased with the ways the various denominations worked freely to support what he saw as the benign, progressive civil religion of American democratic values and institutions.

The nature of religion itself had changed in America, and Bancroft read the past in its new light, even to the point of claiming that "Puritanism constituted not the Christian clergy, but the Christian people, the interpreter of divine will; and the issue of Puritanism was popular sovereignty." In this new day Puritanism might still be celebrated for its cultural significance: "Puritanism was a life-giving spirit; activity, thrift, intelligence, followed in its train; and, as for courage, a coward and a Puritan never went together." And the social weight of Puritanism was undeniable: "I have dwelt the longer on the character of the early Puritans of New England, for they were the parents of one third of the whole white population of the United States as it was in 1834." Yet its religious center was precisely what Bancroft sought not quite to forget but certainly to move beyond through reinterpretation: "On every subject but religion the mildness of Puritan legislation corresponded to the popular character of Puritan doctrines."[5] While John Winthrop would have bristled at such a transmutation of Puritan spirituality and theology into the civil religion of American democracy, by accentuating Winthrop's personal characteristics Bancroft coverted Puritanism into a viable, valuable cultural resource for the new nation. In the process, the Puritan governor became a founding father of the American republic.

Shortly after Bancroft finished the final revision of his great work, John Fiske contrasted John Winthrop with Thomas Dudley to highlight the strengths and weaknesses of the Puritan tradition. In Dudley, wrote Fiske, "we have the typical narrow-minded, strait-laced Calvinist for whom it is so much easier to entertain respect than affection. But Winthrop's character, as we look at the well-known portrait ascribed to Van Dyck, is revealed in a face expressive of what was finest in the age of Elizabeth, the face of a spiritual brother of Raleigh and Sidney." In Fiske's view, Winthrop's personal character made him a man of undeniably heroic proportions: "He was a man of remarkable strength and beauty of character, grave and modest, intelligent and scholarlike, intensely religious and endowed with a moral sensitiveness that was almost morbid, yet liberal withal in his opinions and charitable in disposition. When his life shall have been adequately written, as it never has been, he will be recognized as one of the very noblest figures in American history. From early youth he had that same power of winning confidence and commanding respect for which Washington was so remarkable; and when he was selected as the Moses of the great Puritan exodus, there was a wide-spread feeling that extraordinary results were likely to come of such an enterprise." Indeed, Winthrop's virtues enable Fiske to reclaim a valuable aspect of that largely ignoble Puritan world, beyond which the historian assumes his own more enlightened age has advanced: "Fortunately we can learn something from the stumblings of our forefathers, and a good many things seem quite clear to us to-day which two centuries ago were only beginning to be discerned by a few of the keenest and boldest spirits. The faults of the Puritan theocracy, which found its most complete development in Massachusetts, are so glaring that it is idle to seek to palliate them or to explain them away. But if we would really understand what was going on in the Puritan world of the seventeenth century, and how a better state of things has grown out of it, we must endeavor to distinguish and define the elements of wholesome strength in that theocracy no less than its elements of crudity and weakness."[6] If Bancroft relies on Winthrop's personal character to help him reinterpret the Puritan tradition in a way that will support and serve the civil religion of American democracy, Fiske employs a similar image of the Massachusetts governor to serve the nation's future by leaving most of its Puritan past behind. In a highly ironic way, Mather's hagiography seems to have succeeded in defeating its own purposes.

A more balanced view of the historian's task was articulated by Charles Francis Adams, a contemporary of Bancroft and Fiske, who asserted in his study of the Antinomian crisis that "in the treatment of doubtful historical points, there are few things which need to be more carefully guarded against than patriotism or filial piety. Admirable in their place, these sentiments have less than nothing to do with that impartiality which should be the historian's aim." As shown in his explication of the tangled inheritance that clouded the judgment of James Savage, Adams sought to meet his own high standards. His more balanced overall assessment of the Puritans might thereby provide a less volatile context for his image of John Winthrop. Nevertheless, the historian's point of view is unmistakable: "The judgment seat . . . was, in the minds of the men and women who then lived, just as much an ordeal to be looked forward to and prepared for as, with certain classes, the admission to an academy or college or a profession is looked forward to and prepared for now." Instead of explaining away the Puritan faith, Adams accented the centrality of religion in the Puritan experience in a way that his own readers might understand: "In those days religion meant a great deal. It was no sentiment or abstraction. The superstition which prevailed is to the modern mind well-nigh inconceivable. All shared in it." Thus Adams pictured Winthrop against the backdrop of "the singular condition of religious and theological craze in which early New England existed," and he criticized Winthrop and the other Puritan leaders for being no better than those who had persecuted them in England and for not being great enough to think in advance of their time.[7] Winthrop could not have been the best of the Puritans without being a Puritan, and the Puritans were a deeply—and, in Adams's mind, troublesomely—religious people.

In the main, however, Adams's commitment to balanced judgment only makes Winthrop's character shine forth more nobly, for within the religiously charged Puritan world Winthrop governed with the moderation that Adams later espoused for historians:

Winthrop has been regarded by most of the native New England historians, and notably by Palfrey, with a veneration which has impaired respect for their judgment whenever the authority of the first governor is invoked. They see things only through his eyes, and the ordinary scrutiny of modern historical criticism is laid aside where he is involved. Repeated instances of this indiscriminate adulation will be referred to in the course of this narrative. Nevertheless the difficulty of Winthrop's position, and the skill and high-minded rectitude with which he on the whole demeaned himself, should always be borne in mind. On this point the evidence of a foreign student and investigator carries more weight than that of one to the manor born:— "Every page in the early history of New England bears witness to the patience, the firmness, the far-seeing wisdom of Winthrop. But to estimate these qualities as they deserve, we must never forget what the men were with whom, and in some measure by whom, he worked. To guard the Commonwealth against the attacks of courtiers, churchmen and speculators, was no small task. But it was an even greater achievement to keep impracticable fanatics like Dudley and Endicott within the bounds of reason, and to use for the preservation of the state those headstrong passions which at every turn threatened to rend it asunder."[8]

As portrayed by Charles Francis Adams, the governor was both a Puritan and more than a Puritan: "Winthrop, it is true, shared in the darkness and the superstition, and even—in his calm, moderate way—in the intolerance of his time; but it was just that sharing in the weakness as well as the strength—the superstitions as well as the faith—of his time which made him so valuable in the place chance called upon him to fill. He was in sympathy with his surroundings,—just enough in the advance, and not too much." Yet even

Winthrop, in Adams's view, was not sufficiently advanced to lead his people beyond the fate toward which they were drawn by those characteristics that he shared with them: "It is impossible to ignore the fact, and worse than useless to deny it, that the New England Puritans were a persecuting race. They could not be otherwise. They believed that they were God's chosen people. . . . The Israelites were not an attractive or an amiable or a philosophical race; they were narrow, devout and clannish. . . . Their very imperfections were essential elements of their strength. . . . It was the same with the Puritans of New England. They persecuted as part of their faith. In doing so the Puritan exiles to New England showed that they were not in advance of their times. That they were not, was again an element of their strength; for they were essentially practical men, and not idealists."[9] Such people were definitely not democrats, even in the making.

Unlike Bancroft, whose desire to see everything in colonial times leading smoothly toward the constitutional era led him to argue that Puritanism was actually less theological than democratic, Adams was careful to observe that the later triumphs of American civilization were achieved only when the religious barriers of Puritanism had been overcome: "It is barely possible that New England, contrary to all principle and precedent, may have profited by the harshness and bigotry which for a time suppressed all freedom of thought in Massachusetts; but it is far more likely that the slow results afterwards there achieved came notwithstanding that drawback, rather than in consequence of the discipline it afforded."[10] Thus for Adams, Winthrop's insights and achievements are locked in an irretrievably religious past. Given Adams's negative view of religion, the historian's honesty turns even the most outstanding character from the past into a subject to be admired from a distance rather than a resource to be understood and reclaimed.

A generation later, a historian whose work was interrupted by the First World War examined early New England with broader purposes in mind: "Pride in the valiant work that the Massachusetts leaders did in subduing the wilderness, and in the sacrifices that they made for their religious beliefs, has tended to make their descendants, in the words of the old English saw, 'to their faults a little blind, and to their virtues very kind'; but if the nations of the world are to grow in mutual understanding and brotherly feeling, their histories must be written from the standpoint of justice to all, and not from that of a mistaken national piety."[11] As one of the American historians who had begun to explore the role of economic motivations in the nation's past, James Truslow Adams understood quite clearly how novel his view of the Puritans might seem:

The old conception of New England history, according to which that section was considered to have been settled by persecuted religious refugees, devoted to liberty of conscience, who, in the disputes with the mother-country, formed a united mass of liberty-loving patriots unanimously opposed to an unmitigated tyranny, has, happily, for many years, been passing. In his own narrative of the facts, based upon a fresh study of the sources, the author has tried to indicate that economic as well as religious factors played a very considerable part in the great migration during the early settlement period, in the course of which over sixty-five thousand Englishmen left their homes for various parts of the New World, of which number approximately only four thousand were to join the New England churches. He has also endeavored to show how . . . the domestic struggle against the tyranny exercised by the more bigoted members of the theocratic party was of greater importance in the history of liberty than the more dramatic contest with the mother-country.[12]

An economic perspective led the historian to reassess John Winthrop's reasons for emigration: "His judgment regarding the ending of the opportunity for a public career for such as himself in England was obviously wrong, as events developed there. The England which retained a Pym, a Hampden, and Eliot, and a Cromwell, may well have offered scope for the talents of a Winthrop." Yet Winthrop's character stretched the new interpretive scheme: "In the motives given by him who was the purest, gentlest, and broadest-minded of all who were to guide the destinies of the Bay Colony, we presumably find the highest of those which animated any of the men who sought its shores. As we descend the scale of character, the religious incentives narrow and disappear, as does also the desire for honorable public service, and the economic factor alone remains."[13] Centuries later James Truslow Adams was discovering, as various hard-liners in the Bay Colony had learned, that Winthrop's personality had a way of undoing precisionists of any stripe.

With such chapter titles as "An English Opposition becomes a New England Oligarchy," James Truslow Adams clearly intended to present a new, more realistic view of the Puritan leadership: "We cannot, perhaps, blame men for not being in advance of their age, or even for being behind it. The founders of the Bay Colony were but little qualified, by reason of the narrowness of their views and the intensity with which they were held, to lead men to any higher ground than that which they had been accustomed to tread. Moreover, having changed their place from members of an opposition to members of a government, their new responsibilities would tend to foster even more strongly that fear of innovation which is nearly always characteristic of the middle-class man in power."[14] Centuries of veneration, however, made the Puritan governor's image highly resistant to such demythologizing, and one can almost feel the force of Mather's ghost as James Truslow Adams wrestles with Winthrop's legacy:

Thomas Hooker died in 1647, as the work of the synod was beginning, and John Winthrop in 1649, as it was ending. There is no comparison in the debt that the political thought of America owes to the two men. . . . Hooker led the way along which the people of the United States were to follow, while Winthrop was engaged in the attempt to found a state in a politically impossible form. In spite of his inestimable services in the beginnings of the colony, there was no originality in his contribution to thought, and his subservience to the demands of the theocracy had been foreshadowed by his statement in early manhood that he so honored a faithful minister that he "could have kissed his feet." Of high nobility of character, gentle, forgiving, frequently kindest to those from whom he differed most, there was little in his nature of the born persecutor. Led into acts of intolerant zeal by the ministers whom he so devoutly followed, there is considerable probability in the story related by Hutchinson, that when on his death-bed, being pressed by Dudley to sign a warrant for the banishment of a heretic, he refused, saying that "he had done too much of that work already." His portrait depicts a face of gentleness rather than of strength. His unquestioned integrity, his modesty, and his self-sacrificing devotion to the interests of the colony as he saw them, amply fulfilled the high opinion which the original undertakers of the enterprise had formed of him, although, as in the case of most of the leaders, the effect upon mind and character of the transplanting to America was not wholly a happy one. "He was of a more catholic spirit than some of his brethren before he left England," wrote Hutchinson; "but afterward he grew more contracted, and was disposed to lay too great stress upon indifferent matters."[15]

Finally, even a great man like Winthrop cannot escape his social environment, which was, for James Truslow Adams, formed more definitely by economic considerations than by religious and intellectual traditions: "In England, Puritanism had been grafted upon a national stock of abundant sturdiness and health. In the forests of America, uncultured and ungrafted, the wild fruit grew steadily more gnarled and bitter."[16] The historian's desire to reveal the powerful role of economic factors has reduced the Puritans' religion to an ideological cover for the play of self-interest, thereby rendering even the admittedly virtuous Winthrop merely a contributor to a world well lost. The historian has to struggle somewhat to reduce Winthrop to fit his paradigm, but finally the paradigm prevails.

Readers of Winthrop's journal will recognize an irony here, for Winthrop was acutely aware of the importance of economic motivations in the movement he led. Indeed, his frankness about such considerations in his own life and in the life of the colony, whether or not he always dealt successfully with them, was one of the strengths his contemporaries recognized in his leadership. Nevertheless, for the governor such centrally important matters were not the whole story. For Winthrop, economic factors were one of the aspects—along with religion, morality, and politics—of an integral Puritan way of life. By focusing upon one or another of these elements, each historian presents something less than the full picture, and subsequent historians seek to correct the inherited image by highlighting what their predecessors have left in the background. Unfortunately, the cost of James Truslow Adams's correction was the devaluation of the religious dimension of Puritanism, without which the world would have made little sense to a governor whose personal character could not be wholly reduced to the categories of economics.

In the mid-1960s Edmund S. Morgan observed that "during the past twenty-five years, the economic interpretation of history that seemed so plausible in the twenties and thirties has gradually begun to appear too one-sided. Historians today are wary of attributing events in any period to a single cause. This development came very early to the study of the founding of New England."[17] Historians Samuel Eliot Morison and Perry Miller led the reevaluation by paying close attention to the central role of religious experience and theological ideas in Puritan experience. While neither adopting nor advocating particular Puritan beliefs, these "historians of ideas" argued that modern Americans have something important to learn from "the seventeenth-century mind." Yet these lessons, both historians acknowledged, are antithetical to much that modern people consider important. Morison wrote in 1930:

Even by enlarging the scope of biography beyond the conventional lines of piety and politics, it is not easy to describe these people truthfully, yet with meaning to moderns. For the men of learning and women of gentle nurture who led a few thousand plain folk to plant a new England on ungrateful soil were moved by purposes utterly foreign to the present America. Their object was not to establish prosperity or prohibition, liberty or democracy, or indeed anything of currently recognized value. Their ideals were comprehended vaguely in the term puritanism, which nowadays has acquired various secondary and degenerate meanings. These ideals, real and imaginary, of early Massachusetts, were attacked by historians of Massachusetts long before "debunking" became an accepted biographical mode; for it is always easier to condemn an alien way of life than to understand it. My attitude toward seventeenth-century puritanism has passed through scorn and boredom to a warm interest and respect. The ways of the puritans are not my ways, and their faith is not my faith; nevertheless they appear to me a courageous, humane, brave, and significant people.[18]

Chief among the Puritan leaders to whose virtues Morison wanted to draw his countrymen's attention was Governor John Winthrop.

As one of the principal "builders of the Bay Colony," Winthrop represented what Morison found best in the Puritan tradition: "a high sincerity of purpose, an integrity of life, and an eager searching for the voice of God." The governor was also representative in the sense that his life and the whole Puritan undertaking were so closely intertwined by the time of emigration that "to tell the story of the rest of John Winthrop's life would be to relate the history of the Bay Colony until his death in 1649." Morison does not pretend that Winthrop was perfect, for "superstition, like persecution and coarse language, was part and parcel of the age in which Winthrop lived, and he was no better nor worse than the average educated Englishman of the time." Indeed, in some ways the governor was less able than others: "In his private affairs Governor Winthrop was not what New Englanders would call a good manager. He consistently neglected them for the public business." Nevertheless, "keeping in mind the basis and principle by which he governed, that he and his fellow magistrates were God's vicegerents divinely commissioned to maintain gospel ordinance in a new colony, Winthrop justified those 'extraordinary great commendacions' of him. Without that basis, he would not have been Winthrop. From his fellows of the ruling class, strong and able men, he stands out as a superior man of noble character, with a single eye to the common weal." If "one may regret that he did not more often insist on that comparative mildness and mercy in administration which was natural to him," still "Winthrop's capacity to take advice and yield to the majority, was part of his equipment for leadership."[19] Morison argues, then, that Puritan religious commitments gave the governor's life certain qualities that Morison's own contemporaries unfortunately lacked. The historian was hoping that later Americans, without adopting Puritan religious beliefs as such, might regain Winthrop's moral character and practical wisdom. Morison's Winthrop is more lively and credible than Cotton Mather's saintly governor, but whether the history of ideas could adequately support the reclamation Morison envisioned would depend on a more thoroughgoing revision of the Puritan tradition.

A broad attempt to bring Puritanism back into contemporary discussions about the past and future of American civilization was launched in 1939 with the publication of Perry Miller's *The New England Mind: The Seventeenth Century.* That Americans should take this part of their cultural heritage seriously seemed obvious to Miller: "I assume that Puritanism was one of the major expressions of the Western intellect, that it achieved an organized synthesis of concepts which are fundamental to our culture, and that therefore it calls for the most serious examination." Given the reigning models of interpretation and the generally pejorative assessment of "puritanical" attitudes, however, Miller acknowledged that his task required a carefully balanced style of advocacy:

It ought to be unnecessary in a work of history for the historian to advertise his impartiality, but Puritanism has recently become the center of so many critical storms that any writer upon the subject is greeted at once with the question of whether he be friend or foe. At the risk of appearing too conspicuously before the curtain and stating baldly what ought to be visible in the performance, I should like to make clear that I wholeheartedly admire the integrity and profundity of the Puritan character but that I am far from sharing in its code or from finding delight in its every aspect. Yet I can honestly say that my interest in Puritanism has not been a matter of liking or disliking. Regardless of the repute in which it may be held today, Puritanism is of immense historical importance: it was not only the most coherent and most powerful single factor in the early history of America, it was a vital expression of a crucial period in European development, and those who would understand the modern world must know something of what it was and of what heritages it has bequeathed to the present.[20]

In direct opposition to all of the historians and other scholars who employed a more "scientific" approach such as economics to explain those aspects of Puritanism that appeared repugnant to modern sensibilities, Miller felt "compelled to insist that the mind of man is the basic factor in human history."[21] His goal, therefore, was to elucidate the particular ideas that made Puritanism such a powerful and enduring force in American culture.

In addition to all that the Puritans shared with other seventeenth-century Englishmen, Miller found two basic beliefs behind their desire to reform their nation and its church. First, the Puritans believed that the whole Bible was the revealed word of God, plain and explicit from one end to the other, whereas the Anglicans held the Bible to be the word of God only regarding the broad principles of the Christian religion, in the light of which God intended men to use their reason to deal with the problems of particular situations. Second, the Puritans insisted that the Fall, history, and daily experience demonstrate humanity's ineradicable sinfulness and consequently the need for an experience of the renewal of life that divine grace alone affords, whereas the Anglicans had faith in the human ability to find one's own way to proper behavior and belief.[22] The Puritans, Miller wrote, "could never banish from their minds the consciousness of something mysterious and terrible in life, of something that leaped when least expected, that upset all the regularities of technologia and circumvented the laws of logic, that cut across the rules of justice, of something behind appearances that could not be tamed and brought to heel."[23] Hence they took comfort in the idea of a covenant between God and men, whereby God freely bound himself to sustain the spiritual existence of those sinful men to whom his grace was offered. The idea of such a covenant was the Puritans' way of coping purposefully with the unnerving ambivalence of their spiritual experience, a way of harnessing the contradictions their theology could not honestly overlook. The idea of the covenant, as articulated in the "federal" theology it engendered, was the organizing theme that Miller discovered in the entire Puritan experiment.

Thus Winthrop's understanding of the covenant plays a central role in Miller's view of the governor's leadership: "The colony of Massachusetts Bay, being founded upon a theory that for the comprehensions of ordinary men proved, to say the least, difficult, was supremely fortunate in having in John Winthrop not only a resolute statesman but also a philosopher and stylist." A social interpretation of the covenant was the key ingredient in his "Modell of Christian Charity" sermon, as "John Winthrop, standing upon the deck of the *Arbella*, thinking himself another Moses in a new Deuteronomy, outlined in advance the basis of New England politics." Likewise, when explicating the "little speech" that Winthrop delivered toward the end of his life about the true meaning of liberty as "the culminating expression of the Puritan ideal in New England," Miller observes that "much as historians have praised his speech, few have yet done justice to the large sweep of his argument, and we can appreciate his great artistry only when we remember that his audience had been thoroughly indoctrinated by their parsons with the theology of the covenant. He was deliberately playing upon ideas so fixed in the minds of the populace that they could not possibly be challenged." Indeed, "Winthrop's discourse was unique simply for the dispatch with which he transposed the covenant theory from the soul to the state, and spectacular because he used it to quell an uprising of citizens. He delivered it with such smashing force that for several decades the democratical spirit was hardly anywhere to be seen in Massachusetts Bay."[24] Hence Winthrop's skillful leadership of the Bay Colony, from start to finish, is wrapped together with his power as a spokesman for the covenant, which Miller is convinced is "a constellation of ideas basic to any comprehension of the American mind."[25] Yet a pungent irony emerges when Miller considers what happened to the idea of the covenant that meant so much to Winthrop and his people when the Puritan cause began to triumph in the old homeland that their errand to New England had originally been meant to reform.

Because "Winthrop and his colleagues believed fully in the covenant," Miller argues, "they could see in the pattern of history that their errand was not a mere scouting expedition: it was an essential maneuver in the drama of Christendom." But the Civil War turned English eyes away from the "City vpon a hill," causing immediate economic problems for Winthrop's Puritans and, as England began to move toward a more tolerant religious system than New England had constructed, leaving the next generation of American Puritans with perplexing questions about their identity and purpose. If they were not the advance guard of the Reformation, whch seemed to have outpaced even the prodigious efforts of the founders of the Bay Colony, toward what new end should their still lively sense of purpose be directed? If Massachusetts was not the illustrious outpost of a universal Puritan cause, then their errand into the wilderness needed a new justification: "They looked in vain to history for an explanation of themselves; more and more it appeared that the meaning was not to be found in theology, even with the help of the covenantal dialectic. Thereupon, these citizens found that they had no other place to search but within themselves—even though, at first sight, that repository appeared to be nothing but a sink of inquity. Their errand having failed in the first sense of the term, they were left with the second, and required to fill it with meaning by themselves and out of themselves. Having failed to rivet the eyes of the world upon their city on the hill, they were left alone with America."[26] Just as subsequent generations of

Puritans struggled to discover or invest in America the purposeful intensity of Winthrop's era, so Perry Miller led a generation of scholars who sought by studying the history of New England to find or create a source of cultural significance commensurate with the religious dimensions of Winthrop's world. The search moved in many directions as historians of various persuasions extended or revised the interpretive empire that Morison and Miller's generation founded.[27] In the process, several gifted scholars looked more closely at the life of Governor John Winthrop for clues about Puritanism in early New England and its ongoing contributions, for good or ill, to American life.

Historian Richard S. Dunn, for example, looked at several generations of the Winthrop family to examine New England's movement away from Puritan characteristics and toward the Yankee temperament: "No one family can mirror all aspects of a society in transition, but the seventeenth-century Winthrops do exemplify the most profound cultural development of their era, the secularization of the New England conscience." For Dunn, "the central point is clear enough: John Winthrop was the first American whose keen awareness of human inadequacy drove him to demand responsible action from himself and from all his fellow men. He was the first keeper of the New England conscience." Moreover, the historian's hypothesis about secularization required him to portray the founder of the "dynasty" in stark terms: "For all his self-discipline and sober, shrewd realism, John Winthrop was first and foremost a religious fanatic. It was this devotion to God's purpose which made him such a strong leader in 1630."[28] In this case, a strong hypothesis caused a historian to see too much. As we have seen, Winthrop was indeed devoted to God's purposes as he understood them, and his beliefs could at times lead him to particular actions that might, in today's world, appear fanatical. Yet a balanced temperament guided his more characteristic decisions, and the actual fanatics often challenged Winthrop's leadership precisely because of his leniency. Perhaps if Dunn had read Winthrop as the writer of the history of the colony he governed, he might have been less prone to cast the governor as a one-dimensional actor in the drama of secularization.

Another scholar, Robert C. Black III, also noted the decline of religious intensity in the passage of generations in the Winthrop family, observing that John Winthrop, Jr., never became a Puritan in the thoroughgoing way of his father.[29] While Black's approach was more biographical than sociological, a forthright case for secularization recurred in Darrett Rutman's study of how Boston became a modern, diverse commercial city rather than the medieval ideal expressed in Winthrop's vision of "a Citty vpon a hill."[30] During the 1960s, when these books were written, many scholars—including a number of leading theologians—believed that authentically American experience was secular, rather than religious, in character. When historians investigated early New England, therefore, they did not repudiate the Puritan heritage; they simply interpreted it as incipiently secular.

Even when Rutman wrote a book titled *John Winthrop's Decision for America: 1629,* he was careful to point out that when the Puritan party landed in Massachusetts in 1630, their actual English experience was left quickly behind: "We need not elaborate here upon either the evolving New England Way in town and church or the effect of that way in the subsequent evolution of an American Way. It is enough to say that a peculiar way *did* appear, and that it had an almost immediate effect upon the way men viewed the motivations of 1629. The agonizing, personal decision for America that Winthrop made was forgotten; so, too, were the roots of that decision and the vagueness of his hopes for New England. The New England Way itself was transmuted into the motivation of the founders. In effect, it came to be said that they left Old England with the intention of establishing that which ultimately evolved in New England." While Rutman took pains to point out the simplification that such an interpretation engendered, his own approach to the Puritan experience was inherently secularizing. He speculated that "Winthrop's decision for America was a reaction to his definition of the situation surrounding him at the time of his decision; his definition of that situation was the product of a complex process of successive situational definitions and responses stringing back through his life to—where? childhood? the cradle? the womb?"[31] In such a view, religion was simply one of the factors in the Puritan decision to emigrate from England, and within a generation it was abandoned in New England as well. When the Puritan contribution to American civilization is viewed as the first act in a drama of secularization, religion is seen as only one, presumably minor, motivation in Winthrop's life. Or when religion is considered a major factor, Winthrop is portrayed as a fanatic whose contributions to New England have been well left behind. The hypothesis of secularization leads either to the misinterpretation of the essential role of religion in Puritanism or to its dismissal as a superstitious relic irrelevant to modern American experience.

While historians need to make the past understandable to contemporary readers, we should also beware of that parochialism of the present which results from too conveniently translating alien experience into our own ways of thinking. "We have to caricature the Puritans in order to feel comfortable in their presence," Edmund S. Morgan observed, for "they found answers to some human problems that we would rather forget." Such defensiveness may be a motive in representations of seventeenth-century Massachusetts as "a preposterous land of witches and witch hunters, of kill-joys in tall-crowned hats, whose main occupation was to prevent each other from having any fun and whose sole virtue lay in their furniture." The irony of paying more attention to the actual fanatics in the Bay Colony than to the man who led the Puritan community forward despite internal dissension and external challenges deprived later Americans of crucially needed cultural resources. Morgan wrote: "Actually the central problem of Puritanism as it affected John Winthrop and New England has concerned men of principle in every age, not least our own. It was the question of what responsibility a righteous man owes to society."[32] When society moves in a direction one considers immoral, should a responsible citizen stay or go? To examine this central question of Puritan experience, in 1958 Morgan wrote a biography of John Winthrop, with the explicit goal of making Winthrop's answer available to a generation of Americans who faced their own version of "the Puritan dilemma."

Morgan makes a strong, beautifully written case that John Winthrop's answer came directly from his spiritual experience, relatively early in life, of the Puritan teaching that Christians should be "in the world but not of the world." Winthrop's religious experience in England, in Morgan's view, prepared him admirably to govern the Puritan colony in the New World. Focusing on the exemplary life of an important individual enables Morgan to avoid the pitfalls of such grand theories as the secularization hypothesis and, by virtue of his grace as a biographer, to give his readers a felt sense of a life informed by Puritan beliefs. Yet by viewing Winthrop as one who found an "answer" to a religious question and then skillfully put that answer into practice in his role as governor, Morgan rather ironically falls under Mather's spell, producing a saint's life story for twentieth-century Americans. *The Puritan Dilemma: The Story of John Winthrop* is thus an insightful story of John Winthrop, even an inspiring story about John Winthrop, but it misses the significant way in which the governor's life and work were also a story *by* John Winthrop.

Winthrop's journal does not simply describe his answer to the Puritan dilemma; indeed, telling the story of how the community grappled with such dilemmas became Winthrop's way of being a Puritan. As he chronicled his application of vital Puritan beliefs to his role as governor, Winthrop, in writing the history of the colony he led, gained a crucial angle of interpretation, through which his vision enlarged as he became increasingly open to the meaning of the Puritan project as an ongoing story. In order to understand Winthrop as a representative man, therefore, we must pay attention not only to what historians have said about and made of him but also to his own work as a writer of history.

By the early seventeenth century, of course, other immigrants had come to North America, and in the ensuing years there would be many, many more, for the history of America is the story—or stories—of immigrants. While the early Puritan experience is not unique, then, there were no other immigrants quite like the Winthrop generation in Massachusetts Bay. Certainly there were no models for writing the history of this distinctive community. Therefore, it seems natural to interpret Winthrop's journal by examining its similarities with and differences from other ways of representing the experience of becoming American.

In some significant ways, for example, Winthrop's history of the Puritan community resembles the conversion narratives in which individual American Puritans, like their spiritual kin in England, recorded and examined their religious experiences. Their intense focus often made these narratives uneven in form, for, as Patricia Caldwell observes: "It is hard to reconcile a literary standard of completeness, wholeness, roundness with Puritanism's conviction that the better the man, the more continually he lives on a knife edge in an endless process of wayfaring and warfaring, a ceaseless testing by the vicissitudes of life, a perpetual self-examination, and a vigilant, restless, wide-awake watch against the 'security,' self-deception, and sleepy complacency that—so Thomas Hooker warned—invariably make men 'go to hell with a dreame.'" In examining such writings, Caldwell finds a difference between English and American versions of Puritan spirituality, in that English conversion narratives often refer to individual dreams in which the person subliminally accepts limitations, whereas "to judge by the early conversion narratives of New England, no one, during the first thirty years of the colony, ever had a dream at all—excepting, of course, the one publicly permitted dream: the dream of America." Indeed, this dream was so dominant and widespread that "it is impossible to discount, when reading the conversion stories of New Englanders, the fact of America as a central, even obsessive concern of the imagination, and one that is inextricably bound up with each person's notion of, hope for, and recapitulation of his or her own experience of salvation." Evidently the public rather than merely private cast of Winthrop's faith, particularly the emphasis on the Puritans' common journey in his understanding of their mission, characterized the spiritual life of many New Englanders, for whom migration was "a keystone in the structure of deliverance."[33]

These early Americans described spiritual progress in vast geographic terms, with "an expansion (at least momentary) of the private person into the public figure of Israel," rather than in the personal terms of English narratives. Along with such an orientation came a certain openness toward the future, an impatience with formulas, a willingness to let experience work out its own meanings. As individual men and women examine their lives in the light of the larger Puritan adventure, it seems "as if a certain strain of the collective personality is trying to work itself out in the conversion narrative: a personality that, unlike the English, with its drive toward completion and resolution, is more comfortable with ambivalence and open-endedness. . . . Hence the 'peace, disturbance, peace again' movement never comes to a satisfying close. Like Thoreau walking toward a never-setting western sun, a great number of American Puritans, at least when they express themselves on the subject of their own conversions, either will not or cannot end the story."[34] By writing the history of the Puritan community in the way he did, then, Winthrop accurately represented a characteristic Puritan attitude toward life in America as an ongoing, collective conversion story.

In addition to the journal, Winthrop wrote two narratives, one in his youth and one during the Antinomian crisis, in which he examined his personal spiritual life. Winthrop's judgment had understandably matured between the youthful self-scrutiny of his "Experiencia" and his "Christian Experience," written at age forty-nine during the winter of 1636. Soon to be recalled to office as governor to deal with the Anne Hutchinson affair, Winthrop in his second personal narrative, in the words of Daniel Shea, "shows the impact of events and controversies in which the writer found himself engaged as a public magistrate." Perhaps a series of theological questions in a long letter from Roger Williams spurred Winthrop to examine the condition of his spiritual life, or perhaps he simply needed to articulate his beliefs in response to the tempest into which the Antinomians were stirring the Puritan clergy. Whatever the particular impetus and "whatever his limitations in doctrinal controversy," as Shea observes, "Winthrop knew two things for certain: that Antinomians encouraged impiety when they preached the dangerous doctrine that conviction, repentance, and other preparatory stages of conversion had nothing to do with God's bestowal of free grace; and that the doctrine of free grace, as a cornerstone of Puritan piety, needed to be preached with all the rigor of a John Cotton. The very extremity of Anne Hutchinson's position made it necessary to reaffirm an undistorted yet untainted version of free grace and to allow, autobiographically, that he had just been rescued from creeping Arminianism."[35] If the lawlessness and disrespect for authority her teachings engendered made Anne Hutchinson seem so significant a threat to public order that Winthrop stopped at nothing to banish her, in his private ruminations he seemed almost to welcome the opportunity the Antinomian controversy gave him to assess his personal spiritual estate. In so doing, he distanced himself from Arminian tendencies by affirming that the soul's health cannot be earned or achieved but only gratefully accepted as God's free gift, and then he also resisted Antinomian temptations by acknowledging that Christian saints remain sinners who must work diligently and vigilantly toward spiritual improvement. Honestly recognizing the weakness in his personal spiritual life provided a source of strength for the public battle against the enemies of the Puritan community.

Over the years Winthrop's religious progress had been substantial. As Shea notes, "In the 'Experiencia' he had kept in England, Winthrop located the cause of spiritual depression in his too great attachment to the world, and had attributed his experiences of divine favor to rejection of 'earthly pleasures'; but in the 'Christian Experience' he restates the essential struggle of this period in specifically doctrinal terms." The change in focus signified the mature man's greater insight into the intractable complexity of spritual existence, deepening the voice through which he expressed his more profound understanding: "In a closing paragraph describing how he learned to value both justification and sanctification, the amateur theologian has given way to an autobiographer who is the sole authority for his argument. Shaped to the uses of the present, experience gave the lie to both Antinomians and legalists."[36] Winthrop's maturation as a writer, growing from his spiritual involvement in the religious issues that were at the heart of the politics of his day, is seen clearly but not solely in the distance between his two personal narratives, for an increasingly nuanced and self-conscious voice also informs the public journal in which Winthrop was writing the broader autobiography of the Puritan community's conversion into what we know as an early American culture.

Like all storytellers, autobiographers are selective in deciding what to emphasize and how to interpret the experiences from which their stories are made. On the one hand, autobiographies are arguments about the truth of actual experience, without the fully imaginative freedom of fictional stories. Yet on the other hand, unlike straightforward statements of belief, autobiographies are arguments in the form of stories. Although conventional autobiographies are composed from the vantage point of one who knows how the story will end, in the case of Winthrop's journal, the interconnected story of the governor and the Puritan community seems to be told almost as the events are occurring. At least this is the illusion the writer nurtures, even while his narration becomes increasingly retrospective and controlled.

Winthrop's movement from recording events as they happened and toward a more autobiographical mode was a natural progression, for "when the author enters the complex world of politics," as Roy Pascal points out, "if he puts himself in the center, he falls into rank vanity; it is as an observer that he can make a unity of his experiences, not as an actor." Pascal's observations about autobiography as a literary genre suggest that as a historian Winthrop was discovering a mode of narration that would transcend the particular story of even his illustrious life: "What distinguishes the story of people with an established public achievement and personality is a consistent relationship, a sort of harmony, between outward experience and inward growth and unfolding, between incidents and the spiritual digesting of them, so that each circumstance, each incident, instead of being an anomalous fact, becomes part of a process and a revelation of something within the personality."[37] While Winthrop certainly did not have the explicit autobiographical intention of a Montaigne or a Franklin, in the course of two decades his devotion to writing transformed his journal into a story that surpasses the record of the specific events he recounts.

As Pascal notes, "all good autobiographies are in some sense the story of a calling, that is, they tell of the realisation of an urgent personal potentiality.

165

But in some cases the inner calling merges into a social function, a profession, and a public personality grows out of the private. The autobiography may then be written not primarily for private reasons, but for public, perhaps to satisfy public curiosity about a well-known figure, but, more seriously to illuminate the nature of the public achievement and perhaps to reinforce it."[38] Over the years Winthrop became more self-conscious as a writer, increasingly able to see his own role in the story he was telling and more prone to assess the significance of particular incidents within that larger framework. As he wrote the story of the Puritan community from his unique double vantage point as governor and historian, historiography and autobiography merged, conjoining the meaning of Winthrop's own life with the significance of the ongoing Puritan story and securing thereby Winthrop's identity as the representative American Puritan.

It would be pointless to try to get "behind" his narrative to uncover the "real" John Winthrop, not because the materials do not exist, but because it is in the narrative itself that Winthrop as historian creates the metaphor of Winthrop as governor that is his representative self. "The self expresses itself by the metaphors it creates and projects, and we know it by those metaphors," James Olney observes.[39] He continues:

If autobiography is in one sense history, then one can turn that around and say that history is also autobiography, and in a double sense: the makers of history, or those through whom history is made, could find in their autobiographies the destiny of their time achieved in action and speech; and the writers of history organize the events of which they write according to, and out of, their own private necessities and the state of their own selves. Historians impose, and quite properly, their own metaphors on the human past. History, as almost everyone acknowledges, is not an objective collection of facts but one historian's point of view on the facts: a point of view that, taken as a sum of what he has experienced and understands, reveals to us the historian. As readers we go to history, as to philosophy, to autobiography and poetry, to learn more not about other people and the past but about ourselves and the present.[40]

In the act of representing himself Winthrop becomes representative. The self that we seek not to uncover but to recover from the history of the uses to which the metaphor has been put, therefore, is a writing self—the Winthrop who represents himself by writing autobiography in the form of history.

By telling the story of his own experience and writing the history of early New England in one and the same imaginative act, Winthrop inaugurated a form of writing that became characteristic of a distinctively American literature. Examining Cotton Mather's portrayal of Winthrop as Nehemias Americanus, historian Sacvan Bercovitch finds an imaginative amalgam of "American dream, manifest destiny, redeemer nation, and, fundamentally, the American self as representative of universal rebirth." Although Winthrop's own narrative is far less explicit and certainly less bombastic

than Mather's hagiography of the first Puritan governor, in his journal
Winthrop responds to the problems of his times in a way that adumbrates
what Bercovitch defines as "the genre of auto-American-biography: the
celebration of the representative self as America, and of the American self as
the embodiment of a prophetic universal design."[41] By Cotton Mather's
time, of course, two generations had passed, and the descendants of the
early Puritans were working hard to sustain their hold on the symbols that
shaped colonial American culture.

Mather and others were happy to use their forefathers' images to legitimate their own interpretation of early New England and thereby to
strengthen their attempt to guide the course of American history. Their
success was remarkably enduring: "As the legacy of seventeenth-century
New England," the combination of individual experience and the meaning
of America as a single story of redemption "survived, not by chance but by
merit, because it was compelling enough in content and flexible enough in
form to invite adaptation." Indeed, "every stage of this long development
bespeaks the astonishing tenacity of the myth," and as Bercovitch concludes,
"the persistence of the myth is a testament to the visionary and symbolic
power of the American Puritan imagination."[42] Given the continuing appeal
of the Puritan strategy of cultural interpretation, a way of both responding
to and imposing meaning on experience, Winthrop's rhetorical achievement
is all the more compelling. For his journal shows that the Puritan pattern
began not solely with Mather's interpretation of the saintly governor but
even earlier, with Winthrop's own story of himself and New England on the
way toward becoming America.

Winthrop's full achievement as a historian, and possibly also the maturity of judgment he exercised as governor, depended upon his increasing
self-consciousness as a writer. Because of the "Citty vpon a hill" sermon he
delivered on board the *Arbella*, Winthrop has been remembered primarily as
a man of design. Yet as a writer, he was also a man of interpretation, and it is
through his interpretation of events that we see his originating design evolve
into a sense of purpose that promises to guide the ongoing story of the
community whose early years are recorded in the narrative of his journal.

The linkage between design and interpretation suggests that as a writer
Winthrop was not only a historian and an autobiographer but also a precur-
sor of one of the major traditions in American prose fiction. In *The Interpreted Design as a Structural Principle in American Prose,* David L. Minter
shows how novelists such as Hawthorne, James, Fitzgerald, and Faulkner—
in addition to such autobiographers as Edwards, Franklin, Thoreau, and
Adams—explored the tension between design and interpretation in order to
examine the meaning of American life: "Men of design reflect man's effort,
particularly in America's version of the modern era, to master his world; his
effort (in the twilight of his faith in the providential activity of God in

history) intentionally to shape, according to programs, plans, and designs, his context. They are, to put the matter bluntly, surrogates for (American) formers and reformers dedicated to mastering and portioning out their natural and social environments. Men of interpretation seek, on the other hand, to understand man's curious failures in such endeavors. Put bluntly, and more specifically, men of interpretation are surrogates for those 'poets' dedicated to singing of 'human unsuccess,/In a rapture of distress.'" The tension between Captain Ahab's quest for the white whale and seafaring Ishmael's narrative wonder in Melville's *Moby-Dick,* for instance, and the relationship between Jay Gatsby's glorious attempt to reclaim the past and Nick Carraway's careful self-discovery in Fitzgerald's *The Great Gatsby* exemplify the many American novels in which, as Minter observes, "in interpreted designs, active life is implicitly defined in terms of failure, of failed designs, of unsuccesses, and art is seen as redemptive interpretation."[43] The central drama of American experience, as portrayed in such novels, involves the tragic separation of two fundamental impulses, design and interpretation, that unify the world of John Winthrop's journal.

Winthrop was not a novelist, of course, and his journal does not rank alongside the literary masterpieces of America's great writers. Nevertheless, the comparison suggests another way in which Winthrop contributed to a cultural world that long outlasted the colony he governed. However we evaluate his political leadership, we know so much about Winthrop as governor because he was more than a man of design. However his role as governor has been interpreted or misinterpreted by subsequent historians, and whatever one thinks of his particular actions and beliefs, Winthrop remains a representative man, in Emerson's sense, because he was also a representing man. He stands or falls as "the Puritan Governor" because he was also the Puritan historian. Instead of trying to reclaim his political commitments, moral convictions, and religious beliefs, or attempting finally to dispose of our culture's particular Puritan remnants, therefore, we might more appropriately seek to recover the perspective and principles of inter-pretation that enabled Winthrop to write, and us to read, history as a story. By revealing the Puritan curvature of the "lenses through which we read our own minds," Winthrop offers "some promise of explanation" for the very different America in which we live.

8

Coming Home Again

J OHN WINTHROP'S personal character and experience made him a
natural leader in early New England. Deeply religious, strongly committed to his family and its security, well educated, a lawyer and
justice of the peace, experienced in the business of politics, to the
manor born, eager for public service, yet thwarted by the religious, political,
and economic conditions of his English homeland, Winthrop was strongly
motivated and ideally qualified to lead the Puritans who established a new
society in Massachusetts. As their governor, he experienced the vicissitudes
of politics, learning to see himself as one of the players in the drama of the
history he was recording. Awareness of his own capacity for self-deception,
as a corollary of his abiding trust in the grace and power of the God in whom
he believed, made Winthrop at once scrupulously honest and also quite
tolerant in his dealings with companions whose self-knowledge and discipline were less firm than his own. Because he was so thoroughly committed
to the Puritan project, he dealt forcefully and sometimes stridently with
those whose beliefs or actions seemed to threaten the integrity of the
community he was devoted to building. Occasionally a tough enemy, he was
more characteristically a supportive friend. Self-understanding, relationships
with others, and faith in God were interdependent elements of Winthrop's
essential character, making him an outstanding representative of the Puritan
experience.

Yet some of Winthrop's most characteristically Puritan traits also distanced him from the world of practical affairs in which he played so dominant a role. For example, as a citizen of the seventeenth century, Winthrop
confronted death as a regular feature of life. As a Puritan, however, he
embraced the full gamut of life while recognizing its inherent transitoriness.
He threw himself fully into everyday life even while knowing that its ultimate

direction and significance were beyond human control. Indeed, his staunch religious faith led him not away from but resolutely into the imperfect world of real men and women. Involvement and distance, participation and observation, acting as governor and writing as historian—such combinations were Winthrop's way of living out the Christian injunction to be in but not of the world. Such characteristically Puritan ambivalence suggests an important way in which Winthrop may illumine contemporary American culture by adumbrating alternatives to current patterns of thought. Winthrop's tolerance for ambiguity expresses a seriousness or strength of character far removed from what author Neil Postman describes as contemporary American ways of "amusing ourselves to death."[1] Clues to Winthrop's Puritan ambivalence lie in the way he connected aspects of life that we avoid or lack ways of coherently relating: religion and politics, individual rights and communal obligations, authority and freedom, action and interpretation. Briefly examining these connections may suggest how the man who led the Puritans to a new England might help to guide later Americans back home again.

Winthrop and his fellow Puritans forthrightly stated their beliefs about how religious and political institutions should be connected, and their views provide a historically important perspective that might help to clarify the messy arguments about religion and politics that confuse much current thinking about social morality. Some of today's politicians and church leaders envision "a Christian America," while others argue that church and state should be completely separate. Religion and politics are notoriously touchy subjects, and when they interact, as they have throughout American history, religious and political passions fuel each other's fires. Although American civilization has never had a Church or State in the classic sense developed in European political thought, the debate about the proper relationship between religion and politics is firmly built into American life, and the health of our culture depends in some ways on this continuing argument. The ground rules are given in the First Amendment: "Congress shall make no law respecting an establishment of religion, or prohibiting the free exercise thereof." The framers of the Constitution gave equal scope to two contradictory American traditions, and the tension between these two irreconcilable goods defines the public space in which religion and politics interact in our national life. Each of the religion clauses of the First Amendment expresses a different model of the separation of church and state, and together they define boundaries beyond which we as a people cannot go. Each model has a history and an ideal.

On the one hand, seventeenth-century Puritans—despite caricatures of them as fun-hating authoritarians—championed the free exercise of religion. They saw religion as a cohesive way of life, in which inward spiritual experience, right belief, and social action were harmoniously integrated. In their eyes, religious liberty meant the right of the group to define itself communally and required governmental support. While their explicit functions were clearly separable, church and state could be coordinated without being confused. The Puritans knew the evils of an established church; they came to the New World to reform the Church of England, not to begin a new church. They claimed the freedom to practice their religion as they saw fit and gave others the "freedom" to leave the fledgling Massachusetts Bay Colony and join the Separatist Pilgrims at Plimouth or the free spirits in Rhode Island. For a Puritan leader such as Governor John Winthrop, maintaining the free exercise of true religion was the central goal of government, so long as there was no general government that might deny the freedom the Puritans claimed for themselves. The Puritans' drive toward moral purity in the public realm, limited by their distaste for an established church, introduced an ideal into American political life that long outlived the Bay Colony itself.

On the other hand, eighteenth-century Enlightenment thinkers were less concerned with the free exercise of religion and pressed the cause against an established church. They saw religion basically as a matter of conscience, which was useful for morality but which worked against the public good as soon as ritual, clerics, and dogma were introduced. For them, liberty meant the right of individuals to hold whatever principles they chose, so long as they did not lead to actions which disrupted public order. In the private sacred realm, religion was free, but in the public secular realm churches should be curtailed by the state. For an Enlightenment leader such as Thomas Jefferson, the prevention of an establishment of religion was an important goal of government, so long as the private beliefs of all men remained free. The commitment to keep America free from an established church likewise endured as an ideal long after the Enlightenment waned.

Soon after the ratification of the Constitution, new religious organizations grew and prospered between the boundaries of free exercise and no establishment. These "denominations" became America's distinctive contribution to church history, bounded by the dead hand of an established church on one side and by the anarchy of cults on the other. Subsequent generations of Americans have construed all "normal" churches as denominations and considered others from either side to be outside the mainstream of American life. On the one hand, a society that accentuates one religious group's right to define its way of life in the public realm verges upon totalitarianism. Hence Jefferson and the Enlightenment stood for negative rights, for the freedom from a dominating church. On the other had, a society that radically undercuts the contributions all religions make to public life drifts toward anarchy. Thus Winthrop and the Puritans stood for positive rights, for the freedom to exercise religion. As the framers of the Constitution seem to have known, both ideals are necessary for a healthy democracy.

There were not many "religion cases" in the federal courts until the United States Supreme Court determined in the 1920s and 1930s that the "due process" and "equal protection" clauses of the Fourteenth Amendment mean that the freedoms stipulated in the First Amendment apply to state legislation as well as to congressional actions. Since then, the number of religion cases has increased dramatically, and the Supreme Court's rulings have defined a space for religious freedom between the Enlightenment and the Puritan heritages. "No establishment" cases tend to protect the rights of individuals and minorities from the domination of a religious majority, while "free exercise" cases tend to protect the rights of groups and the majority to practice their religion in the public realm. The Court accentuates sometimes the one and sometimes the other as it tries to maintain a balance between the two clauses.

While compromises are never universally satisfying, the vitality of the religiously pluralistic society that America has become requires both kinds of religious freedom. Advocates of individual rights have long pointed effectively to Jefferson's articulation of the ideal of separation between church and state. Just as accurately, the defenders of the rights of religious groups and communities can ground their side of the issue by tracing a tradition from the Puritans' quest for the free expression of religion. Certainly both positions, as well as the views of those who assess the variety of moral questions that involve religious beliefs, will be more constructively articulated when the connections between religion and politics are understood as part of the natural groundwork of a free society. One does not have to adopt particular Puritan positions in order to regain the directness with which they faced such issues. If a democracy's vitality can be gauged by the nature and quality of the debates it sustains, then contemporary American arguments about religion and politics could be enlivened, complicated, and enriched by recovering this aspect of Winthrop's Puritan vision.

Along with his willingness to honor the prerogatives of both church and state went Winthrop's tendency to see an inextricable bond between individual rights and community obligations. In one sense, Winthrop's respect for his companions both as individuals and as a community was rooted in his characteristically Puritan conjunction of private spirituality and public religious expression. Puritan religiosity was at once intensely personal and broadly social in ways that may elude the comprehension of many contemporary Americans, whose churches prosper by encouraging inward spiritual self-development while accepting their diminished relevance as social institutions. Yet in another sense, Winthrop's insistence on linking the integrity of the individual with the coherence of the community was focused far more broadly than the specifically religious domain is generally considered today.

Along with their strong emphasis on the corporate nature of Christian life, the importance of the church and its proper relationship with government, and the moral quality of society as a whole, the Puritans were also intensely individual people. Careful self-scrutiny was cultivated as a lifelong habit in Puritan spiritual life, and self-interest was recognized—however ineffectively regulated—as a primary economic motivation. Such qualities were active elements in Winthrop's character, and he believed so deeply in fully regarding the personal considerations of individuals in legal matters that he acquired a reputation for leniency of judgment that antagonized moralistic hard-liners such as Thomas Dudley. Despite the political troubles his leniency cost Winthrop as governor, people remembered his generosity and kindness to individuals within the Puritan community. But Winthrop had no sympathy as governor or historian for those whose individualism threatened the colony's cohesion, and he was personally offended by those whose self-interest led them to abandon the community during hard times.

Winthrop defended the individual rights of Puritans within the Bay Colony, but those who did not honor their reciprocal obligations to the community drew his scorn. In September 1642 he wrote in his journal:

For such as come together in a wilderness, where are nothing but wild beasts and beastlike men, and there confederate together in civil and church estate, whereby they do, implicitly at least, bind themselves to support each other, and all of them that society, whether civil or sacred, whereof they are members, how they can break from this without free consent, is hard to find, so as may satisfy a tender or good conscience in time of trial. Ask thy conscience, if thou wouldst have plucked up thy stakes, and brought thy family 3000 miles, if thou hadst expected that all, or most, would have forsaken thee there. Ask again, what liberty thou hast towards others, which thou likest not to allow others towards thyself; for if one may go, another may, and so the greater part, and so church and commonwealth may be left destitute in a wilderness, exposed to misery and reproach, and all for thy ease and pleasure, whereas these all, being now thy brethren, as near to thee as the Israelites were to Moses, it were much safer for thee, after his example, to choose rather to suffer affliction with thy brethren, than to enlarge thy ease and pleasure by furthering the occasion of their ruin.

For Winthrop, individual interests and rights made sense only insofar as they contributed to strengthening the life of the colony, for the ongoing commitments that bound individuals into community were the social form of the covenant between the Puritans and their God.

Thus Winthrop's respect for individual rights cannot merely be reduced to the self-interest championed by contemporary libertarians; nor can his regard for communal obligations be honestly transposed into the authoritarianism so often espoused by modern communitarians. Moreover, because he saw individual rights and community obligations together as expressing a faithful relationship with God, Winthrop's Puritan vision provides richer, albeit more complex, resources for social renewal than may be found in current attempts to stake out a secular middle ground between individual interests and community responsibilities. Despite the good intentions behind such efforts as sociologist Amitai Etzioni's founding of the new journal *The Responsive Community: Rights and Responsibilities,* for example, without a religious dimension "the moral voice of the community" sounds a thin note. Likewise, without something akin to Winthrop's willingness to broaden the base of the Puritan community and his conviction that the ongoing story of New England transcended the particular reforms that had inspired the initial Puritan errand, attempts such as Robert Bellah's to reinvigorate social commitments by resuscitating earlier American "habits of the heart" read more like defensive manifestos on behalf of a once dominant subculture than inclusive visions in concert with the pluralistic society America has become.[2] Again it appears that the principles of interpretation guiding Winthrop's work as a historian telling the story of early New England may provide richer resources for revisioning America than do any of the specific ideas of Puritan theology or any of Winthrop's particular actions as governor.

John Winthrop devoted the final twenty years of his life to guiding and preserving the Puritan community in New England, relying on deeply held convictions about leadership that seem quite remote from the political culture of late twentieth-century America. Since the authority of an elected government came from God, the governor could be called to account by the people, Winthrop believed, only for breaches of his oath of office, certainly not for errors of judgment, lack of skill, or any of the shortcomings of human nature. The covenant between the magistrates and the people was a sacred trust; therefore, to challenge the governor on any other grounds revealed a dangerous mistake about the relationship between authority and liberty. Because of the agreements between them, neither the people nor their governors were free to act without restraint. The governor's authority and the people's liberty were fully interdependent. Winthrop asserted a higher respect for the governor's authority, along with a broader tolerance for his human infirmities, than is in fashion today. Conversely, in his journal entry for 14 May 1645, he affirmed an idea of civil liberty far different from the simple notion of the absence of restraint that generally passes for freedom today: "This liberty is the proper end and object of authority, and cannot subsist without it; and it is a liberty to that only which is good, just and honest. This liberty you are to stand for, with the hazard (not only of your goods, but) of your lives, if need be." The true liberty of a free people, he believed, must be protected by the full authority of their governors, "wherein, if we fail at any time, we hope we shall be willing (by God's assistance) to hearken to good advice from any of you, or in any other way of God; so shall your liberties be preserved, in upholding the honour and power of authority amongst you." The crucial point for Winthrop was that authority and liberty actually exist only in relationship with each other.

Political morality, for such a way of thinking, depends centrally upon a just balance of authority and liberty within the community, rather than on expecting personal perfection from individual leaders or providing unmitigated opportunities for everyone's self-interest. Working out such a vision inevitably requires tolerance for ambiguity and a willingness to compromise in order to preserve the integrity of the community. Winthrop's religious beliefs made it possible, indeed imperative, for him to champion such commitments. Without his faith in an ongoing covenant between a gracious God and sinful men, neither authority nor liberty would have made sense or mattered much to him. It may be difficult, then, to see how Winthrop's sense of the relationship between authority and liberty can be recovered in a culture whose irreducible pluralism relativizes the political agendas of all religious faiths. Yet we do not have to adopt Puritan theology to recognize the validity of Winthrop's political morality and the importance of grounding the relationship between authority and liberty in an ideal of community that transcends immediate situations. The recovery of such a sensibility depends ultimately upon our capability simultaneously to pursue a dream ("wee shall be as a Citty vpon a hill") and its continual interpretation ("for history must tell the whole truth"). In Winthrop's double role as governor and historian lie Puritan resources that are at once renewable and renewing.

As the Puritans' governor, Winthrop was involved in many of the arguments that defined the course of life within the Bay Colony. He had definite ideas and was not hesitant about asserting them. While his was often one of the voices in the debate, Winthrop was also a skilled mediator of disputes, and the people usually relied on him to keep the colony on an even keel. Without his gradual moderation, the political battles between the magistrates and the deputies might have stalled the colony's development. Without his firm guidance, the sharp antagonism between the antinomianism of Anne Hutchinson and the authoritarianism of men like Thomas Dudley might have torn the community apart. Likewise, Governor Winthrop was central in protecting the Bay Colony's interests in conflicts with neighboring colonies, with their foes in England, with Indians who asserted ancient rights, and with Europeans who sought a share of New England's land and trade. The Puritans were fortunate to have their internal and external affairs in Governor Winthrop's hands.

As the Puritans' historian, Winthrop recorded the events and squabbles of daily life, along with larger trials and successes, during the colony's first two decades. He wrote their history as a story shaped by conflicts and resolutions, as though continuing reformation were part of an unfolding future, unlike his colleague, William Bradford, whose history of Plimouth interprets the Pilgrims' problems by looking backward to pristine but increasingly remote origins. While Governor Winthrop sought consensus and argued for an ideal of communal coherence, Winthrop the historian described the conflict of interpretations as a natural part of life in the New World. The combination of these two roles—as governor the guardian of the Puritan design and as historian the shaper of its interpretation—gives Winthrop's journal its lasting authority. In contrast to the more conventional distinction, then and now, between those who act and those who interpret, such doubleness suggests a way of transcending the division between politics and culture that has bedeviled American history. As a historian, Winthrop made it possible for later Americans to understand, if not to inhabit, the colony he governed. Thereby he created a world wherein today's quite different Americans may learn to conjoin commitment and interpretation by envisioning history as a story.

Notes

Selected Bibliography

Index

Notes

INTRODUCTION

1. Anya Seton, *The Winthrop Woman* (Boston: Houghton Mifflin Co., 1958), vi, 513.

2. Cotton Mather, *Magnalia Christi Americana; or, The Ecclesiastical History of New-England; From Its First Planting, in the Year 1620, unto the Year of Our Lord 1698* (1852; New York: Russell and Russell, 1967), 1:36.

3. Ibid., 118.

4. Ibid., 119, 120, 121, 122, 123.

5. Sacvan Bercovitch, *The Puritan Origins of the American Self* (New Haven: Yale University Press, 1975). Bercovitch includes the complete text of Mather's "*Nehemias Americanus*. The Life of John Winthrop, Esq., Governor of the Massachusetts Colony" as an appendix, pp. 187–205.

6. Louis Auchincloss, *The Winthrop Covenant* (Boston: Houghton Mifflin Co., 1976), 22, 244, 245.

7. Robert C. Winthrop, *The Life and Letters of John Winthrop*, 2 vols. (Boston: Ticknor and Fields, 1864–67), 2: 2–4; hereafter cited as *LL*.

8. Quoted by Cynthia Harrison, in "The 'City on a Hill' Cliché: Puritans' Winthrop Was No Advocate of Liberty," *Los Angeles Times*, 21 January 1989, pt. 2, p. 14.

9. For an insightful recent discussion of the continuing role in American culture of nostalgia for primordial purity, see Richard T. Hughes and C. Leonard Allen, *Illusions of Innocence: Protestant Primitivism in America, 1630–1875* (Chicago: University of Chicago Press, 1988) 1–24, 205–32.

10. Vera Lee, "Crime among the Puritans . . . and the Penalties Therefor," *Harvard Magazine*, July–August 1986, pp. 48A–H.

11. Lewis H. Lapham, "Notebook: Powdered Roses," *Harper's*, December 1985, p. 10.

12. Edmund S. Morgan, *The Puritan Dilemma: The Story of John Winthrop* (Boston: Little, Brown, and Co., 1958).

CHAPTER 1. ENGLISH ROOTS

1. *LL* 1:14.

2. The "Grant of Groton Manor" may be found, in Latin, in Arthur Meier Schlesinger, ed. chair, *Winthrop Papers*, 5 vols. (Boston: Massachusetts Historical Society, 1929–47), 1:7–11; hereafter cited as *Papers*.

3. *LL* 1:20.

4. "Will of Adam Winthrop, 1562," *Papers* 1:17–24.

5. The records and writings of Adam Winthrop, the governor's father, are collected in *Papers* 1:1–7, 29–154, 169–78. Cf. 1:25–51.

6. *Papers* 1:5. Colons were used as a convenient mode of abbreviation, as here in "Qu:[een] Eliz:[abeth]." An admirably succinct explanation of the calendar is provided in the excellent biography of John Winthrop, Jr., by Robert C. Black III: "The dates herein are of the 'Old Style' in common use among the English in the seventeenth century. They are *ten days* behind the more accurate dating of the Gregorian Calendar. It should also be borne in mind that the New Year was ordinarily commenced on Lady Day (Annunciation to the Virgin Mary), which was March 25." This means that dates in January, February, and the greater part of March were reckoned by the early Winthrops and their contemporaries as falling in the final months of the "old" year, instead of in the first months of our "new" year. While persistent, this discrepancy need not be a source of major confusion. Unless otherwise noted, therefore, we shall simply follow the calendar that was used to organize time in the world of John Winthrop. See Black, *The Younger John Winthrop* (New York: Columbia University Press, 1966), 4n.

7. *LL* 1:52.

8. *Papers* 1:154.

9. Ibid., 78.

10. Ibid., 87–88.

11. Black, *Younger John Winthrop*, 5.

12. *Papers* 1:91.

13. Ibid., 97, 99.

14. Ibid., 168.

15. Ibid., 173.

16. Ibid., 155

17. Ibid., 88n.

18. Ibid., 161–62; Robert C. Winthrop describes this notebook as "an imperfect manuscript, stained and torn in many places, and quite illegible in others; many pages missing and many passages effaced, and plainly intended for no eye but his own." *LL* 1:63–64.

19. *Papers* 1:161–64.

20. Ibid., 165.

21. Ibid., 166–67.

22. Ibid., 167–69.

23. Ibid., 169.

24. Ibid., 182–83.

25. Ibid., 186–90.

26. Ibid., 192–93.

27. Ibid., 193.

28. Ibid., 196, 197, 204–5, 208.

29. Ibid., 207, 209.

30. Ibid., 214–15.

31. Ibid., 221–23.
32. Ibid., 224–25.
33. Ibid., 226–29.
34. Ibid., 221, 229–30.
35. Ibid., 268.
36. Ibid., 282, 281.
37. Ibid., 282–83, 289.
38. Ibid., 287, 286.
39. Ibid., 268, 295–310.
40. Ibid., 311.
41. Ibid., 317, 330, 336–37.
42. Ibid., 385.
43. Ibid., 2:57–58.
44. Ibid., 91–92.
45. Ibid., 94, 99–100.
46. For the various drafts of considerations, observations, reasons, and objections relative to emigration, see *Papers* 2:114–49.
47. Ibid., 151–52.
48. Ibid., 161.
49. Ibid., 224–25.
50. Ibid., 225–26.
51. Ibid., 228.
52. Ibid., 228–29.
53. Ibid., 231–33.

CHAPTER 2. LAYING FOUNDATIONS

1. Citations from Winthrop's journal are from the authoritative two-volume edition edited by James Savage, *The History of New England, from 1630 to 1649* (Boston: Phelps and Farnham, 1825; Boston: Little, Brown, and Co. 1853), and will be made in the text rather than in notes. For ease in correlating citations from this edition with others, references are made by date of entry, according to Winthrop's calendar, rather than by page numbers in the Savage edition.
2. *Papers* 2:282–95.
3. Ibid., 302.
4. *LL* 2:28.
5. Ibid., 29–30.
6. *Papers* 2:312–13.
7. *LL* 2:31.
8. *Papers* 2:331–32.
9. For Winthrop's essay "On Reformation without Separation," ca. March 1631, see *Papers* 3:10–14.
10. Ibid., 20.
11. Ibid., 25–26.
12. Ibid., 171.
13. Ibid., 167.
14. Ibid., 174.
15. Ibid., 172.

CHAPTER 3. A TIME OF TESTING

1. *Papers* 3:314.
2. Ibid., 404.
3. Ibid., 451.
4. Ibid., 445.
5. Ibid., 475, 473.
6. Ibid., 4:182–83.
7. Ibid., 183.
8. Ibid., 3:343–44.
9. Ibid., 344.
10. The complete text can be found in David D. Hall, ed., *The Antinomian Controversy, 1636–1638: A Documentary History* (Middletown, Conn.: Wesleyan University Press, 1968), 199–388.

CHAPTER 4. LOOKING STEADILY FORWARD

1. *Papers* 4:391, 392.
2. Ibid., 401–2.

CHAPTER 5. THE PERILS OF THE TEXT

1. Richard S. Dunn, "John Winthrop Writes His Journal," *William and Mary Quarterly*, 3d ser. 41, no. 2 (April 1984): 186, 185, 204.
2. Ibid., 212.
3. James Kendall Hosmer, ed., *Winthrop's Journal, "History of New England,"* *1630–1649* (New York: Charles Scribner's Sons, 1908; New York: Barnes and Noble, 1966), 1:3, 5, 17, 16, 17, 18.
4. Charles Francis Adams, ed., *Antinomianism in the Colony of Massachusetts Bay, 1636–1638; including "The Short Story" and Other Documents* (Boston: Prince Society, 1894), 17.
5. Ibid., 26.
6. Ibid., 31.
7. Ibid., 31n, quoting Masson's *Life of Milton*.
8. Hall, *Antinomian Controversy*, 199. Adams's reprinting of the third edition of the text is reprinted again by Hall, pp. 201–310.
9. Adams, *Antinomianism*, 40.
10. Ibid., 42.
11. Ibid., 39–40.
12. Ibid., 42, 39.
13. James Savage, Preface to *The History of New England, from 1630 to 1649*, by John Winthrop (Boston: Phelps and Farnham, 1825), 1:iii, iv.
14. *LL* 2:465.
15. Ibid., 466.
16. Ibid., 422.

CHAPTER 6. WAYS OF MAKING HISTORY IN EARLY NEW ENGLAND

1. William Bradford, *Of Plymouth Plantation, 1620–1647*, edited by Samuel Eliot Morison (1952; New York: Modern Library, 1967), chap. 4, p. 23.

2. Ibid., chap. 7, p. 47.

3. Ibid., chap. 32, p. 320.

4. Romans 6:23, KJV.

5. For his account and interpretation of the case, see Bradford, *Of Plymouth Plantation*, chap. 32, pp. 320–22.

6. Ibid., pp. 324–30, for Bradford's account of Brewster's life and death.

7. Ibid., chap. 34, p. 334.

8. *Proceedings of the Massachusetts Historical Society* II (Boston, 1870), 402.

9. Peter Gay, *A Loss of Mastery: Puritan Historians in Colonial America* (New York: Random House, 1966), 18.

10. Edmund S. Morgan, *Visible Saints: The History of a Puritan Idea* (Ithaca, N.Y.: Cornell University Press, 1963), 115.

11. Quoted by Raymond J. Cunningham, in Cotton Mather, *Magnalia Christi Americana; or, The Ecclesiastical History of New England,* edited and abridged by Raymond J. Cunningham (New York: Frederick Ungar Publishing Co., 1970), iv.

12. Cotton Mather, *Magnalia Christi Americana; or, The Ecclesiastical History of New-England: From Its First Planting, in the Year 1620, unto the Year of Our Lord 1698* (1852; New York: Russell and Russell, 1967), 1:25, 27.

13. Ibid., 36–37.

14. Ibid., 105.

15. Ibid., 113.

16. Ibid., 118.

17. Ibid., 119.

18. Ibid., 121, 122.

19. Ibid., 122.

20. Ibid., 124, 128, 126, 131.

21. Edmund Wilson, *Patriotic Gore: Studies in the Literature of the American Civil War* (New York: Oxford University Press, 1966), 8–9.

22. Ibid., 84–85.

CHAPTER 7. THE GOVERNOR AND THE HISTORIANS

1. Ralph Waldo Emerson, *Representative Men,* vol. 4 of *Emerson's Complete Works* (Cambridge, Mass.: Riverside Press, 1897), 11, 12, 29, 30, 31.

2. George Bancroft, *History of the United States of America: From the Discovery of the Continent* (1859; New York: D. Appleton and Co., 1882), 1:3, 221.

3. Ibid., 233–34.

4. Ibid., 312, 317.

5. Ibid., 318, 321–22, 320.

6. John Fiske, *The Beginnings of New England; or, The Puritan Theocracy in Its Relation to Civil and Religious Liberty* (1889; Cambridge: Riverside Press, 1899), 103, 102, vi–vii.

7. Charles Francis Adams, *Three Episodes of Massachusetts History: The Settlement of Boston Bay, the Antinomian Controversy, a Study of Church and Town Government* (1892; New York: Russell and Russell, 1965), 561, 433, 387–88, 472–73, 560–78.

8. Ibid., 378 n. 1, quoting Doyle, *English in America: The Puritan Colonies.*

9. Ibid., 465–66, 575.

10. Ibid., 578.

11. James Truslow Adams, *The Founding of New England* (1921; Boston: Little, Brown and Co., 1949), 163.

12. Ibid., x.

13. Ibid., 137–38.

14. Ibid., 147.

15. Ibid., 258–59, quoting Thomas Hutchinson, *History of the Colony of Massachusetts-Bay.*

16. Ibid., 174.

17. Edmund S. Morgan, ed., *The Founding of Massachusetts: Historians and the Sources* (Indianapolis: Bobbs-Merrill Co., 1964), 88.

18. Samuel Eliot Morison, *Builders of the Bay Colony* (1930; Boston: Houghton Mifflin Co., 1958), v–vi.

19. Ibid., 58, 79, 101, 104.

20. Perry Miller, *The New England Mind: The Seventeenth Century* (New York: Macmillan Co., 1939), vii, viii.

21. Perry Miller, *Errand into the Wilderness* (Cambridge: Belknap Press of Harvard University Press, 1956), ix.

22. Perry Miller and Thomas H. Johnson, eds., *The Puritans: A Sourcebook of Their Writings* (1938; New York: Harper and Row, 1963), 40–55.

23. Miller, *New England Mind,* 487.

24. Ibid., 422, 419, 425, 427.

25. Miller, *Errand* 49.

26. Ibid., 11, 15.

27. See, for example, the commentary and works cited in Michael McGiffert, "American Puritan Studies in the 1960's," *William and Mary Quarterly,* 3d ser., 27 (1970): 36–67; and David R. Williams, "New Directions in Puritan Studies," *American Quarterly* 37, no. 1 (Spring 1985): 156–61. A more complete listing of recent works on Puritanism is found in the bibliography of the present work.

28. Richard S. Dunn, *Puritans and Yankees: The Winthrop Dynasty of New England, 1630–1717* (Princeton: Princeton University Press, 1962), vi, 4, 9.

29. Black, *Younger John Winthrop.*

30. Darrett Rutman, *Winthrop's Boston: Portrait of a Puritan Town, 1630–1649* (New York: W. W. Norton and Co., 1965).

31. Darrett Rutman, *John Winthrop's Decision for America: 1629* (Philadelphia: J. B. Lippincott Co., 1975), 51, 55.

32. Morgan, *Puritan Dilemma,* xi, xii.

33. Patricia Caldwell, *The Puritan Conversion Narrative: The Beginnings of American Expression* (Cambridge: Cambridge University Press, 1983), 15–16, 26, 27.

34. Ibid., 30, 34.

35. Daniel B. Shea, Jr., *Spiritual Autobiography in Early America* (Princeton: Princeton University Press, 1968), 102, 105.

36. Ibid., 109, 110.

37. Roy Pascal, *Design and Truth in Autobiography* (Cambridge: Harvard University Press, 1960), 6, 10.

38. Ibid., 112.

39. James Olney, *Metaphors of Self: The Meaning of Autobiography* (Princeton: Princeton University Press, 1972), 34.

40. Ibid., 36–37.

41. Sacvan Bercovitch, *The Puritan Origins of the American Self* (New Haven: Yale University Press, 1975), 108, 136.

42. Ibid., 186.

43. David L. Minter, *The Interpreted Design as a Structural Principle in American Prose* (New Haven: Yale University Press, 1969), 30.

CHAPTER 8. COMING HOME AGAIN

1. See Robert McGinn's comments on Postman's *Amusing Ourselves to Death* in *The Stanford Magazine,* December 1989, p. 8.

2. See John F. Wilson's insightful review of Bellah's important book, *Habits of the Heart: Individualism and Commitment in American Life* in *Religious Studies Review* 14, no. 4 (October 1988): 304–6.

Selected Bibliography

PRIMARY SOURCES OF JOHN WINTHROP'S WRITING

Hosmer, James Kendall, ed. *Winthrop's Journal, "History of New England,"* 1630–1649. 2 vols. New York: Charles Scribner's Sons, 1908; New York: Barnes and Noble, 1966.

Schlesinger, Arthur Meier, ed. chair. *Winthrop Papers.* 5 vols. Boston: Massachusetts Historical Society, 1929–47.

Winthrop, John. *The History of New England, from 1630 to 1649.* 2 vols. Edited by James Savage. Boston: Phelps and Farnham, 1825; Boston: Little, Brown, and Co., 1853.

Winthrop, Robert C. *The Life and Letters of John Winthrop.* 2 vols. Boston: Ticknor and Fields, 1864–67.

OTHER HISTORICAL AND SECONDARY SOURCES

Adams, Charles Francis. *Three Episodes of Massachusetts History: The Settlement of Boston Bay, the Antinomian Controversy, a Study of Church and Town Government.* 1892; New York: Russell and Russell, 1965.

Adams, Charles Francis, ed. *Antinomianism in the Colony of Massachusetts Bay, 1636–1638; including "The Short Story" and Other Documents.* Boston: Prince Society, 1894.

Adams, James Truslow. *The Founding of New England.* 1921; Boston: Little, Brown, and Co., 1949.

Auchincloss, Louis. *The Winthrop Covenant.* Boston: Houghton Mifflin Co., 1976.

Bancroft, George. *History of the United States of America: From the Discovery of the Continent.* 10 vols. 1859; New York: D. Appleton and Co., 1882.

Battis, Emery. *Saints and Sectaries: Anne Hutchinson and the Antinomian Controversy in the Massachusetts Bay Colony.* Chapel Hill: University of North Carolina Press, for the Institute of Early American History and Culture, 1962.

Bellah, Robert, et al. *Habits of the Heart: Individualism and Commitment in American Life.* Berkeley: University of California Press, 1985.

Bercovitch, Sacvan. *The Puritan Origins of the American Self.* New Haven: Yale University Press, 1975.

Bercovitch, Sacvan, ed. *The American Puritan Imagination: Essays in Revaluation.* London: Cambridge University Press, 1974.

Black, Robert C., III. *The Younger John Winthrop.* New York: Columbia University Press, 1966.

Bozeman, Dwight. *To Live Ancient Lives: The Primitivist Dimension of Puritanism.* Chapel Hill: University of North Carolina Press, for the Institute of Early American History and Culture, 1988.

Bradford, William. *Of Plymouth Plantation, 1620–1647.* Edited by Samuel Eliot Morison. 1952; New York: Modern Library, 1967.

Caldwell, Patricia. *The Puritan Conversion Narrative: The Beginnings of American Expression.* Cambridge: Cambridge University Press, 1983.

Cohen, Charles. *God's Caress: The Psychology of Puritan Religious Experience.* New York: Oxford University Press, 1986.

Conkin, Paul. *Puritans and Pragmatists: Eight Eminent American Thinkers.* New York: Dodd, Mead, and Co., 1968.

Delbanco, Andrew. *The Puritan Ordeal.* Cambridge: Harvard University Press, 1989.

Dunn, Richard S. "John Winthrop Writes His Journal." *William and Mary Quarterly,* 3d ser., 41, no. 2 (April 1984): 185–212.

Dunn, Richard S. *Puritans and Yankees: The Winthrop Dynasty of New England, 1630–1717.* Princeton: Princeton University Press, 1962.

Emerson, Ralph Waldo. *Representative Men.* Vol. 4 of *Emerson's Complete Works.* Cambridge, Mass.: Riverside Press, 1897.

Erikson, Kai. *Wayward Puritans: A Study in the Sociology of Deviance.* New York: John Wiley and Sons, 1966.

Fiske, John. *The Beginnings of New England; or, The Puritan Theocracy in Its Relation to Civil and Religious Liberty.* 1889; Cambridge, Mass.: Riverside Press, 1899.

Forrer, Richard. *Theodicies in Conflict: A Dilemma in Puritan Ethics and Nineteenth-Century American Literature.* New York: Greenwood Press, 1986.

Gay, Peter. *A Loss of Mastery: Puritan Historians in Colonial America.* New York: Random House, 1968.

Gunn, Janet Varner. *Autobiography: Toward a Poetics of Experience.* Philadelphia: University of Pennsylvania Press, 1982.

Hall, David D. *Worlds of Wonder, Days of Judgment: Popular Religious Belief in Early New England.* Cambridge: Harvard University Press, 1990.

Hall, David D., ed. *The Antinomian Controversy, 1636–1638: A Documentary History.* Middletown, Conn.: Wesleyan University Press, 1968.

Harrison, Cynthia. "The 'City on a Hill' Cliché: Puritans' Winthrop Was No Advocate of Liberty." *Los Angeles Times,* 21 January 1989, pt. 2, p. 14.

Hawke, Daniel. *The Colonial Experience.* Indianapolis: Bobbs-Merrill Publishing Co., 1966.

Heimert, Alan, and Andrew Delbanco. *The Puritans in America: A Narrative Anthology.* Cambridge: Harvard University Press, 1985.

Hughes, Richard T., and C. Leonard Allen. *Illusions of Innocence: Protestant Primitivism in America, 1630–1875.* Chicago: University of Chicago Press, 1988.

King, John Owen, III. *The Iron of Melancholy: Structures of Spiritual Conversion in America from the Puritan Conscience to Victorian Neurosis.* Middletown, Conn.: Wesleyan University Press, 1983.

Lapham, Lewis H. "Notebook: Powdered Roses." *Harper's,* December 1985, pp. 9–10.

Lee, Vera. "Crime among the Puritans . . . and the Penalties Therefor." *Harvard Magazine,* July–August 1986, pp. 48A–H.

Leverenz, David. *The Language of Puritan Feeling: An Exploration in Literature, Psychology, and Social History.* New Brunswick, N.J.: Rutgers University Press, 1980.

McGiffert, Michael. "American Puritan Studies in the 1960's." *William and Mary Quarterly,* 3d ser., 27 (1970): 36–67.

McGinn, Robert. Review of *Amusing Ourselves to Death,* by Neil Postman. *The Stanford Magazine,* December 1989, p. 8.

Mather, Cotton. *Magnalia Christi Americana; or, The Ecclesiastical History of New England.* Edited and abridged by Raymond J. Cunningham. New York: Frederick Ungar Publishing Co., 1970.

Mather, Cotton. *Magnalia Christi Americana; or, The Ecclesiastical History of New-England; From Its First Planting, in the Year 1620, unto the Year of Our Lord 1698.* 2 vols. 1852; New York: Russell and Russell, 1967.

Miller, Perry. *Errand into the Wilderness.* Cambridge: Belknap Press of Harvard University Press, 1956.

Miller, Perry. *The New England Mind: The Seventeenth Century.* New York: Macmillan Co., 1939.

Miller, Perry, and Thomas H. Johnson, eds. *The Puritans: A Sourcebook of Their Writings.* 1938; New York: Harper and Row, 1963.

Minter, David L. *The Interpreted Design as a Structural Principle in American Prose.* New Haven: Yale University Press, 1969.

Morgan, Edmund S. *The Puritan Dilemma: The Story of John Winthrop.* Boston: Little, Brown, and Co., 1958.

Morgan, Edmund S. *Visible Saints: The History of a Puritan Idea.* Ithaca, N.Y.: Cornell University Press, 1963.

Morgan, Edmund S., ed. *The Founding of Massachusetts: The Historians and the Sources.* Indianapolis: Bobb-Merrill Co., 1964.

Morison, Samuel Eliot. *Builders of the Bay Colony.* 1930; Boston: Houghton Mifflin Co., 1958.

Mulder, John, and John Wilson, eds. *Religion in American History: Interpretive Essays.* Englewood Cliffs, N.J.: Prentice Hall, 1978.

Olney, James. *Metaphors of Self: The Meaning of Autobiography,* Princeton: Princeton University Press, 1972.

Pascal, Roy. *Design and Truth in Autobiography.* Cambridge: Harvard University Press, 1960.

Pettit, Norman. *The Heart Prepared: Grace and Conversion in Puritan Spiritual Life.* New Haven: Yale University Press, 1966.

Reinitz, Richard. *Tensions in American Puritanism.* New York: John Wiley and Sons, 1970.

Rutman, Darrett. *American Puritanism: Faith and Practice.* Philadelphia: J. B. Lippincott Co., 1970.

Rutman, Darrett. *John Winthrop's Decision for America: 1629.* Philadelphia: J. B. Lippincott Co., 1975.

Rutman, Darrett. *Winthrop's Boston: Portrait of a Puritan Town, 1630-1649.* New York: W. W. Norton and Co., 1965.

Seton, Anya. *The Winthrop Woman.* Boston: Houghton Mifflin Co., 1958.

Shea, Daniel B., Jr. *Spiritual Autobiography in Early America.* Princeton: Princeton University Press, 1968.

Simpson, Alan. *Puritanism in Old and New England.* Chicago: University of Chicago Press, 1955.

Solberg, Winton. *Redeem the Time: The Puritan Sabbath in Early America.* Cambridge: Harvard University Press, 1977.

Vaughan, Alden. *New England Frontier: Puritans and Indians, 1620-1675.* Boston: Little, Brown, and Co., 1965.

Vaughan, Alden. *The Puritan Tradition in America, 1620-1730.* Columbia: University of South Carolina Press, 1972.

Von Rohr, John. *The Covenant of Grace in Puritan Thought.* Atlanta: Scholars Press, 1986.

Wertenbaker, Thomas Jefferson. *The Puritan Oligarchy: The Founding of American Civilization.* New York: Charles Scribner's Sons, 1947.

Williams, David R. "New Directions in Puritan Studies." *American Quarterly* 37, no. 1 (Spring 1985): 156–61.

Wilson, Edmund. *Patriotic Gore: Studies in the Literature of the American Civil War.* New York: Oxford University Press, 1966.

Wilson, John F. Review of *Habits of the Heart: Individualism and Commitment in American Life,* by Robert Bellah et al. *Religious Studies Review* 14, no. 4 (October 1988): 304–6.

Ziff, Larzar. *Puritanism in America: New Culture in a New World.* New York: Viking Press, 1973.

Index

Adams, Charles Francis, 123–26, 151–53
Adams, Henry, 167
Adams, James Truslow, 153–56
Allen, Bozoun, 107
Allen, John, 117
Allerton, Isaac, 45
Ames, William, 26
Aspinall, William, 46
Auchincloss, Louis, 6

Bancroft, George, 148–50, 151, 153
Bellah, Robert, 174
Bellingham, Richard, 71, 73, 87, 89, 90, 94
Bercovitch, Sacvan, 166–67
Black, Robert C. III, 160
Blackstone, William, 44
Bradford, William, 51, 57, 67, 68, 87, 130–39, 143, 146, 147, 149, 175
Brewster, William, 57, 133–34

Caldwell, Patricia, 163–64
Cartwright, Thomas, 26
Child, Robert, 111
Coddington, William, 56, 82
Conant, Roger, 44
Cotton, John, 39, 59, 64, 67, 68, 80, 81, 83, 84, 85, 86, 104, 105, 117, 118, 164
Coytmore, Martha, 118
Cradock, Matthew, 41, 44, 66
Culverwell, Ezekial, 19–20, 29

De Aulnay, (Charles de Menon, Sieur d'Aulnay de Charnise), 99–102
Davenport, John, 85, 104, 105
D'Ewes, Simonds, 65
Downing, Emmanuel, 29, 35

Dudley, Thomas, 46–47, 53–56, 61, 64, 65, 66, 73, 74, 75, 82, 87, 89, 107, 150, 173, 175
Dummer, Richard, 82
Dunn, Richard S., 121–22, 160
Dyer, Mary, 86

Edwards, Jonathan, 167
Eliot, John, 112
Emerson, Ralph Waldo, 148, 168
Emes, Anthony, 107
Endecott, John, 37, 44, 45, 51–52, 67, 77, 82, 107
Etzioni, Amitai, 174

Faulkner, William, 167
Fiske, John, 150–51
Fitzgerald, F. Scott, 167, 168
Fones, Thomas, 30, 31–32
Franklin, Benjamin, 167

Gager, Wulliam, 46
Gorges, Ferdinando, 58
Gorges, Robert, 44
Gorton, Samuel, 103, 114
Granger, Thomas, 132

Hackett, William, 131–32
Hawthorne, Nathaniel, 167
Haynes, John, 59, 61, 64, 71, 73, 74
Higginson, John, 76
Hooker, Thomas, 59, 61, 68, 72, 75, 76, 104, 117, 118, 128, 163
Hopkins, Mrs. Edward, 116
Hosmer, James Kendall, 122–23
Humfrey, John 47–48, 56

Hutchinson, Anne, 71, 73, 74, 76, 78, 79, 81, 82, 83, 84–86, 92, 93, 113, 117, 123, 124, 126, 137, 164, 175
Hutchinson, Faith, 126

James, Henry, 167
Jefferson, Thomas, 171, 172
Johnson, Arbella, 41, 46
Johnson, Isaac, 35, 46

Keayne, Robert, 94–96

La Tour (Charles de Saint Etienne de la Tour), 99–102
Ludlow, Roger, 64
Luxford, (John Winthrop's bailiff), 87

Mason, John, 58
Mather, Cotton, 5–6, 127, 141–46, 149, 151, 154, 166, 167
Maverick, Samuel, 44, 82
Melville, Herman, 168
Miller, Perry, 156, 157–60
Minter, David, L., 167–68
Morgan, Edmund S., 156, 161–62
Morison, Samuel Eliot, 156–57
Morton, Thomas, 44, 46, 113

Norton, John, 106
Nowell, Increase, 46

Oldham, John, 77
Olney, James, 166

Pascal, Roy, 165–66
Peirce, William, 59
Perkins, William, 26
Peter, Hugh, 74, 88, 105, 106
Postman, Neil, 170

Rich, Nathaniel, 65
Rogers, Ezekiel, 102
Rogers, Richard, 26
Rutman, Darrett, 160–61

Saltonstall, Richard, 82
Sands, Henry, 22
Savage, James, 122–28
Savage, Thomas, 126
Seton, Anya, 4–5
Shea, Daniel, 164–65

Shepard, Thomas, 91
Sherman, Mrs., 94–96
Skelton, Samuel, 45, 60
Smith, John, 47
Smith, Ralph, 67
Stone, John, 76, 77, 79, 83
Stone, Samuel, 59
Story, George, 95, 96
Stoughton, Israel, 78, 79, 82, 106
Stowe, Harriet Beecher, 145–46

Thoreau, Henry David, 163, 167
Tilley, John, 77–78
Twain, Mark, 112
Tyndal, John, 27, 118

Underhill, John, 113

Vane, Henry, 74, 75, 80, 82, 113, 124, 125

Walford, Thomas, 44
Ward, Nathaniel, 89
Weld, Thomas, 93, 105, 125, 126
Weston, Thomas, 44
Williams, Roger, 48, 49, 57, 60, 61, 62, 67, 71–72, 76, 78, 113, 114, 124, 125, 164
Wheelwright, John, 80, 81, 82, 83, 84, 85, 113, 124
Wilson, John, 34, 46, 49, 57, 61, 67, 78, 81, 85, 86, 125, 131
Winslow, Edward, 67, 134–35, 136
Winthrop, Adam (the elder), 13–15
Winthrop, Adam (the younger), 13, 15–19, 29, 30
Winthrop, Forth, 19, 33, 51
Winthrop, Henry, 18, 33, 41, 45
Winthrop, John, writings in addition to *The History of New England*: "Christian Experience," 17, 19–20, 92, 164; "Experiencia," 20–26, 164; "Common Grievances," 32; arguments for the Puritan plantation, 35–36; personal considerations for emigration, 36–37; "Humble Request," 39–40; "Modell of Christian Charity," 42–44, 50, 137; "Short Story," 93, 123–27
Winthrop, John, Jr., 18, 30–31, 32, 33–34, 38, 50, 51, 71, 76, 99, 111, 150, 160
Winthrop, Margaret Tyndal, 27–29, 30, 31, 32, 34–35, 38–39, 45, 47, 50–51, 87, 118
Winthrop, Robert C., 6–7